Time on Target: The World War II Memoir of William R. Buster

Time on Target

The World War II Memoir of William R. Buster

Jeffrey S. Suchanek
and
William J. Marshall, Editors

Library of Congress Cataloging-in-Publication Data

Buster, William R.
    Time on target: the World War II memoir of William R. Buster/Jeffrey S. Suchanek
and William J. Marshall, editors.

        p. cm.

    Includes index.
    ISBN 0-916968-26-C
    1. Buster, William R. 2. World War, 1939-1945--Personal narratives, American. 3.
Generals--United States--Biography. 4. United States. Army--Biography. I.
Suchanek, Jeffrey S., 1955- II. Marshall, William J., 1944- III. Title.

    D811 B856 1999
    940.54'8173--dc21
    [B]

                                                                            99-049950

Order from Kentucky Historical Society
100 W. Broadway, Frankfort, KY 40601-1931
Phone (502) 564-1792; fax (502) 564-4701

TABLE OF CONTENTS

FOREWORD

Perhaps it is trite to say that the most intimate accounts of any undertaking come from the participants in it. This seems to be especially true of discourses on war because, of all human endeavors, war is the furthest removed from the daily happenings of life. Only one who has engaged in combat can adequately describe it, for it is the sole experience that pits man against both man and nature in an unremitting struggle for survival.

William Robards Buster, born in Harrodsburg, Kentucky, October 10, 1916, knew a soldier's combat experience and left his firsthand account of it. He received appointments to both the Naval Academy and the United States Military Academy. After failing the color perception test at the Naval Academy, he passed the physical examination at West Point and entered the Military Academy in the fall of 1935.

He was a good cadet, but not a "file-boner," the West Point equivalent of both a "brain" and a spit-and-polish tin soldier. He was obliged on a number of occasions to "walk the yard" in order to erase certain demerits. But he took his studies seriously and graduated in the top third of the class of 1939. That year he served as associate editor of the Academy yearbook, *The How-itzer*. He played football all four of his cadet years, mostly on the "B" squad; the most exhilarating episode of his gridiron career occurred when he played strong end for three minutes in the Army-Navy game of 1938. He later said West Point life was not always fun but "It taught me orderliness, discipline, and gave me more self-confidence. I'll be forever grateful for having had the opportunity to attend."

He graduated from the Academy just in time to serve as a soldier through one of the most crucial periods in national and world history, that of World War II. Thus his story includes accounts of the incredible expansion, arming, and training of the United States Army for its ordeal by fire, as well as his experience in the great conflict itself.

Posted initially as a second lieutenant in the 7th Mechanized Cavalry Brigade at Fort Knox, Kentucky, he was a participant in the very formation of the armored branch of the army. His brigade possessed only light tanks armed with 37mm guns, hardly more than toys compared with the Germans' medium and heavy tanks armed with their 75mm and 88mm guns. He was assigned to the armored field artillery, where his battalion was supposed to be equipped with medium-caliber (155mm) howitzers, but the only cannon the unit possessed were 75mm pieces. His battalion's first 155mm cannon was a non-serviceable World War I piece "appropriated" from a local courthouse lawn; its parts were rusted together, and it could be used only for visual instruction and drill. When in 1940 his organization moved from Fort McClellan, Alabama, to take part in the Louisiana maneuvers (field exercises), it was armed with 155mm pieces borrowed from the Alabama National Guard.

Buster went through the usual whirl of postings and assignments as the army grew. He served at the Infantry School at Fort Benning, Georgia, and the Artillery School at Fort Sill, Oklahoma, where he later said, "You learned to fire out of your hip pocket, not with sophisticated computerized gadgetry." He learned also that the most effective artillery fire is Time-On-Target fire, in which the shells of many guns are timed to strike the target simultaneously.

He participated in maneuvers in Tennessee, twice in North Carolina, and again in Louisiana. His description of the Louisiana maneuver area is of keen interest to me, because two years after he was there I endured maneuvers there as a junior-grade infantry officer. Buster's account evokes a feeling of bittersweet nostalgia. He says, "Just going through a maneuver in Louisiana was the best survival training in the world, because we experienced just about all the discomfort that you'd find outside of the South Pacific. Louisiana had every insect and reptile ever classified, I think." The trouble with this training for both him and me was that our severest living conditions in combat would come in sub-zero temperatures in Europe instead of the heat of Louisiana or the South Pacific.

After the first Louisiana maneuvers Buster was transferred to the newly created 2nd Armored Division commanded by the soon-to-be-renowned General George S. Patton. Eventually (in January 1942) Buster was assigned to the division's 92nd Armored Field Artillery Battalion, in which he remained throughout World War II. His battalion was armed with 105mm howitzers mounted on thinly armored, full-tracked vehicles that were whimsically nicknamed "Priests" because the design of the machine gun position reminded them of a pulpit.

Shortly after the Japanese attack on Pearl Harbor, Buster was sent back to Fort Knox, where he participated in writing the manual for the employment of armored artillery. Thus, having lived through the experimental and practical stages of the early development of techniques and tactics for his arm, he contributed to the exposition of the theoretical doctrine for the employment of it.

On December 11, 1942, the 92nd Armored Field Artillery Battalion sailed from New York to join its sister components of the 2nd Armored Division (now commanded by General Ernest Harmon) which were engaged in Operation Torch, the Allied invasion of North Africa. After landing at Casablanca, the 2nd Armored Division moved to a position near the border of Spanish Morocco, where it remained as a strategic deterrent to prevent Spanish forces from joining with Axis forces in the theater. The following spring the division moved forward into Algeria, but the war in North Africa ended in May without the unit's having been committed to battle.

The division began at once preparing for the invasion of Sicily, which was launched on July 10, 1943. Buster was now a major serving as the battalion's operations officer. To his considerable agitation, the 92nd was again held in reserve. He recalled, "I just sat on the beach at Port-aux-Poules with the rest of my unit and gritted my teeth." His unit did not get into combat in the brief time required for Allied forces to take the island.

From Sicily the 2nd Armored Division sailed to England. There Buster was promoted to lieutenant colonel and assigned to command his battalion, the youngest officer of this responsibility in the division. The unit participated in the Overlord Operation (the Normandy invasion), landing at Omaha Beach five days after the initial lodgment there. Still again the unit found itself temporarily in reserve. Not until July 1 did it fire its first shots in battle. From this time forward Buster and his comrades were not obliged to grit their teeth for want of action.

They participated fully in the furious combat that scourged the "bocage" (hedgerow) country, which lay inland from the coast. In the third week of July the division spearheaded the American breakout in the famed Cobra operation and in the subsequent smashing of the German counterattack designed by Hitler to cut off the American penetration at Avranches. The division then joined in the headlong Allied drive to the Seine River, which Buster's battalion crossed on August 28. That evening he shaved off the talismanic mustache he had grown and pledged to wear until Operation Overlord was completed.

From the Seine the division moved northeast into Belgium, then into Holland, and in late September into Germany. Here the unit attacked the vaunted Siegfried Line, a belt of concrete bunkers and antitank "dragon's teeth" defended by rifle, machine gun, and artillery fire. The division, along with the entire Allied force, now found itself halted by a shortage of gasoline, combat exhaustion among the troops, and desperate enemy resistance. Day after day the 92nd Battalion fired hundreds of shells in support of the division's operations; during the fourteen-day period beginning November 18 it fired over eighteen thousand rounds.

The mood of high confidence among the troops that had been kindled by the speed and relative ease of the dash across France now started to evaporate. Buster remembered, "We began to realize that the war certainly wasn't over. We went from betting on the day the war would end to the stark realization that the Germans still had a lot of fight left in them . . . What we still didn't realize, however, was that not only were the Germans prepared to defend their homeland, but that they were still thinking of winning the war offensively."

In mid-December the Germans translated into action their thoughts of winning offensively (actually, Hitler's thoughts) by launching their great attack in the Ardennes. The 2nd Armored Division was moved south to join in defeating it. After weeks of hard fighting in bitter winter weather, the organization participated in the successful American attack on the town of Houffalize, Belgium, the last objective in ironing out the deep German penetration. At the climax of this action Buster's battalion fired almost three thousand rounds in a single day. His account of this fighting strikes a familiar chord; my own division, the 99th Infantry Division, was the first unit assaulted by the Germans in their counteroffensive, and during the entire operation we held the apex of the vital northern shoulder of the bulge in the line from which the encounter received its popular name, "Battle of the Bulge." The Elsenborn Ridge, on which we were located, has been designated by historian Stephen Ambrose as the "Cemetery Hill" of the battle of the Ardennes.

Buster's description of the bone-chilling winter cold arouses in me a memory that still sends a shiver up my spine. He recounts how he was able to combat the cold by calling upon a legendary Kentucky substance. He had been fortunate enough to obtain a sheepskin-lined leather jacket, pants, and flight boots from an Air Corps crew. How did he do it? He explains that he had a particularly aggressive battalion supply officer, then he divulges, "I think it may have cost me a few bottles of Kentucky bourbon that Mildred (his wife) managed to surreptitiously supply me with periodically through the mail."

With the German campaign in the Ardennes smashed, the 2nd Armored Division joined in the American offensive across the Roer River and the Erft Canal, and advanced to the Rhine, the last formidable terrain barrier to the heartland of Germany. At midnight of March 29, 1945, the 92nd Battalion crossed the historic river. After participating in trapping an entire German army in the Ruhr River Valley "pocket," the 2nd Armored joined in the Allied sweep eastward to the Elbe River, where the American troops met the Russians and were halted by an order from General Eisenhower. The division headed for Berlin when it received the order. Buster obviously was disappointed by it; he speaks of receiving the "bad news" contained in it. He believes he may have been the first Allied ground soldier to sight the Elbe; he saw it from an American observation airplane that was engaged in spotting targets for the artillery.

Shortly after the end of European hostilities Buster was promoted to the position of division artillery commander. He received many awards and citations for his wartime service, including the Silver Star with Oak Leaf Cluster, the Bronze Star, the Air Medal, and the French Croix de Guerre with Palm.

He ended up getting to Berlin after all. General Eisenhower selected the 2nd Armored Division to be the occupying unit in the American sector of the city. The division provided security for the historic Potsdam Conference in which the Allied leaders made the final decisions concerning the war against Japan and the occupation of Germany and the area of Europe that had been held by the Germans. What most completely captured Buster's attention in Berlin was the devastation of the city, which he describes in vivid detail. The dead lay buried in the rubble. He recalled: "The smell of (human) death has a very peculiar odor. It's not like the odor of decaying livestock or vegetation. It's a very distinctive smell and it hung over Berlin like a cloud." How true! The smell of dead horses and cows did not particularly upset me; the smell of dead humans could make me vomit.

Shortly after the end of the war in Europe, Buster was ordered back to the United States, where he served in the Pentagon in the section that was concerned with war refugees and displaced persons. In pursuit of his duty, in January 1946 he accompanied a commission to Europe for three months and toured many of the refugee camps there. In December 1947 he received an extended leave from the army in order to take over the management of his wife's farm near Midway, Kentucky. In March 1948 he submitted his resignation from the army.

This book is good reading. General Buster was a soldier, not a literary person. His memoir is expressed in a soldier's manner. Like the narratives of Caesar or Grant, it is neither elegant nor sophisticated. But it is terse, straightforward, and clear.

It is not philosophical or judgmental; its strongest statement of condemnation is an incidental reference to Hitler as an "s.o.b." Buster's tone reveals the outlook of a serious and dedicated man working diligently to complete an onerous task as quickly and efficiently as possible. It reveals also the spirit of a courageous soldier who was willing to risk his life repeatedly in the performance of his duty.

The memoir is peppered with technical military terms, their meaning either explained in the text or made clear by the context. Buster occasionally resorts to the colorful idiomatic language of barracks and field. For example, in discussing how the unusual mobility of the armored units required the artillery to displace forward repeatedly and rapidly after firing a mission, he uses such terms as "shoot and scoot" or, more pungently, "harass, bypass, and haul ass."

To my mind, this memoir rings as true as steel. Any former combat soldier will recognize the episodes and experiences recounted here, and the shifting moods of exhilaration, anger, frustration, and fear. Anyone possessing a grain of empathy with the human being caught in the toils of war will find the story interesting in detail and moving in emotional effect.

February 1998   Charles P. Roland

EDITORS' PREFACE

This is not the story of a high-ranking commander, with thousands of troops at his disposal, making momentous strategic or tactical decisions during World War II. Rather, William Robards Buster, from Mercer County, Kentucky, was a mid-level artillery commander responsible for more than eight hundred men. He would attain his stars long after the war was over while he served in the Kentucky National Guard. His World War II experiences were not by themselves unique or extraordinary. Indeed, his wartime experiences were undoubtedly rivaled by countless thousands of Americans who served in all branches of the military during the war. What makes his story compelling and important in the retelling, however, is the period in which he served, beginning with his enrollment at the United States Military Academy at West Point in 1935 and ending with his retirement from the Army in 1948. During these years the United States went from a minor player in world affairs to the foremost superpower. The nation's newfound political and military status was supported by the expansion of its armed forces, an evolutionary process designed and implemented by men like William Buster. During the time Buster served, the United States Army evolved from a force of 186,000 enlisted men and officers still utilizing horse cavalry to one over ten million strong with more than 100,000 tanks and 372,000 artillery pieces. Inside Buster's personal memoir is the story of a nation growing to maturity and assuming its role as a leader on the world stage. This book joins Philip Ardery's *Bomber Pilot* (1978), Col. Arthur L. Kelly's *Battle Fire! Combat Stores from World War II* (1997), Alvin C. Poweleit's *Kentucky's Fighting 192nd Light G.H.Q. Tank Battalion* (1981), and Frank F. Mathias' *G.I. Jive* (1982) among accounts of World War II written by Kentuckians.

This book is based on a series of oral history interviews with General Buster conducted initially by William J. Marshall over a three-year period (1985,1986,1988), and completed by Jeffrey S. Suchanek (1993-95). By combining these oral recollections with diary entries Buster kept during the war, the official 2nd Armored Divisional Artillery Operational Log, and an operational log kept by "B" Battery of the 92nd Armored Field Artillery Battalion, he and the editors were able to reconstruct his experiences and movements during the war. Any factual errors are the fault of the editors.

The editors would like to thank the following for their proofreading skills and editing advice: Tom Appleton, Clayton Barnett, Terry Birdwhistell, Dan Bundy, Ken Cherry, Dave Fleming, Gretchen Haney, Melba Porter Hay, Lindsay Herkness Jr., Edwin Hoopes Jr., James C. Klotter, David Nichols, Robert Pryor, Charles P. Roland, Jeanne Ontko Suchanek, and Kenneth Tomlinson. The encouragement and determination provided by Mildred and Kate Buster made the completion of this book possible.

"Billy" Buster, age five, in a suit made from a WWI military uniform.

CHAPTER ONE: A MILITARY CAREER

William Robards Buster was born in Mercer County, Kentucky, in 1916 during World War I, "the war to end all wars." In the same year, the first tanks were employed by the British Army during the Battle of the Somme. This new technology did little to alter the "meat-grinder" nature of the war as French, British, and German casualties amounted to over one million in just this one battle. The Treaty of Versailles, which officially ended the tragic conflict in 1919, coupled with economic depression and the shame of defeat, sowed the seeds for a second conflict and eventually led to the rise of a new Reich led by a megalomaniac named Adolf Hitler.

These events had little effect in small towns or in rural areas like Mercer County, Kentucky. Influenced by an uncle, a veteran of "The Great War," who raised him, William Buster prepared himself for a military career from an early age. While in high school he attempted to join a newly formed National Guard unit, but was refused because of his age. Following a year at Centre College, he attended a school which prepared young men for service-academy entrance examinations. In 1935, after failing to pass the Naval Academy physical, Buster accepted an appointment to the United States Military Academy at West Point, New York.

I trace my roots to Harrodsburg, one of Kentucky's most historic towns. In October 1916, my father and mother, John Buster and Martha Lillard Nooe Buster, moved their family into Harrodsburg, the oldest town west of the Alleghenies, from their farm near Burgin, Kentucky. Since a disastrous flu epidemic had struck Mercer County the year before, my father took the advice of his brother-in-law and family doctor, Dr. John Robards, and moved his pregnant wife and three sons to a comfortable brick house on Hillcrest Avenue adjacent to Clay Hill, the birthplace of Beriah Magoffin, one of Kentucky's Civil War governors. They found living more convenient and the doctor closer in Harrodsburg.

The Buster family first came to Kentucky from Virginia, where in 1720 they had been among the early settlers of Goochland County, now Albemarle, near Charlottesville. Several generations later part of the family migrated down the Cumberland River to Wayne County, Kentucky, arriving about 1800. One of them was a surveyor and helped General Joshua Jones lay out the town of Monticello, Kentucky. My paternal grandparents, Nimrod and Sally Buster, moved to Boyle County in 1873. He owned a considerable amount of land about three miles north of Danville. My father owned part of that land until his death, and then my older brother Jack bought it.

The Lillards on my mother's side of the family trace their ancestry back to France in the 1600s. Captain John Lillard married Susanna Ball, a cousin of Martha Washington, and fought with the Virginia Militia under the command of George Washington during the American Revolution. Following the war, Captain Lillard moved from Culpeper County, Virginia, to the Kentucky Territory and settled in the vicinity of Harrodsburg.

His great-great-granddaughter, my mother, Martha Lillard Nooe, grew up known as "Mattie" by family and friends. Her father was John Augustus Nooe, a prominent farmer in Mercer County. He was a graduate of the old Kentucky University, a forerunner of Transylvania University, and one of the founders of the school system in Burgin. The Nooes came to Kentucky sometime in the early 1800s and lived in Jessamine County. The old Nooe homestead was located on the Lexington-Harrodsburg road. The house is still there and the Nooe family cemetery is behind it. My mother died of edema, or "dropsy" as it was called then, when I was eighteen months old, and I did not have much contact with her side of the family thereafter.

It was into this lineage that I was born on 10 October 1916, the youngest of four boys. My oldest brother was Nimrod Shelby Buster, the next was John "Jack" Ingram Buster, and the third was Granville Robards Buster. I was christened William Lillard Buster, and after my mother's death I lived with my aunt and uncle, Dr. John B. and Emma Robards. They had no children of their own, and since my father already had three sons to raise, they agreed to take me in upon the death of my mother. Growing up as I did practically as their son, I became so closely associated with them from an early age that, more often than not, many people called me by their name. Eventually I adopted their name as my middle name and had it changed legally.

My father's farm was located on the Buster Pike between Burgin and Danville. I adored my father. He was a great man and really one of the fairest and finest people I've ever known. He was a tobacco and livestock farmer. Even though I lived with my aunt and uncle, I saw him all the time because his farm was just four miles outside of Harrodsburg. My father served as sheriff of Mercer County and worked in the sheriff's office for a total of sixteen years. Back in those days and up until just recently, the sheriff couldn't serve consecutive terms of office, so my father was the High Sheriff for four years and then one of his deputies would take the office for the next four and my father would be his deputy. They maintained the line of succession to the sheriff's office in this way, which was very effective, but in reality my father ran the office the whole time.

My aunt and uncle built a brick house on College Street in Harrodsburg. We moved into that when I was four or five years old and lived there until 1927. While the new house was being completed we lived at historic "Diamond Point," a lovely old house that guarded the northern approach to Harrodsburg and is located where the road divides to become North Main and College Streets. I lived with my aunt and uncle on College Street until I went to West Point. My uncle, a country doctor and a good one, had a wide practice. I spent many hours going on calls with him, and later when I was old enough to drive, fourteen or fifteen years old, sometimes he would root me out of bed in the middle of the night to drive him to his emergency calls. If it was an obstetric case, sometimes that meant waiting for hours in the car while he was attending to the patient inside the home. Much of his medical practice consisted of home visits. The local hospital was used only for very serious cases. Many of his cases were old patients with minor illnesses. Of course, some were hypochondriacs, and they would call when there wasn't anything wrong with them. They just wanted him to come out and visit, and most of the time he would go.

With my uncle being a doctor we lived comfortably, but we felt the Depression like everyone else. Many of his patients would pay him in vegetables and produce, and many others just couldn't pay at all. When he died in 1938, the amount that people owed him totaled thousands of dollars. Although Harrodsburg was fairly insulated from extreme want, I also remember the severe drought of 1930. I don't think agricultural communities suffered nearly as much during the Depression as the urban areas. It didn't change lives a great deal in Mercer County, but I do remember one instance that was rather horrifying. After the stock market crash in 1929, when the banks closed, Bush W. Allen, the president of the Mercer County National Bank and one of the community's leaders, committed suicide. That was our family's bank and he was a family friend, so that was a blow to everyone. But even though we felt the stress and strain of the Depression, we lived comfortably compared to other people. Everyone felt that the hard times were just something you had to live through and that economic conditions would eventually improve. If the tobacco farmers had a good crop, although prices were low, that movement of money, which was very unusual then, was encouraging.

Both my father and my uncle were leaders in the Democratic Party in Mercer County. That was back in the days when the feeling between Democrats and Republicans ran pretty strong. Mercer County was a Democratic community. I think people exercise their judgment a lot more now than they did in those days. Party affiliation was much more important at that time than it is now. My uncle ran for the state legislature and served a term in the state senate. He was a great political opponent of John Young Brown Sr., although they were friends otherwise. He was a great favorite among the legislators and had a fair amount of influence. I can remember helping him during his campaigns. I would go house to house and knock on doors and introduce myself and hand out cards and tell people, "Please vote for Dr. Robards." Since many people owed my uncle money for services rendered, I don't think it was too difficult a job for me! While I don't know whether I helped him or not, I disliked doing it. Campaigning was always very distasteful to me.

I spent the year 1925 in Florida. That was during the real estate boom, and Dr. Robards decided that he was going to get involved in the real estate business. We were there until the boom became a bust and my uncle decided to return to Kentucky. I didn't enjoy Florida. The place we initially rented while we were building a house was rather cramped. Once we got into our own house conditions improved. But I remember that everything in Florida was crowded. The school system was vastly overloaded. They had to have double classroom sessions. I would go to school from eight o'clock to twelve, and then there would be another group of students who would arrive and would stay until four o'clock. I didn't make any close friends there. It was another interesting experience for me, though, and I did enjoy the visits we made to Clearwater Beach and Tarpon Springs.

Back home in Kentucky I attended the Harrodsburg public schools, which were excellent. I felt like I received a good education. The teachers were excellent and although I was not always a good student, I received good grades. I didn't work as hard as I should have, yet I ranked near the top of my class. I guess I absorbed information quickly, but I certainly didn't tax myself. In high school my favorite subject was geometry. I also liked history and the sciences. I did not like foreign languages. I had no problems with English, but it was not a favorite subject.

After graduating from high school, I entered Centre College in the fall of 1934. I had determined to try for one of the service academies, and in those days a year of satisfactory college work precluded the need to take an entrance exam. Also a year of college was good preparation. In addition to the college work, I also felt I needed some extra preparation for what I thought would be an appointment to the Naval Academy at Annapolis, Maryland. I took additional instruction at the Kavanaugh Academy in Lawrenceburg, which offered a night course to instruct those students who thought that they might like to attend one of the military schools.

Rhoda Kavanaugh, the principal, was a real character. Kavanaugh was the name of the school established by her family, which had been chosen to be a county high school. But she also had some special students who came to her for preparation for Annapolis or West Point. These students lived at the school and were called "house boys." They were instructed in the evenings as well as in the daytime. She had a study hall in the evening that she supervised. She would sit there in her long black dress, rocking back and forth in a chair by an old potbellied stove. If anybody lifted their head from their book, she would crack down on them either verbally or with the cane she always carried. She was tough, but I also remember that she had a wonderful sense of humor.

I went there to sharpen my ability in algebra and to learn what to expect at the academy. She would give us assignments and if we had questions she was there to help. We would go over the military academies' previous year's entrance exams and work the problems so that we became familiar with the system. The entrance exams were printed and distributed by the Government Printing Office and were available by request. Kavanaugh had been requesting the entrance exams for years and had prepared a number of students who went on to become admirals. Admiral Edmund Tyler Wooldridge (Class of 1920), Vice Admiral Charles K. Duncan (Class of 1933), and Rear Admirals John Huston Brady (Class of 1923), Rhodam Yarrott McElroy (Class of 1935), Andrew Irwin McKee (Class of 1917), Logan McKee (Class of 1921), and Elliott West Shanklin (Class of 1924) all had attended the Kavanaugh Academy to help prepare them for Annapolis. Two other attendees of the Kavanaugh Academy went on to West Point and later became generals: William Breckinridge, who later was one of my instructors at the Military Academy, and me. Most of the "house boys" who attended the Kavanaugh Academy were trying to get into the Naval Academy, although the entrance requirements were the same as those for West Point.

My uncle had served in World War I in the Medical Corps and was very interested in the Army and a military career for me. It was his influence more than anything else that put the idea of a military career in my mind, and I worked toward that goal. While I was still in high school the Harrodsburg National Guard unit (the one that later endured the Bataan Death March during World War II) was organized. I tried to join but I was too young. I also tried to take some Civilian Military Training Corps courses but, again, I was told I was too young.

My father and my uncle had the right connections to get me an appointment to the Naval Academy. They were great friends of Virgil Chapman, who was the U.S. congressman representing Mercer County. My father handled all of the political patronage in the county for the Democrats, so it was not difficult to get an appointment from Congressman Chapman. Back in those days, anyone who attended either one of the service academies was held in high esteem by his peers and by the people in the community. It was considered quite an achievement to get an appointment. But it took a lot of preparation in order to qualify and stay once you got there. There are many stories of boys from Kentucky who received an appointment only to fail the entrance examination or, once accepted, were dismissed for academic failings later.

I actually had a choice of attending the Naval Academy or West Point, and my first choice, after much deliberation, was the Naval Academy. A great friend of mine, Ralph Kercheval, one of my heroes and a football player for the University of Kentucky, outlined for me on several occasions the advantages of a naval career over that of the Army. He told me that in the Navy I would be able to see the world and wouldn't have to get dirty. So I chose an appointment to the Naval Academy and reported there on 1 July 1935. I took the physical examination and passed all of it except the color perception test. My color perception was borderline. The doctors were a little unsure whether I was actually color blind, so they gave me four sets of tests, three more than they normally gave. The last test, which involved pinpoints of light at twenty feet with variations in shades of red and green, got me. I flunked that one. So although I qualified academically, I failed the physical.

My uncle had accompanied me to Annapolis for my physical examination. On our way back to Kentucky through Washington we called Congressman Chapman and told him that I had failed the physical at the Naval Academy and that he could give the appointment to someone else. I went home prepared to enjoy the summer before reentering Centre College in the fall. I was home about two weeks when I received a telegram from Congressman Chapman which ordered me to report to the United States Military Academy at West Point on 1 August. It seems Congress had passed an act that expanded the enrollment of the service academies and many of the new slots were still unfilled. Needless to say, I was delighted to have received a second chance, but apprehensive about having to pass another physical examination. When I arrived at the Military Academy, I was greatly relieved to learn that the color perception test was not nearly as stringent as it had been at Annapolis. Besides, I had learned a few tricks from my previous experience, which I will not divulge. So I passed the physical with flying colors and became a cadet.

In all honesty I had not been devastated when I failed the physical at the Naval Academy because the atmosphere there was not what I had expected. I wasn't expecting brass bands or anything like that, but for me the attitude there was too low key and casual. When you entered the grounds of the Military Academy at West Point, you knew immediately that you were in a military installation and that discipline and orderliness were the orders of the day. That's what I expected and wanted to be a part of, and I have never been sorry.

Cadet William R. Buster, 1939. "When you entered the grounds of the Military Academy at West Point, you knew immediately that you were in a military installation and that discipline and orderliness were the order of the day. That's what I expected and wanted to be a part of, and I have never been sorry."

CHAPTER TWO: THE UNITED STATES MILITARY ACADEMY

The years from 1935 to 1939 were eventful and ominous internationally. In 1935, Italy's fascist dictator, Benito Mussolini, led that country into war with Ethiopia. In 1936, Germany's own Nazi dictator, Adolf Hitler, reoccupied the Rhineland and began supplying men and material to the fascist side during the Spanish Civil War. In 1937, Japan and China officially declared war against one another, an event that had been brewing since the Japanese takeover of Manchuria six years earlier. In 1938, Hitler forcibly annexed Austria as a province of Germany and also bullied Czechoslovakia into handing over the Sudetenland.

The political and military developments in Europe prompted the United States Congress to initiate a small buildup of the nation's armed forces, including the Corps of Cadets at the United States Military Academy at West Point. The Military Academy, not unlike the nation itself, was undergoing great change during the four years (1935-39) that William Buster attended. New academic buildings and cadet living quarters were constructed, and a widely expanded curriculum was initiated to meet changing military technology and tactics. Buster attended West Point during the brief period when upper (first) classmen were allowed to tour military facilities during the summer recess to witness maneuvers and the firing of weapons firsthand. The summer tours, which left hazing of the plebes to underclassmen (yearlings) at Beast Barracks and summer camp, were discontinued in 1939.

Classes that graduated during the late 1930s and early 1940s provided the Army with the junior officers who served during World War II and Korea. Others, like Creighton W. Abrams, Andrew Goodpaster, Bruce Palmer Jr., and William C. Westmoreland, later rose to prominence during the Vietnam War.

Beast Barracks

Henry Riggs Sullivan, a classmate from Centre College, had also received a late appointment to the Military Academy. The two of us rode the train together to West Point and entered the Academy at the same time. We even roomed together for the first year. Riggs had an excellent mind and was a good student and a natural-born leader. I think he had attended summer training in the Marine Corps one summer prior to his Academy appointment, so he was more familiar with the military lexicon and system than I was. He eventually went into the Army Air Corps and, like most people who went into the Air Corps early, advanced up the chain of command very rapidly. After the war he was with the Strategic Air Command for many years. He was one of Curtis LeMay's fair-haired boys. I think he also became the first Commandant of Cadets at the Air Force Academy when the Air Force split from the Army and became its own service branch.

Riggs and I took the "George Washington" from Lexington, Kentucky, to Grand Central Station. We had to go across the Hudson River on the Weehawken Ferry to get to the West Shore Railroad Station. I recall that the train to West Point rode the tracks along the shore of the Hudson River. The Military Academy itself sits way up on the hill overlooking the river. From the train station I couldn't even get a glimpse of the Academy. All I saw was a long, steep road that wound up to the top of that hill. I discovered very quickly that I had brought along far too much luggage, which I had to lug up the hill because they did not roll out a red carpet for us at the train station.

Those of us who arrived at West Point by virtue of the congressional act that enlarged the service academies were given the moniker of "Augustines" by the regular cadets, because we entered the Academy on 1 August instead of the normal 1 July entry date. Our class, the Class of 1939, was the largest class that had ever entered the Military Academy up to that time. The Cadet Corps went from twelve hundred cadets to eighteen hundred in one year, so it was an unusually large plebe class.

The Academy had to organize a completely new "Beast Barracks" detail and a whole new reception committee for the two hundred of us additional cadets. Prior to our class, "Augustines" had been looked down upon because they did not undergo the rigors of "Beast Barracks," which helped to acclimate new cadets to life at the Academy. But for our class, because there were so many of us, they organized a special "Beast Barracks" detail that was just as tough as the normal one. Consequently, when we were accepted into the Corps it was without the denigration that had usually accompanied the late arrivals in some of the previous classes.

When Riggs and I arrived at West Point it was a very, very hot day and the humidity was hardly bearable. We were immediately organized into squads and given our physical examination. After passing the physical we were sent to the Cadet Store to draw our bedding and clothing. By the evening of the first day I was a very tired cadet. There is no question that I was intimidated the first few days by the whole experience. The reception committee really bore down on us after we had drawn our equipment. They were called the "Beast Detail" for good reason. It was the job of the upper classmen to show us that instilling discipline was one of the main objectives of the institution. They impressed that idea upon us every waking moment by utilizing clean but very forceful language.

When we entered the Academy we were "sized." When we reported to our assigned company we were "sized" again. If you've ever seen movies of old cadet parades, everyone appeared to be the same height. They did that by making sure that all the people in each company were relatively the same height. "A" Company and "M" Company consisted of the tallest cadets and, conversely, "E, F, G" and "H" companies were the shortest, or the "runts." (It is not so true these days.) I was assigned to "M" Company, the last lettered company in the Corps. "M" Company was known as the "lost battalion" because of the location of our barracks—and perhaps because of our outlook on life. We were "sized" so that it would be pleasing to the eye of on-lookers as we passed in review. The cadets in "A" and "M" companies, called the "flankers," didn't associate very much with the "runts" because it appeared that the "runts" had an entirely different life philosophy. In terms of cadet lingo, the "runts" were "file boners." In other words, they worked real hard to improve their class ranking, or at least that was the impression they created. When a "flanker" would get caught in an area where the "runts" were quartered, these little men would come out of the barracks from all directions and haze the hell out of him on the spot. The tall and short cadets seemed to develop mental complexes because of their size.

The first day at the Military Academy we attended all the formations in the clothes we had on, but the next day we got an issue of what they called "plebe skins." This consisted of a pair of gray trousers and a gray shirt. Of course, we also had to draw shoes and socks, underwear, and toilet articles, and we had to carry all of that back to our barracks. Our military training began the next morning. Reveille was at 5:50 a.m. Ordinarily an upper classman had about ten minutes to get dressed and report to ranks, but plebes were expected to be there within three minutes. When we arrived in ranks we were meticulously inspected by the upper classmen. Their job was to make our life miserable until roll call, and some of them became really adept at it.

After reveille we were allowed to return to our room to make up our beds and get everything back in our lockers. Then we fell out in front of the barracks in company formation and were marched by company into the mess hall for breakfast. The company was seated together at tables that sat ten. Breakfast took about thirty or forty minutes. When we got back to our room after breakfast we were allowed to finish straightening up before our military training began.

The purpose of "Beast Barracks" was to instill military discipline into incoming cadets in the shortest possible time. It was also designed to get our attention so that we knew this was serious business and not something to be taken lightly. We were drilled in all phases of military life as a cadet. During that period of time we were taught not only close-order drill and the manual of arms, but also the "courtesy and customs" of the service. We were instructed in all of the things we needed to know in order to exist at the Academy and eventually in the world of the military.

The discipline was rigidly enforced. "Beast Barracks" was very tough on a young fellow who had had no training of that kind. There was a certain amount of hazing, but it had been downgraded by law to the point where there was no physical punishment allowed. For small infractions the upper classmen would "drive you down to their room." That meant they would order you down to their room immediately after reveille and before breakfast in full uniform. They would then stand you up against a wall and make you brace very severely. They would try to put their hand behind your back to make sure that you were getting your back flat up against the wall.

They also made us memorize various facts about the Academy, such as the number of gallons of water Lusk Reservoir would hold. These facts were usually published in the plebe bible called "Bugle Notes," which incoming cadets received with their equipment.

Initially we were given only very basic military training such as close-order drill and turning movements, just to give us a feel of what it was like to be a soldier. Later on we were taught how to execute squad movements, which was a more difficult exercise back then than the system they use now. The squad formation was fairly complicated. The cadets who were not adept at picking up ideas quickly, or who were not as physically coordinated, were put into the "Awkward Squad." Some cadets had difficulty mastering the manual of arms exercise, which was also far more complicated back then. Most of the cadets who found themselves assigned to the "Awkward Squad" were put there to sharpen up their ability to handle a rifle.

We had the same amount of time in "Beast Barracks" as those cadets who had arrived in July, but our time in the summer camp portion of our training was reduced. After participating in "Beast Barracks," the incoming cadets were then assigned to summer camp that was located on the eastern portion of the drill field known as "The Plain." It was over across from the barracks but completely separate. Summer camp was a training period designed to bring the new cadets slowly into the Corps. They trained with the "yearling class," or sophomores, who had been there all summer. The "yearlings" took the new cadets under their wings and taught them the rudiments of being a cadet. Although the "Augustines" had a month's less time in the summer camp phase of our training, I realized after "Beast Barracks" that I had mastered all of the rudimentary military skills necessary to exist at the Academy. I was ready to begin my academic military education.

Plebe Year

After "Beast Barracks" and summer camp were over, there was a tremendous sense of relief because the constant pressure directed towards us by the upperclassmen decreased dramatically. During "Beast Barracks" two "yearlings" were in charge of our squad. They oversaw all that the squad did. When we went to summer camp we lived in a tent with several "yearlings." They were on our back all the time. When academics began we were assigned a permanent room in barracks. Most of the plebes were assigned to rooms on the fourth floor, while the upperclassmen populated the other three floors. Thus there was a degree of separation between us plebes and the people who could make our lives miserable. The Academy's administration designed this arrangement on purpose because they knew the world of a plebe was difficult enough as it was without undue harassment by upperclassmen. The harassment still persisted throughout the first year but not to the extent that we experienced during "Beast Barracks" and summer camp. We would invariably screw up and draw the ire of an upperclassman, and he would make our life pretty unbearable for a few minutes. But if you minded your own business, did what you were told, and didn't draw any attention to yourself, you were able to exist without too much harassment.

Riggs Sullivan and I roomed together during "Beast Barracks" and that first academic year because we were fortunate enough to get assigned to the same company. At one point during "Beast Barracks" after a particularly hard week of harassment by the upperclassmen, Riggs and I really got fed up. Riggs was particularly upset because he had ranked very high academically at Centre College, was a star football and basketball player there, and was the top man in his fraternity. He was not mentally prepared for the kind of verbal abuse we encountered during "Beast Barracks." Perhaps this happens to all plebes, I don't know. But at any rate the two of us discussed the situation one night and decided that we just didn't think that this was the right career for us. So we asked our squad leaders if we could go down to their room and talk to them. They agreed, and we had a heart-to-heart talk with them and told them how we felt. Fortunately for us they were, at heart, two very nice young men, and they took the time to give us a pep talk. They pointed out all of the lifelong advantages that would accrue from having graduated from West Point, that "Beast Barracks" and the constant harassment would end soon, and that life there really was pretty good. They asked us to think it over very carefully before we made any decision. Riggs and I owe a lot to those two young men because we did think it over and decided to stick it out. I guess other plebes didn't have such understanding upperclassmen because the attrition rate during "Beast Barracks" was pretty high.

As a plebe you could only speak to an upperclassman when spoken to and only to answer questions, never to shoot-the-breeze. If you had a question you had to raise your hand and be acknowledged before you could speak. Most of the time you didn't dare ask a question because it might indicate that you didn't know something that you were supposed to know. Talking out of turn was not a problem for me.

The conditions in the mess hall were particularly trying because during our entire plebe year we had to sit at a brace during the meals. This meant that you had to sit on the front half of your chair with your back absolutely straight with your chin tucked in. Try eating that way and you'll realize how difficult that is! Generally eight cadets sat at a table, four or five of whom were upperclassmen. Plebes were assigned duties at the ends of the table. The water corporal was seated at one end of the table and the coffee corporal at the other. An upperclassman would bang his glass or coffeecup down on the table and then flip it down to the water or coffee corporal, who would then fill it up and pass it back. The bang was the first and only indication the plebe would have that the glass or cup was on the way. He would have just enough time to look up and catch it.

This practice was frowned upon by the administration, but it took place all too often. The cadet officers assigned as guards in the mess hall to keep order overlooked it unless they saw it directly, and then they were honor-bound to report it. But the Officers of the Guard would generally walk around the mess hall looking straight ahead so they wouldn't see violations they would be forced to report. It made eating pretty hectic that first year.

The food was tasty, healthy, and well prepared. I don't recall that we ever complained about it. The only problem was getting enough of it because, due to the vigorous life we led, we were almost always hungry. There was the Cadet Store where we could get snacks and candy to take back to our room to eat. There was also a place called "The Boodlers" that was located in the Visitors Center. This was where our guests would call. They had a little cadet restaurant in there that served soft drinks and ice cream. It was not open during the week, only on weekends. To supplement our diet we were pretty well restricted to what we could buy from the Cadet Store. Cadets weren't allowed to have money. We had to use a "Boodle Book," which was an allocation of ten dollars a month divided into coupons with which we could pay for whatever we got at "The Boodlers." The word "boodle" means something that is highly treasured. The "Boodle Book" was a way of leveling the playing field between cadets who came from rich and poor families, as well as ensuring that cadets did not overindulge.

Plebes were forced to participate in a lot of "details," or drills, which were designed as harassment. For example, to amuse themselves a group of upperclassmen might order what was called a "clothing formation." They would tell us to appear in front of the barracks wearing a specific uniform at a designated time. Usually they'd give us about three to five minutes' notice, whereupon we would run up to our room and put on the prescribed uniform—generally some outlandish combination—and report down to ranks for inspection. If everything was in order we were dismissed. But if anything was not right or in proper order they would prescribe another ridiculous uniform which would be completely different, and we'd have to root through our locker to find something that we had undoubtedly packed away. After you went through this "clothing formation" several times in a matter of thirty minutes, your room was in absolute, complete chaos. Then just to cheer us up they would order an inspection within the hour and everything had to be back in perfect order.

We lived by the honor system. On weekends there was a sentry posted in the hallway of each barracks. As we left our room and passed his post we had to say, "All right, sir." The "all right" meant that we would not indulge in alcohol, gambling, go off-limits—which meant leave the grounds of the Academy or go into certain areas that were restricted—and that we were telling the truth. And then when we returned we also had to repeat the "all right," which indicated that everything was "all right" as far as those five elements of our conduct were concerned. But if you could sneak out of the window and crawl down the drainpipe, you were not under any obligation. You were subject to being caught, of course, and being punished. On the other hand, you had not declared an oath that you would behave by certain standards, and so that was different.

The barracks sentry was taken off duty at eleven o'clock on weekends. There was not a sentry in the hall during the week, only on weekends. During the week we were not supposed to go out. Period. We could visit other cadets in our barracks but could not go outside the barracks area unless we had a valid reason. But on weekends after the sentry retired, if you'd gone down the drainpipe, for example, you might be able to sneak back in through the front door because there wouldn't be anybody there. A cadet was always on duty, though, in the Orderly Room. Each division of barracks had an Orderly Room by the entrance door. The orderly was supposed to stay up all night, but occasionally he'd fall asleep and you could sneak by.

I pretty much adhered to the rules and regulations, and there were not very many instances where I deliberately circumvented them. But I had many classmates who resorted to all sorts of things, and some of their escapades are legendary. James Elmer "Moose" Mather did everything in the book in violation of regulations during his cadet career. Many times he crawled out the window and slid down the drainpipe and made his way to Highland Falls or some other town nearby where a dance was being held and then managed to creep back in undetected. He seemed to have really flourished on being a daredevil because he and his two cohorts, William Patterson and Victor Leroy Johnson Jr., were always up to something. Johnson didn't start out wild, but his two companions contaminated him. Another classmate of mine who violated a good number of regulations was Michael Shannon Davison. He later became a four-star general, so I guess that questionable conduct as a cadet did not necessarily portend an unsuccessful career.

Enforcement of the honor system was left to the cadets. The "Honor Committee" was composed of cadets. The punishments were meted out by the "Honor Committee." The provisions of the Honor Code were very rigidly enforced. The Honor Code also covered cheating in the classroom. Any violation was subject to instant dismissal from the Academy. There were several cadets who were dismissed for honor violations. I think most of them were violations that involved being off-limits. They were discovered in areas designated "off limits" after they had given their oath—the "all right" to the sentry—that they would not go there. In several instances we thought the violation had been accidental, but apparently the "Honor Committee" felt duty-bound to punish the offenders. In some cases a cadet was punished for what was called "quibbling," which meant being charged with an infraction and then using a very lame reason to account for it. Honor Code matters were handled very quietly, and violators simply disappeared from the Military Academy.

We had eight-man squads for drill and training. When we went to class we would report to the designated location where the cadets attending that particular class formed, would line up by section, and be marched in military formation to class by the section leader. All academic classes were divided into sections, and it depended on your grades as to what section you were in. Cadets receiving the highest grades were in the first section, and the ones that were the lowest in academic averages would be in the bottom section. In some subjects there might be eight sections and in some there might be twelve; it depended on the course and the way that the class was divided. There were many divisions in French, for example. There might be four different divisions that would attend at different times because we had twelve companies. In order to accommodate all of us the schedule was arranged so we could attend the appropriate number of times. But "A" Company would attend at a different time than "M" Company, for example.

The squad leader was chosen by academic rank. West Point was a very competitive society because your class ranking determined your access to just about everything in your entire Army career. I didn't necessarily study hard to earn a better grade than the next guy, but I studied hard to earn the best grade I could. After "S.I." (Saturday Inspection) and after passing in review, we were dismissed. The first thing we did was stream to the board where the grades were posted as well as the latest class rankings. These were displayed in one of the sally ports, a different sally port for each class. Your rank in the class determined what section you were going to be in, which meant what instructors you were going to get. Eventually your class rank determined your branch of service and even the post where you would be assigned. We were re-ranked according to our academic averages at the end of specified periods of time, and these rankings could change but usually not drastically. I don't think there was any great fluctuation in our class ranking after the first year because as you went along you amassed a grade-point average and you'd have to do something pretty drastic to change that.

We were assigned seats in each classroom. There were rarely more than twelve individuals in a class but some had sixteen, and we were seated by academic rank. We were re-sectioned every six weeks. We had a battery of what were called "writs," which really were written examinations. At the end of that time our grades were averaged for the examination and our class standing was reassessed and we were re-sectioned. You might stay in the same section or you might go up or down. It depended on how well you had done.

During plebe year you had a course in mathematics every day, and we had English and first-year French. We also had drawing, actually basic architecture and learning how to draw figures. It was called "descriptive geometry." That was part of the course. We had a lot of military subjects as well. We had courses on the tactics and technique of infantry where we studied military formations and their uses, and we were given tactical problems to solve.

There were no lecture classes at West Point. Because of the small sections every cadet was called upon to recite every day. You could never get by without preparation. The few lectures we had were mostly incidental. Lectures were not the main thrust of the instruction. Instead we were required to go to the blackboard for foreign language classes, mathematics, and the sciences to solve problems or diagram sentences or scientific formulas. In English class we sometimes had to give extemporaneous speeches. On one occasion a classmate of mine, Fidelis Newcomb, who had a droll sense of humor, was called upon to give such a speech. He stood up and stated, "Sir, I believe that public speaking is a constipation of thought and a diarrhea of words." I think Fidelis had problems making a decent grade in that class afterwards.

I found that my academic work required my constant attention and much studying. I was never in any academic trouble. I had more trouble with French than any other subject. To a large degree learning a language depends on the ability of the instructor. Because I was down in the fifth or sixth section, way below the middle of the class, I got an instructor who took an interest in me and helped me out. His name was William Breckinridge and his family was from Lexington, Kentucky. With Bill Breckinridge's help I ended up in the third section. Under his tutelage I began to catch onto the language a little bit faster and somehow tried a little harder. Most of the classroom instructors were graduates of the Academy and officers in the Army.

Certain instructors at West Point, like instructors everywhere, by their enthusiasm and teaching ability would be able to motivate average students to do better. And then there were the instructors that, when you got them, boy, you were dead. They were just not stimulating instructors. I mention Bill Breckinridge not only because he was a Kentuckian but also because he was a good instructor.

Roscoe Wilson was a particularly good physics instructor and I enjoyed having him. He married a Louisville woman and retired there as a four-star general. During his military career he was involved in aircraft design for the Air Force. Most of the Academy instructors had been chosen because of their teaching abilities. By and large they were all good. The poor ones were weeded out very quickly. The instructors were evaluated by their superior officers and by the cadets.

History was a subject that I really enjoyed. A lot of it, of course, was military history. We studied military campaigns from ancient history down through World War I. We studied many of the great military leaders, their strategies and tactics, including Alexander the Great, Hannibal, Napoleon, Robert E. Lee and Stonewall Jackson, Ulysses S. Grant, and "Black Jack" Pershing. We spent a considerable amount of time studying the American Revolution, the Civil War, and World War I. Military history was the subject that I enjoyed more than any other.

The curriculum at West Point was pretty thorough. The classes were tough and extended most of us to our intellectual limit. Fulfilling the requirements didn't allow much time to pursue our own special interests. We had many examinations and quizzes that kept us on our toes. If you weren't prepared or if the professor didn't think you were prepared, you would get demerits, as well as a poor grade. Upperclassmen were allowed nine demerits a month. A plebe was allowed twelve demerits because we could acquire them more easily than an upperclassman. Upperclassmen were looking over our shoulders all the time and would sometimes "skin us" for a small infraction that normally would be overlooked.

If we accumulated more than the allotted demerits we had to "walk them off" around the quadrangle area, which meant walking back and forth outside the barracks at a hundred and twenty steps a minute carrying a rifle. You had to be dressed in full uniform and had to carry the rifle at a military angle just as if you were going to a drill or a parade. We were assessed one hour for each demerit over the allotted amount, and we "walked them off" during the time that we otherwise would have had free on Saturday afternoons. It really hurt.

The way we could acquire demerits beyond the classroom varied. Sometimes we wouldn't have our room straightened up properly or were late for a formation. You generally would be assessed demerits at the Saturday Inspections. If your breastplate wasn't polished or you had lint on your rifle or dust on your cartridge box, you could very easily acquire one, two, or three demerits, depending on the infraction.

The worst difficulty I got into was during Second Class year on a Saturday night. We had a friend who was a waiter in the mess hall, and we frequently asked him to acquire a few bottles of beer for us. He would take the beer down to the basement of the barracks and put it in the reservoir of the toilet where the water was real cold. On this particular night six or eight of us had gone to the cadet "hop." By the time we got back to the barracks the sentry had been dismissed, so we went down to the basement where the latrines were and each of us quietly had a bottle of beer and then went to bed.

Well, one of the upperclassmen had been in confinement for a "slug," which was a serious disciplinary punishment including demerits and confinement to quarters. He'd had twenty tours of walking the area and had been in confinement for a month. This particular night was his last night in confinement. He went down to the basement and got four or five of those beers and drank them in his room. During the night he got sick and vomited in the hall mop sink. Unfortunately, the officer in charge, a regular Army tactical officer, picked that night to inspect our barracks and noticed the odor. When he went into the upperclassman's room he found the cadet passed out and the beer bottles in the wastebasket.

That initiated an investigation. It's the only time that I felt that the honor system was abused. They called in the upperclassman and asked him where he got the beer. He was told that, according to the honor system, he would have to reveal his source for the beer. Under protest he told them. They then asked him to reveal who else was involved. By the time the interrogation was over, all of us had been brought into it. This was in April 1936. Many of us were cadet officers. We were all busted on the spot and had our rank taken down. Because we had not been caught red-handed, we were not given any demerits or any confinement. But the next year none of us were ranked as cadet officers. Practically all of us would have had rank of some type, Riggs Sullivan in particular, because he was the highest-ranking "yearling" in the company. He later became the company commander and ranked very high in the Cadet Corps.

I "walked the area" a few times as a cadet. It was a very boring thing to do. I walked the area mostly as a plebe, as most cadets do. I don't recall that I was required to walk the area as an upperclassman, although I may have once during my "yearling" year. I know that there have been several cadets who have graduated with perfect academic records, a straight 3.0 all the way through the Academy. There were some, I suppose, who were real "file-boners" as we called them. A "file-boner" is a cadet who is really striving to get to the top, and I suppose there were a number of "file-boners" who were able to escape without having to walk the area even once.

Our First Captain, Tom (Harry Thomas) Smith, got busted once because of his actions after one of the Army-Navy games. He was the number-one man in the Corps, a six-striper. The Corps was given free time in Philadelphia after the game, which we had won. When we formed up at the railroad station at midnight, Tom took his place at the head of the Corps of Cadets and called the battalions to attention and took the roll. Afterward, in executing his "about-face" to report to the Commandant of Cadets, who was the officer in charge supervising the formation, he tripped over his feet because he'd had a little too much to drink. Of course, the Commandant found out he'd been drinking and busted him right on the spot. One could get into deep trouble pretty quickly at West Point.

Athletics and physical training was also a part of our regular curriculum. Every cadet, particularly during plebe year, had to take boxing and wrestling. We also had to meet certain requirements in track. For example, we had to run a half-mile within a specified time, climb a rope that hung from the gymnasium ceiling using only our hands, do a specific number of chin-ups, and qualify in gymnastics. Cadets also had to learn to swim if they didn't already know how because you had to meet certain swimming requirements. We were taught fencing and even had to pass a dancing class. They taught us dance-floor etiquette and the dance steps. Most of the time your partner was another cadet, so that made it a little difficult to learn!

I was on the football team, which did not take dancing lessons with the other plebes of their company. The team took dancing lessons only on certain days. My dancing partner was Frankie Joe Kobes, who was part Native American and an end on the team. He was about six feet six inches tall and weighed about 240 pounds. He lived right down the hall from me in the barracks so we practiced our dance steps in the hall at night. With big Frankie Joe as my partner, the other cadets knew better than to make any disparaging remarks toward us as we whirled our way down the hallway. I'll tell you, leading Kobes around the dance floor was a little difficult, but we both managed to pass.

We always loved it when Army was victorious on the football field because that meant that the plebes could "fall out." For that whole weekend after an Army victory we could sit down and eat like the rest of the Corps and not have to sit at a brace. Football victories were eagerly awaited by plebes. I had played football in high school and also on the freshman team at Centre College. Naturally I was very interested in the game. Although my football abilities were not of the caliber that made the coaches salivate, I nevertheless tried out for the team and was fortunate enough to make the squad all four years.

I played end and loved playing defense. I think that's the reason I stayed on the Corps squad because I could play defensive end pretty well. I played strong end on the strong side of the line. My job was to dash across the line of scrimmage and take out the blockers. If the play was designed to come to my side of the field, the coaches didn't care whether I actually tackled the ball carrier or not so long as I wiped out the interference. It was the linebackers' job to tackle the ball carrier.

Football was a less sophisticated game back then. We wore a leather helmet with no facemask. I know I cut my face around the eyes two or three times and had other injuries that would have been prevented had we had facemasks. I suffered a serious shoulder separation in spring practice during my "yearling" year that took a little of the joy out of playing the rest of my career at the Academy because it never did heal completely. We didn't have cantilevered shoulder pads like they do now. Our shoulder pads were just leather with a little canvas backing. On this particular play I hit the blocking back, Wingfoot Jung, on the point of my shoulder. Wingfoot was a tough guy of Chinese descent who weighed about 175 pounds. I hit him a good lick to take him out of the play, and as soon as I hit the ground, terrific pain began shooting up my shoulder. I managed to get up and walk off the field, and the trainers took me right to the hospital. The only thing the doctor could do was put straps of adhesive tape down my chest and back to hold my shoulder down to keep it from popping in and out of place. They kept me in the hospital for ten days.

In those days players were "two-way" players. In other words you played both offense and defense. You couldn't just play one or the other. I hated playing offense, particularly when it came to blocking those big defensive tackles. If we had had a two-platoon system in those days like they have now, I might have ranked a little bit higher on the squad. I liked playing defense very much, particularly the type of smashing defense Army played in those days. I loved to charge across the line of scrimmage and just blast into the blockers or take out the ball carrier when I could. It was a rough-and-tumble style, not one where I floated back and waited for the play to develop and then reacted. It's amazing that we didn't get hurt a lot more than we did. Of course, back then unless you had a bone sticking out of your skin you didn't consider yourself injured.

Gar Davidson, the football coach, was from the old school. He was in the Army Engineers and was a fine person but not a great football coach. He certainly was inspirational as an officer and a gentleman, and fortunately he had some able assistants. One of them was Harvey Jablonski, who was the biggest chunk of man I ever saw. He was the line coach and quite a guy. Another assistant was Paul Burlingame, a character of the first order.

I used to play quite a bit on the "B Squad." "B Squad" didn't get to take many trips, but we did go up to Cornell to play their "B Squad" one afternoon as a reward for the beating we took practicing against our "A Squad" all week long. It was "B Squad's" job to run the upcoming opponent's plays against our "A Squad" in practice during the week so the "A Squad" could prepare for the Saturday game. For the game against Cornell's "B Squad," Burlingame was our coach. "Old B-game" was from Louisville and was a former All-American end, or at least he was a top end in the country on the Army football team in his day. On the bus to Cornell Paul got up and began reading the pre-game and post-game itinerary to us. "This paper says you're all supposed to be in bed by twelve o'clock." And then he kind of smirked and said, "But it doesn't say whom with!" Paul treated us like men, and we would have followed him to the gates of Hell if he had wanted to go. I remember during that game against the Cornell "B Squad," our own "A Squad" was playing Harvard or Yale. Whenever there was a break in the action we'd run over to the sideline and listen to the radio broadcast of the "A Squad" game. As I recall we beat the Cornell "B Squad" handily and had a wonderful time that evening under the less-than-watchful eye of Coach Burlingame.

I did get to play for the "A Squad" against Navy for about three minutes at Franklin Field in Philadelphia in 1938, which was quite an achievement as far as my football career was concerned. Army won that game too, but I can't remember anything about how I played. I was so excited I was in a fog! I never got to play against Notre Dame, but I did play against Harvard, Yale, Holy Cross, and some of the other lesser powers of college football during that era. Army, of course, was one of the national powerhouses.

Every cadet had to participate in a sport. If you were not on the Corps squad you had to play intramural sports. We called it "intramurder" sports. They had intramural football, basketball, track, swimming, and baseball. In the fall I played football and in the winter I was on the "B Squad" basketball team, too. I never made the "A Squad" in basketball but I was good enough to sit at the training table and enjoy the training table meals that were served to the athletes. In fact, I don't recall resting during the academic year. We would always seek every moment for rest that we could. Sometimes having a nap on Sunday afternoon was much more important than having a date. I recall becoming very upset with myself on several occasions for having asked a young woman to meet me in "The Boodlers" on a Sunday afternoon because it ate into my naptime. We used to call naptime "boning red comforter," the red comforter being one of the covers on your bed.

When you made your bed in the morning, the mattress was folded back and the sheets and covers were stacked on it very neatly. The purpose of folding the mattress back was to discourage the cadet from lying on it until after classes were over. The rooms were subject to inspection any time after breakfast until three o'clock in the afternoon. After three o'clock you could take your mattress down and grab a nap. But the red comforter, being on top of the folded mattress, could be spread on top of the springs and you could lie on it and take a nap. And if you were interrupted or word came that the tactical officer was in the barracks, the comforter could be folded up and put back very quickly.

Our spare time was very dear to us. Weekends were very, very important. Of course, we had assigned duties on weekends. There was a parade on Saturday morning. There was always a Saturday Inspection, usually conducted in ranks and followed by a parade review. Saturday Inspection was an inspection in ranks by the tactical officer and some of the senior cadet officers. They'd inspect the state of our uniform, the polish of our brass, the cleanliness of our rifle, the polish on our "tar bucket," which was the name that was given to the cadet shako that we wore, and the polish on our shoes.

Each cadet would be inspected individually, but the individual inspection usually took less than a minute unless they discovered something wrong. Most of the time they could find something wrong just to make sure you didn't get too cocky. One of the cadets accompanying the inspector wrote down the infraction and your name would be posted on the bulletin board along with the number of demerits that had been assessed. Inspections created a lot of anxiety because your disciplinary record was at stake. The more demerits you accumulated the lower your ranking in that phase of your training.

On Sunday afternoon, except during the winter months, there was a full dress parade. We also had chapel in the morning at which attendance was not optional. The rest of the time we had free, provided you didn't have to bone up on some academic work. It made us appreciate our freedom a lot more. Nowadays cadets are given all kinds of free time, and I think it's a mistake. They don't operate under nearly the same restrictions that we did. Our day was so planned that we had very little time for leisure, and when the academic year started we had almost no time for leisure except on weekends. We were restricted to the grounds of the Military Academy at all times unless we were on leave or on a trip with a Corps squad to a football game or some other activity of that sort. When you became a first classman you received six weekends free and were allowed to go anywhere you liked. At the time that I was there, that was the rule. The lower classes were restricted to the Academy grounds.

During our plebe year, for example, after class we were free to visit the library or go to the bookstore or "The Boodlers," but we had to go directly to our destination. We were not allowed to wander around or gaze at the sights at West Point and things of that nature. After our plebe year, of course, we were totally free in the afternoon and could visit other cadets or go swimming in the gym or at the cadet pool. We had a great deal of freedom after our first year. The first year was the only one that was terribly restrictive. Of course, I suppose every old graduate invariably says, "The Corps has gone to hell!" when we see how things have changed, but I think there's some truth to that.

We had a pretty busy day at the Academy. We got up at 5:30 in the morning and it was lights out at 10:00 in the evening, although under most circumstances we could get "late lights" that would give us legal lights in our room until 10:30. That made a pretty full day. When we were at summer camp we paraded every day, and then we generally paraded twice on weekends during the academic year. As a plebe it was absolute hell because we got ridden from the time we formed for the parade until we were dismissed. There was always an upperclassman or two telling us to brace or to straighten our rifle and to stare straight ahead.

It was a real chore getting ready for a review. Those white pants we wore were very stiffly starched, and when I took them out when they had just come back from the laundry I had to "break" them very carefully by making a very smooth triangle so they'd break at just the right places. Then to keep from wrinkling them I'd stand on a chair and slide them on. You'd never sit down in them unless you didn't intend to wear them on parade again. Then I'd have to put on all of the accouterments like the crossbelt, sash, and "tar bucket," and then we'd fall out and wait. I was in "M" Company and, of course, "A" Company went first, followed by all the others in alphabetical order. We'd have to wait for our company's turn and then we'd stand out there at attention on the parade ground for a full thirty minutes while they played various marches and went through all of the procedures of reporting.

Taking off the pants after the review was an ordeal, too. I'd sit stiff-legged in a chair and my roommate would pull them off so that they wouldn't get any wrinkles in them, and then I'd do the same for him. Parading was a chore and a bore, but every time we passed in review I still got a thrill. I think the reviews were much more striking in those days than they are now because the lines were just two deep. They were not mass formations like they have today, and our alignment had to be perfect.

Those were some of the activities that taught us to do things quickly, properly, and instilled discipline. The training was all designed for a purpose or it would not have been organized that way. All of us hated it. I've often said that I wouldn't go through another plebe year again. But on the other hand I wouldn't take anything for the experience because it taught me to make decisions quickly and to accept orders without question, especially in times of intense stress and confusion. In combat, if you're lucky enough to survive, you may have time to second-guess or ponder the wisdom of orders later. But in the heat of battle I found it was usually best to follow the orders I had been given as closely as possible.

Life As An Upperclassman

One of the first things that happened to a "yearling," or a sophomore, was that we were assigned certain duties in "Beast Barracks" for the incoming class of plebes. I was appointed a squad leader. This assignment allowed us to sharpen up the skills that we had learned as plebes. It also allowed us to heap upon the poor plebes the same indignities that we had received the preceding year. It taught us how to instruct, how to lead, and how to make decisions. That was how our "yearling" year began. The plebes came in 1 July, and for six weeks we directed all of our efforts into their training.

I believe that I was always fair and tolerant. By that time I understood the reasons for many of the things that plebes were forced to go through. Life at the Military Academy is very demanding, more so than at any public or private university in the country. You learn many things

Cadet William R. Buster (fifth from right). *"Our class, the class of 1939, was the largest class that had ever entered the Military Academy up to that time."*

at the Academy that help you survive in combat and in life. But certain types of individuals also abused "Beast Barracks." There were members of my class—and of every class—who had certain characteristics that caused the "beast" to come out in them and caused them to be unfair and overbearing. I tried to avoid that, and to the best of my knowledge I was not too hard on the plebes. Peer review was part of the program, too. The first classmen were the guardians of the discipline of the Corps, and they would straighten out anyone who got out of line as far as hazing went.

I had some great classmates. Ned Kirby Smith, a great-grandson of General Kirby Smith, roomed next door to me in the barracks, and Julian Ewell, a descendant of General Richard S. Ewell, was another classmate. My roommate for a couple of years was Thomas Jonathan Jackson Christian Jr., a great-grandson of Stonewall Jackson and one of the finest young men I ever knew. My roommates were the ones I became the closest to. One of them was Ed Hoopes from Pennsylvania. He was a very handsome guy, very smart, and had a great personality and was well liked by everyone.

Another roommate was Mart Bailey, an "Army brat" from Georgia. His father had been a colonel in the regular Army. Mart was an entirely different type of individual. He was particularly handsome and quite a ladies' man. Bailey and I were in the same division during the war. He was killed in France. George B. Pickett, the great-great-grandson of General George E. Pickett of Pickett's Charge fame, was also a classmate. One cadet whom we knew was marked for greatness was Andy Goodpaster. Andy chose the Corps of Engineers as his specialty, and after the war he was President Eisenhower's chief of staff and became the head of NATO.

Another interesting descendant of a famous individual who was at the Academy at the same time I was but not as a cadet was Simon Bolivar Buckner, the son of the Civil War general. He was a pretty tough old bird. He was a brigadier general and the Commandant of the Military Academy during my plebe year. General Douglas MacArthur visited the Military Academy while I was there. Omar Bradley was a major then and was on the battalion board that heard the disciplinary cases involving the cadets. He was also a member of the Tactical Department. There were many future World War II generals who were instructors or members of the Tactical Department while I was there.

The children of Army officers were known as "Army brats." They did quite well at the Academy simply because they knew the routine and many of them had been through special prep schools to prepare them. They came in with certain qualities that those of us country boys from the "sticks" didn't have. They had an understanding of Army life and had grown up on Army posts. Many of them knew one another. Except for Riggs Sullivan, I didn't know anybody there when I arrived. Of course, I made many friends, but the "Army brats" certainly had an early advantage.

General William D. Conner was also a superintendent of the Academy when I was there. He was known familiarly as "Dugout Willie," and I think he'd gotten that nickname during World War I. General Jay L. Benedict succeeded him. Lieutenant Colonel Charles W. Ryder was the Commandant of Cadets. I had to appear before Colonel Ryder once because of an incident that I got involved in. It's very rare that a cadet ever has to appear before the commandant but in this case it was an unusual circumstance. It was one of those things that begins innocently but turns bad before you know it.

One classmate had been promoted to cadet rank after he had been a buck private for a long time. His promotion called for what was known as "dragging," where we did humiliating things to people like dump water on them and drag them through the mud. It was not quite as bad as being tarred and feathered, but it was not too far removed. These things usually took place during summer camp. In this case it occurred during the winter, and so the hazing took place in the barracks. A number of us carried this classmate down to the basement where the showers and latrines were located. We threw him fully clothed into one of the bathtubs and then dumped a bottle of jet oil in the water. Jet oil was what we used to shine our shoes with, and it was a stronger chemical than we had counted on because it caused his more sensitive parts to become swollen. He had to be taken to the hospital and that, of course, is when the incident came to the attention of the authorities. There really wasn't any particular punishment for it because "dragging" was a common hazing practice, but the commandant thought the incident was serious enough to warrant his personal investigation.

One by one we were all summoned to the commandant's office, where he dressed us down for our indiscretion, poor judgment, and unbecoming conduct. When I was summoned to his office I felt sure that my days at the Academy and certainly my military career were over. Upon entering his office he proceeded to berate me up and down for my stupidity in participating in such a childish act and to insist that the Army was no place for pranksters. I was convinced that I was about to be drummed out of the Corps in disgrace. Imagine my surprise and vast relief when he concluded by saying, "None of this will go on your record. You are dismissed." I was just as relieved when our classmate was discharged from the hospital after a few days, completely recovered with no ill effects or hard feelings. We all learned our lesson that time, and I pretty much stayed out of trouble after that.

My second year I was made a cadet corporal, the only rank a third classman could attain, and with it I acquired one stripe on my sleeve. My third year I was made company supply sergeant, which was the fifth-ranking grade in the cadet company. The sergeants were all second classmen. I was busted from that because of the beer incident and ended the year with a clean sleeve. My stripe was restored the next year. Then they changed the way they ranked the cadets, and some of the top sergeant grades were retained by first classmen, so I ended up as the company supply sergeant.

As the company supply sergeant I was responsible for all of the equipment that was issued to the cadets in my company. I didn't actually have to issue it, but I maintained the records. I was also responsible for the company supply room and everything in there, such as the weapons, the officer sashes, all the footlockers, and the office supplies. I had the normal responsibilities that a supply sergeant has in the Army today.

Before graduation after my first year at the Academy, I moved over to the summer camp location. In those days the summer camp was just across the plain at the Fort Clinton parapet. There was a big area with tent frames supporting the traditional Army squad tents, and that was our home for the summer unless you were assigned to the "Beast Detail." If you were on "Beast Detail" you went over to the barracks and lived with your squad so that you were right next to them. Summer camp was where we received intensive military training. During the academic year there were two drill periods and two intramural athletic periods a week. Since I was on the football and basketball teams, I didn't participate in intramural athletics, but I still had to attend the military drill period.

During the summer we received concentrated instruction with various weapons. We spent two weeks on the rifle range, which involved firing on the range every day, and we spent an equal amount of time in the artillery stables learning how to hitch up the artillery horses to the caissons and cannon. We spent some time learning about the Army Air Corps, as it was called in those days. We learned how to operate coast artillery pieces. At that time, there were many coast artillery guns around the Academy that had been set up to guard the Hudson. During the summer training period we really learned the basics of military tactics and techniques.

During summer camp of our senior year we got to visit various posts around the country for more specialized training. For example, we went to Tobyhanna, Pennsylvania, for artillery training; Fort Benning, Georgia, for infantry training; Mitchell Field, New York, for an introduction to aviation; and Fort Monroe, Virginia, for coast artillery training. Visiting these different posts was not always a pleasant experience, but it was certainly interesting and varied enough that I never had an opportunity to get bored. It also gave me time to consider what specialty I might choose upon graduation.

It was while I was in transit between Fort Benning and Fort Monroe that I was notified that my uncle and surrogate father, Dr. Robards, had died. I was allowed to go home for the funeral. One of the reasons I eventually chose Fort Knox as my post was so that I could be closer to my Aunt Emma for as long as possible. Once she passed away I lost most of my connections with my hometown of Harrodsburg.

My senior year I volunteered to be associate editor of *The Howitzer*, the Military Academy's yearbook, to add to my extracurricular accomplishments. I got to work with a couple of other cadets, James B. Knapp, who was editor-in-chief, and Orin H. Rigley Jr., who acted as business manager. Jim Knapp was a file-boner of the first order but a nice guy, and Rigley could crunch numbers with the best of them. One of the perks for working on *The Howitzer* was that we were given time off from some other activities, and although it took a lot of hard work, I found it quite enjoyable and satisfying.

At the Academy we also had to take a rigorous equestrian training course. To graduate we had to pass what was called the "Monkey Drill," which was everything you've seen cowboys and stunt men doing in the movies. We had to rear mount over the horse's rear end and then swing from one side to the other in the saddle. Then they put the horse in the chute and we had to take two or three jumps with no reins and our feet out of the stirrups. This exercise was supposed to teach us balance, and it got pretty hairy sometimes. I remember that on one occasion I relaxed after making the third jump only to have my horse jump the gate at the end. Fortunately, I managed to stay on, but it was as close as I ever got to breaking my neck. A lot of cadets suffered displaced shoulders and broken arms and legs during equestrian training.

There was a detachment of cavalry and artillery stationed at West Point. In fact, when I attended the Military Academy there were over four hundred horses stabled there. The cavalry earned a bad reputation at West Point because of the attitude of the cavalry officers. I found out that, like most cavalrymen, they were pretty hard-nosed, hard boots, and they didn't make many friends among the cadets. They all seemed to have abrasive personalities. They put a lot of emphasis on the value of the horse over the value of the cadet. In our graduating class, the cavalry was the last branch that anyone chose for his specialty.

At the time I graduated, the cadet who ranked number one in the class had his choice of branch and post. Then the cadet ranked second had his choice and so on until all the vacancies in a particular branch or specialty were filled. The most popular branch was the Corps of Engineers. Most of the "brains" chose the Corps of Engineers. Some of the brightest would also choose the artillery. The glory-hounds or more ambitious types who wanted to make the Army a career chose the infantry because that was the branch which generally led to the top ranks. These cadets were "boning general" even as cadets because the combat branches were the ones where most of the generals eventually came from. Some cadets chose one of the technical branches if they had a particular interest in that area. In most classes the infantry was the last branch that most cadets chose because of its lack of glamour. Most of the "goats" in the class, which is what they called the cadets with the lowest academic ranking, were ranked into the infantry. Well, in our class the "goats" were ranked into the cavalry, so that is an indication that it was not too popular.

Of course, the cavalry in those days was still horse cavalry. A horse has to be cared for, and the really successful horsemen were the ones who put the welfare of the horses first. I remember we were on a cavalry hike one time and one of the horses slipped over the side of a trail and fell into a ravine. The instructor, an old cavalryman, went galloping up and asked, "Is the horse all right? Is the horse all right?" He didn't ask about the unfortunate cadet. Cadets were expendable as far as he was concerned, but horses weren't. At the time I graduated the only cavalry that wasn't strictly horse cavalry was the 7th Mechanized Cavalry Brigade stationed at Fort Knox. It was considered a bastard organization and something to be avoided by the true cavalryman.

Artillery was going to be my choice regardless of my class ranking. I liked horses but I didn't want to be in the cavalry. I liked the tactics and technique of artillery. It was more challenging to me than being in the infantry. To be in the artillery required more technical knowledge and technique. It was more complicated as far as the function and control of the weapon and required more coordinated effort. The infantry was more of an individual activity. The artillery was the branch that I wanted; it seemed to suit my nature and personality more. Besides, I didn't want to have to walk my way through my military career when I could ride.

I ranked high enough in the class that I really was never in any doubt that I would be able to get into the artillery. Our rank in the class not only helped determine our choice of branch, but it also determined where we would be stationed. At that time the Army had only 186,000 officers and men and the units were scattered over the country. Vacancies or new slots were allotted for each particular post and each particular unit, and the graduating class from the Academy filled those vacancies or slots in the officers' ranks. The man ranked number one in the class had his choice of wherever he wanted to go and whatever branch he wanted. The farther down your class ranking was, the more your opportunities diminished. I ranked 147th in my class of 456 and chose Fort Knox. I was lucky to get Fort Knox because up until then the Army was very selective as to who went to Fort Knox, and they didn't have any second lieutenants there. Apparently, the plan to increase the size of the Army was in the works, so they allowed four second lieutenants to go there, and I was one of them.

As I recall we started out with 750 people in my class at West Point. About two hundred were eliminated by Christmastime our plebe year. Another eighty or so were eliminated by the end of the academic year in the spring. After plebe year was over we lost only a handful more, and 456 of us graduated. That was fairly normal for any entering class. The greatest attrition occurred before the first Christmas, and then in the spring a few more left. From then on most of the rest made it. Academics, particularly mathematics and English, was the main reason for the high attrition rate. A few were eliminated because of disciplinary reasons and various and sundry other things. Of course, each cadet who left had an opportunity to retake the examination and come back the following year. That's how George Patton made it. It took him five years. He was dismissed and had to come back and be re-examined. There was one guy like that in my class, Edward MacDonald Serrem. We called him "Father" Serrem because he was about three or four years older than the rest of us and had come back twice. I think he graduated with my class. He had determination and he made it.

At our graduation ceremony President Franklin D. Roosevelt delivered the commencement speech. He awarded us our diplomas and shook hands with each one of us. I couldn't tell you a word he said during his address because I was so excited I didn't listen very intently.

Out of the 456 young men in the graduating class of 1939, over 10 percent were killed during World War II. The war was particularly hard on lieutenants and captains, and by the time the United States entered the war in 1941 most of my classmates were first lieutenants or captains. So many were killed because they were usually in command positions close to the front lines or were flying combat missions with the Army Air Corps. The leadership role for which we had been trained put us into positions that required our technical expertise and know-how and, unfortunately, put many of us in harm's way.

That was my experience at the United States Military Academy. Life at "Hell on the Hudson" was not always fun, but it taught me orderliness, discipline, and gave me more self-confidence. It gave me a firm foundation upon which to build my military career, and I'll be forever grateful for having had the opportunity.

2d Lt. Buster commanding Battery B, 21st Field Artillery, on review at Fort Knox, 1940.

CHAPTER THREE: THE PREWAR ARMY

Following World War I, the U.S. Army had badly neglected armored warfare tactics. The Army was populated by many hide-bound traditionalists who did not foresee the enormous potential of armored units. Those visionaries in the Army who did recognize this potential were paralyzed by Congressional budget restraints that did not encourage the military to develop or purchase the latest in military hardware. When Nazi Germany unleashed its armored units during the blitzkreig of the Low Countries and France in 1940, the Roosevelt administration awakened to the obsolescence of the U.S. military forces and the Army quickly established armored divisions at Fort Knox, Kentucky, and Fort Benning, Georgia.

After spending a short time at Fort Knox with the 7th Mechanized Cavalry Brigade, William Buster was eventually assigned to the newly organized 2nd Armored Division stationed at Fort Benning. Shortly thereafter, Congress federalized the National Guard and implemented the Selective Service system, actions which sent thousands of men pouring into army bases as the military began a rapid buildup. Equipped with obsolete weapons, including World War I-vintage 75mm artillery pieces and tanks that were no match for the German panzers, Buster and his peers hastily organized new units and trained thousands of soldiers.

The Japanese surprise attack on Pearl Harbor on 7 December 1941 galvanized a nation and an army. During the next two years the 2nd Armored Division participated in a series of maneuvers in Tennessee, Louisiana, and the Carolinas that, for the first time, tested the tactical and logistical capabilities of armored units. George S. Patton, a long-time proponent of armored warfare, rose to prominence during this period. His unorthodox tactics, hands-on leadership, and flamboyance propelled him into the limelight of a nation desperate for a military hero. Other more junior officers, like William Buster, learned armored warfare tactics by the seat of their pants and gained valuable experience. It was during these maneuvers that the 2nd Armored Division received its nickname as the "Hell On Wheels" Division. In 1942, Buster was ordered to Fort Knox to put down in writing the knowledge he had gained in the field. He helped write the basic field manual for the employment of armored field artillery that the army utilized for the remainder of the war.

In 1942, Buster's unit, the 92nd Armored Field Artillery Battalion, was sent to Fort Bragg, North Carolina, for invasion training. Buster himself was sent to Quartermaster School in Norfolk, Virginia, to learn the art of combat loading transport and supply ships. He learned his job so well that he was featured in a War Department training film. The film was used by all the services, including the Marine Corps.

Reporting For Duty

My scheduled date for reporting to my first post was 12 September 1939. In the meantime I had three glorious months to play.

My aunt (and foster mother), Emma Robards, and my oldest brother, Nimrod, along with several friends came up for graduation and delivered my new car, which was a Pontiac convertible that cost almost $1,200 brand-new. Following the graduation ceremonies my family left for home and I began my leave. After a few days on Long Island visiting my then-OAO (One And Only) Bobbie Eden, who had been too ill to attend June Week, I departed for Washington to spend several days with Jack Christian, my roommate during our yearling year. Our second year Jack was promoted to the Regimental Staff and went to live in the 8 1/2 Division with the rest of the cadet brass. Jack was not only an outstanding student as well as a model cadet in looks and deportment, but a fascinating friend and companion. He was an Army brat whose father was serving in Washington with the War Department.

While in Washington I learned something about politics, too. None of the Army and Navy personnel who were stationed in Washington were allowed to wear their uniforms on duty, even in the War and Navy Departments. Isolationism in the U.S. had gained such influence that the Armed Forces were required to minimize their presence even in our nation's capital by appearing in public only in civilian attire. I guess the administration did not want to antagonize the strong "America First" lobby and endanger the military-aid programs that were so desperately needed by Great Britain.

Jack's dad, Lieutenant Colonel Thomas Jonathan Jackson Christian, was a delightful character. He showed us the sights in Washington including the wharf area where I was introduced to the joys of delicious seafood dishes, which were rare in Kentucky and non-existent at West Point. I had been there a couple of times before but didn't have the time or the proper guide to enjoy the Washington area.

After seeing the sights in Washington, I drove Jack to Kentucky to visit my family and to introduce him to the Bluegrass State. After a few pleasant days at home we departed for Atlanta, where we met up with two other classmates, Joe Kingsley and my ex-roommate at West Point, Ed Hoopes. Joe was a great friend even though he was in another part of the Corps. After an enjoyable visit with Joe's sister in Atlanta, we took off for Miami Beach, where Joe's family had a cottage. We had a ball. Finally I bid farewell to my friends and drove back to Kentucky alone for my last summer of fun. I put over 30,000 miles on my new Pontiac by the time I reported for duty at Fort Knox.

At Fort Knox I found that the prewar Army was like a country club. It was more of a social organization than a combat force even at a busy post where new tactical principles were being introduced. There was a lot of emphasis on spit and polish. We were given Wednesdays and Saturday afternoons off and things moved at a relaxed pace. We drilled in the morning, had light duties in the afternoon, and knocked off at four o'clock. The units of the 7th Mechanized Cavalry Brigade at Fort Knox were all under-strength even though they were considered a priority outfit. For example, the companies in the artillery units that would ordinarily have four or five officers were lucky if they had one, and that rarely was a captain. The officer in charge was usually a first lieutenant because the captains were relegated to staff duty or were assigned to some special project.

We had some capable officers, but then we had some who had gone to seed. Up until the time I came in, promotion was almost at a standstill. The number of vacancies for each grade was established by the War Department, and until somebody retired or died no one was promoted. I knew some first lieutenants who were teaching at West Point who had been second "looies" for thirteen years or longer before being promoted. There were some captains with twenty-five years of service teaching there. Some majors with thirty years' service retired because they had no chance for promotion. The lieutenant colonels who served at the Academy were veterans of long service. Even so they were far ahead of their contemporaries.

This static situation, which occurred in the Army just after World War I, created a martinet type of officer, one who was very ambitious yet frustrated. General George S. Patton was an example of that type of officer. He was always very aggressive and at times could be very unreasonable. But there also were others who were complete gentlemen, knew what they were doing, went about it quietly, and got the job done just as effectively.

I found that the soldiers themselves were well trained and knew their job because most of them had been in the Army for a number of years. Most of the enlisted men were there because during the Depression there wasn't anything else for them to do. To a lot of them the Army was a job. Twenty-one dollars a month was not much income, but at least they didn't have to worry about being fed and clothed. I also had my problem soldiers—some payday drunks—and I had to learn how to deal with them. As I came to know them better I had to decide whether the situation was something I could deal with myself or if it needed to be sent up the chain of command. It didn't take me long to know the difference. But I later found out that some of those who gave me the most disciplinary trouble were often times the best soldiers in combat and were the ones I could really count on.

Before I reported to Fort Knox I had been told at the Academy a little about what to expect. The officers at West Point tried to give us a little practical advice. They taught us the courtesies and customs of the service and gave us tips on how to navigate through polite society. For example, we were told that when making formal visits it was polite to leave a calling card. It was like signing a guest register. Things were much more formal in those days than they are now. There were a number of things that the officers made us aware of so that when we reported to our first post we would know what to do and wouldn't embarrass ourselves.

I had been to Fort Knox once before for a preliminary physical prior to reporting for active duty in September 1939, but I really hadn't had time to look around much. A classmate of mine, Sterling R. Johnson, and I were the only ones who were assigned there out of the Class of '39. Johnson selected Fort Knox because he was engaged to a girl who lived in nearby Louisville.

Fort Knox itself in 1939 consisted of a series of brick buildings positioned around the parade ground in front of Post Headquarters. There was a tent area with concrete floors and metal tent frames, and World War I tarpaper shacks scattered over the whole compound that were used in the summer by the National Guard. The Army didn't have Reserve units as such in those days. The Officer Reserve Corps was all they had. The 1st Cavalry and the 13th Cavalry were stationed at Fort Knox and they later built brick barracks, which still exist. But the rest of Fort Knox was World War I cantonment and really too small for a large concentration of troops.

The outfit Johnson and I were assigned to was the 7th Mechanized Cavalry Brigade, a new organization and a very elite and highly trained group. It was a great experience for me, although I initially had misgivings about being assigned to that unit because it was not a traditional artillery unit. I knew that the Army was not completely committed to the concept of armor at that time. The 7th Mechanized Cavalry Brigade was the only armored unit of any size in the whole Army. There had been a lot of discussion among some of the young majors in the cavalry and the infantry during the 1930s that a highly mobile armored force was necessary, and the mechanized unit at Fort Knox was entirely experimental. George Patton, in particular, I'm sure, had something to do with the brigade's formation, and the people at the Infantry School at Fort Benning saw the need for it, too. They had some tank companies there that worked with the infantry in the development of tactics. It was through their activities and, in some cases, personal friendship with the Chief of Staff that they were able to get a unit like the 7th Mechanized Cavalry Brigade created.

Prior to our entry into the war the concept of innovation was largely foreign to the old Army commanders. For example, the chief of cavalry thought that the formation of armored units was outlandish and that they should be abolished or ignored. After the 2nd Armored Division was organized at Fort Benning in 1940, he did not willingly send any cavalry officers to command its cavalry elements. It was several months after the 1st and 2nd Armored Divisions were organized before any cavalry officers were ordered to the divisions. The Army was populated by a lot of hard-headed old birds back in those days who stubbornly held onto their antiquated beliefs which put us at a temporary disadvantage against the enemy.

The 7th Mechanized Brigade was equipped with the latest material in the Army's inventory, but it certainly was anything but modern compared to the type of equipment the Germans were unleashing in Europe. The heaviest armament that the 7th Brigade had was the light tank. It had no medium tanks. In fact, there was only one medium tank company, consisting of nineteen tanks, in the whole Army. The light tanks we had at Fort Knox had a puny 37mm gun, which would hardly punch a hole in a Model T Ford. The Army, just prior to World War II, had not been provided with the most modern equipment. I reported for duty just as the Army was given the go-ahead to begin gearing up and modernizing. Over the next several years I participated in the full integration of armor into the Army's tactics. My arrival at Fort Knox at that particular time had a definite impact on my military career. The Army's new emphasis on the use of armor was the reason that I was eventually assigned to the 2nd Armored Division at Fort Benning, Georgia. My rank rose from that of a second lieutenant to a lieutenant colonel during the course of the buildup and prosecution of the war.

In September 1939 the 7th Mechanized Cavalry Brigade numbered about 3,500 men. There were not many other troops at Fort Knox at that time. Soon after I reported for duty the strength of the post began increasing rapidly, but no provision had been made for housing the new troops. New buildings weren't constructed for a couple of years. The old buildings were, of course, used to quarter the troops, and tents were used in the summertime. The lack of adequate permanent housing restricted the number of troops that could be stationed there year-round. That's one reason the Army built most of the new training facilities in the South. When I eventually went to Fort Benning we lived in tents for two winters, and even though it got pretty cool down there in the wintertime it was a lot better than it would have been in a tent at Fort Knox. I remember when I was at Fort Knox we had a visit from the Inspector General in mid-January 1940. The morning of the scheduled inspection the temperature was nineteen degrees below zero. We were inspected outdoors, including vehicles and guns. Needless to say, it was a very short inspection and, fortunately, we weren't too closely scrutinized.

When I reported for duty in September 1939, I reported directly to my regiment. In those days that was the proper reporting procedure. Back then young officers had to wait several years before they were sent to their branch schools. In my case it was the Artillery School at Fort Sill, Oklahoma. Today they immediately send you to Artillery School or to the branch school you choose upon graduation. It's only after you complete that training that you are sent to your post. But in those days I was sent to my post first, and in many ways I think it had certain advantages. I had had no intensive artillery training before I reported to Fort Knox and so I had to learn a lot of basic things. This was useful to me because these were things I knew I needed to know and so I paid more attention. I acquired the knowledge of how to do things without knowing why they were done that way. I think sometimes that it's better to be exposed to something and to learn the mechanics of it first, and then be sent to school to find out why it's done that way. That way you really remember and you're able to learn a lot quicker. At least that was my experience.

When I reported to my regiment it was away on maneuvers at Pine Camp, New York. The only officer on duty at the Regimental Command Post was a lieutenant I had known at West Point. The 7th Mechanized Cavalry Brigade consisted of the 1st Regiment and the 13th Regiment of Cavalry. In addition to the two regiments of armor, it had a regiment of artillery—the one to which I was assigned—and various support units. The 68th Field Artillery was a strange sort of regiment. It had no battalions. It was a regiment of four batteries. It had sixteen guns, which at that time were towed 75mm howitzers. These were pack howitzers mounted on wheels. They did not have a great deal of firepower. We also did not have half-tracks. The howitzers were drawn by scout cars.

When the regiment returned from Pine Camp, I was assigned to "B" Battery. The Battery Commander, Louis Freidersdorf, was the only officer in "B" Battery. Captain Freidersdorf immediately turned me over to the first sergeant for guidance and instruction. It was he who taught me how to "lay a battery" with an aiming circle, which was a transit with a compass. The deviation of the direction of fire from compass north had to be set and an aiming stake erected for each artillery piece so that they knew where the center of their sector of fire was. That was called "laying a battery." With the first sergeant's help I also directed the routine training for the enlisted people in the battery and in the battalion. I learned a great deal just by watching the experienced noncommissioned officers.

The morale in the 7th Mechanized Cavalry Brigade was tops. Our men fought at the drop of a hat. They were the elite and they knew it. It was something of which every one of the soldiers was very proud. The brigade was made up of experienced people. We were a show and demonstration outfit so the soldiers were some of the best in the Army. Unfortunately, I didn't stay with this unit very long. Sterling Johnson and I were transferred to the 5th Infantry Division, a brand-new unit being activated at Fort Knox, on 15 October 1939. Within the 5th Infantry Division a new artillery regiment was activated that was designated the 21st Field Artillery Regiment, and that's where I was sent. I guess they picked out several people whom they thought they could spare from the 7th Mechanized Cavalry Brigade, and not surprisingly Johnson and I, being the newest and rawest, were the ones who were sent to this new organization.

When I reported to the 21st Field Artillery Regiment I found that there were only five officers in my whole battalion, which is a big unit. Others were to come. I reported in to Major Douglas Crane, a very crusty character I had met socially. We had become friendly because we were both bachelors and lived across the hall from each other in the Bachelor's Officers Quarters. The BOQ was the old central mess hall and was right across from the Brick Club. When I had first reported to Fort Knox in September it was hot as hell and the only room available at the BOQ was one upstairs. Even with a fan on, it would be two or three o'clock in the morning before I could get to sleep. By the time Major Crane arrived and moved in I had managed to get a room on the first floor and that was when I lived across from him. Those quarters were much more bearable.

When I reported to him on 15 October I expected a friendly reception. Instead you would never have known that he'd ever seen me before because he said, "Buster, am I glad to see you! You're commanding 'A' Battery *and* 'B' Battery, you're the regimental adjutant, you're T.J.A.— Temporary Judge Advocate—of a Special Court, and we want a football team on the field next Saturday." So I immediately acquired five jobs during the first two minutes of my assignment to my new outfit. It was quite an experience.

I reported to "A" Battery and found that all I had were thirteen enlisted men, all of whom were sergeants except for one corporal. They all had anywhere from eight to eighteen years of service and came from the field artillery at Fort Myers, Virginia. This was one of those red-hot demonstration battalions that did all of the things for the VIPs in the War Department. Here I was, a green second lieutenant, and I was supposed to tell these old soldiers not only what to do but how to do it.

When I went to "B" Battery I found the same situation, only this group was from the 6th Field Artillery at Fort Hoyle. Some of them wore decorations from World War I. This was my cadre. However, I didn't have time to feel insecure. I never stopped to worry about my inexperience. A certain amount of confidence was instilled in me when I was at West Point that carried over and I felt that I could cope with most anything, or at least give it one hell of a try. Major Crane had told me that one of my responsibilities was to hold a NCO school for these old noncoms so that they would learn their responsibilities and duties. Well, I held the school for the NCOs, but you can imagine who learned the most. After I had established good rapport with them, those old sergeants took me in hand and taught me a lot. Because of that, I had no major problems even though I was the rawest shave-tail you can imagine. They had seen shave-tails come and go before, so they knew what to expect.

Initially our regiment was nowhere near combat-ready. We were supposed to be a 155mm-artillery outfit but we had no 155mm guns. Almost no one in the battalion save the old major had ever seen a 155mm artillery piece. The most common artillery weapon used by the Army at that time was the 75mm cannon. A lot of the Army was armed with French 75mms. The American 75mm gun was really inferior to the French version. We finally found a 155mm-GPF artillery piece from World War I on some town's courthouse lawn, which we "appropriated" and moved to the training area at Fort Knox. Even though all of the moveable parts were rusted together and it was incapable of actually being fired, we were able to take a pointer and point out what the mechanisms were and what they were supposed to do. We also practiced the cannoneer's drill and explained what each crewman was supposed to do. The men would then pretend they were actually firing the weapon.

The equipment shortage lasted for several months after the formation of the 21st Field Artillery Regiment. We simply could not get all of the equipment we needed because there were other new units being formed around the country and the existing stockpiles had to be spread out until American industry could catch up with the demand. However, that didn't always mean that we went without. There were certain enlisted people and officers who were known as "scroungers," and they could come up with most anything. I'm sure it was not always legal, and many times it was not according to regulations, but nevertheless they got the job done.

Sergeant Brinley was the supply sergeant for "B" Battery of the 21st Field Artillery when I was the battery commander. He had received the Silver Star in World War I but was a payday drunk. He would work his way up to sergeant and then would get in trouble and get busted down to private again. Many times we would need something and there would be no way to get it through official channels. But the next day or week I would find that somehow or other we had "procured" whatever it was that was needed. One day I took Sergeant Brinley aside and said, "Brinley, where did you get this?" He screwed up his face and squinted at me and said, "Lieutenant, don't ever ask me where I get anything!" He was trying to tell me that if I asked too many questions I might not like the answers I received. So I took the hint and quit asking.

The new troops we received in late 1939 and early 1940 were all raw recruits, and we had to take them and clothe them and train them from scratch. There were no training units then. Each unit received its quota of troops directly from the induction centers and then had to train them. The Army now began to call many Reserve officers to active duty. Early in 1940 we began to receive them. Most of them were products of college ROTC programs and were relatively inexperienced. As soon as these officers arrived the administrative duties were spread out. I finally ended up as the second in command of one battery instead of commanding two batteries.

I also had other responsibilities. I was appointed the battery's executive officer, and my responsibilities were to supervise the training of the troops in the battery. I was also assigned to be T.J.A. of the Special Court—prosecutor for a court martial—and was responsible for setting up the court, summoning all witnesses, and instructing the officers that sat on the court on procedure. Fortunately, a full year's course in military law was required at West Point. We went into all the ramifications of the law. I had read McKelvey and had studied criminal law. I also had had training on the operation of courts martial and had participated in moot courts so I had some background in military justice. In most military courts the T.J.A. and defense counsel usually came from the ranks of the Reserve officers who were attorneys in civilian life. Fortunately, most of the cases I was involved in as T.J.A. were run-of-the-mill cases of the drunkenness or AWOL variety and were not of a serious nature.

As a second lieutenant I made $125 dollars a month, which I found did not go very far. In fact, I had to take my monthly bills and decide which ones I had to pay immediately and which ones could wait. I was required to eat at the Officers' Mess and that cost me $30 a month. Then I had $95 left to pay for all the other expenses I had accumulated over the month. For example, one of the first things I had to do when I arrived at Fort Knox was buy a white dress uniform. I had all the other kinds but I didn't have a white one, which was required for social affairs in the South. So my first paycheck was pretty much spent before I had been there a week.

As executive officer of the battery I was responsible for many things. For example, it was my responsibility to be up before reveille and to take the reports in the battery area. After reveille I would outline the training schedule for the day, which I had drawn up the previous evening. The men would be put through calisthenics before breakfast and then after breakfast had close-order drill, which was emphasized a great deal more in those days than it is now. Then the men would be broken up into section groups, and the different NCOs would take their sections and instruct them in the finer points of the things they were supposed to do. At the battery level we would spend a lot of time practicing what we called the "cannoneer's hop," which meant getting the cannoneers accustomed to their individual duties and responsibilities and drilling them just like a football team running plays. This usually took up most of the morning.

In the afternoon we would put the individual sections together and teach them cooperation and coordination so that the entire battery became a cohesive unit. Of course, many times we'd schedule a field exercise where the battery would be taken out into the field and given a problem to solve. As time went on we spent most of our time in the field executing field maneuvers intended to sharpen our skills.

During the winter of 1940 we were sent to Fort McClellan, Alabama, to conduct basic maneuvers. From Fort McClellan we went to Fort Benning and participated in some larger-scale maneuvers. It was at Fort Benning that we began receiving newer equipment. I recall that four days before we were to leave Fort Benning for the first Louisiana maneuvers we were issued four-ton trucks to move the 155mm artillery pieces, which the Alabama National Guard had loaned us. None of our soldiers had ever seen a four-ton truck before. They were enormous and were specially designed. We had only four days to orient ourselves on the maintenance and operation of those vehicles. We found that they had not even been greased properly at the factories. All the wheels had to be removed and the grease seals checked so that we would be able to depart for Louisiana on time.

During the first Louisiana maneuvers the 21st Field Artillery Regiment was an experimental unit. Our "antitank weapons" were wooden posts that we mounted on sawhorses. We put them into position and pointed them down the roads or across fields as if they were real weapons. We taught the soldiers what the mission of our unit was by utilizing the crude "weapons" that we had. But we were never discouraged by the lack of equipment. We always felt the shortage was just temporary and that we would eventually be supplied with top-of-the-line material. We had all the confidence in the world that the government was going to provide us with whatever we needed before we would be required to go into combat.

There is no doubt that the initial buildup of the Army actually weakened our combat effectiveness. During that time the experienced troops were divided up among the new units and became the cadre responsible for training the new people. It was a time when young officers like myself were forced to learn things in a hurry, and it sharpened the skills of the more experienced people as well.

The 2nd Armored Division

During the initial buildup of the Army I kept being transferred to different units. I participated in the first Louisiana maneuvers with the 21st Field Artillery Regiment of the 5th Infantry Division. We had scarcely returned to Fort Knox from those exercises when I was ordered to Fort Benning, Georgia, to the hitherto unheard of 2nd Armored Division that was being activated there. The new division was to be activated on 15 July 1940. I joined it on 1 July, so I was with it two weeks before it was officially activated. I had a set of transfer orders that had information on them that the provisional division headquarters hadn't even seen, so they were very interested in my orders when I arrived. I would remain in the 2nd Armored Division until I returned to the United States after the war.

I was a second lieutenant when I reported to Fort Benning. I had just a little under one year's service at that time. In September I was made a first lieutenant, but it was a temporary rank and did not include an increase in pay. At Fort Benning I was sent to the 14th Field Artillery Regiment, which had been created from half of the old 68th Field Artillery Regiment that I'd served with briefly at Fort Knox. So I had come home, so to speak, because I knew most of the officers and men. I think that was one of the reasons I was transferred from an infantry division artillery unit into an armored division artillery unit. I had previous experience in an armored artillery unit, even though my "experience" consisted of only one month.

On 27 August 1940 Congress passed a joint resolution that federalized the National Guard. On 16 September the Burke-Wadsworth Act was passed, by just one vote, authorizing the implementation of the Selective Service System, or the draft. These actions by Congress were part of the initial effort to build up the Army to full peacetime strength. The 2nd Armored Division began receiving the first "selectees" by the end of October. Fort Benning was the Infantry School of the Army and this initial buildup had an immediate impact on the camp. Newly created units were encamped all over the reservation. The headquarters and some of the initial elements of the 2nd Armored, for example, started out in an area called the "Frying Pan," which was an accurate description of the place due to the heat and humidity. Our camp was on the main post not very far from the post headquarters. It consisted of buildings that were leftovers from World War I. Some of the troops were put in these old barracks, others were put in pyramidal tents that were pitched in the area. For well over a year I lived in a pyramidal tent. The only break that officers got was that each officer got a pyramidal tent of his own.

The 14th Field Artillery Regiment later was sent out to what was known as the "Harmony Church" area that was about fifteen miles outside of Fort Benning. Eventually new barracks were constructed at a place called "Sand Hill," which got its name from a railroad siding by that name. At that time I was assigned a ten-by-ten room in a barracks building. It was very important that the headquarters for an armored division be located near a railroad because the amount of supplies and equipment that continuously arrived was enormous. Without a railroad nearby it would have been a logistical nightmare.

U.S. Army light tank on maneuvers in Louisiana, 1941.

The first Jeeps I ever saw came in a long convoy through the front gate at Fort Benning. That was the first time any of us had ever seen a Jeep. Actually, the name was derived from the first vehicle that came out called a command and reconnaissance car, or "C & R" car. The official Army name for it was GP, which meant "General Purpose." Well, the soldiers quickly shortened that to "Jeep." It was a high-wheeled, three-quarter-ton vehicle and a very clumsy thing. Later on when the smaller one-quarter-ton vehicle was produced we called them "Peeps" in the Armored. We were the first ones to get them. The rest of the Army called them "Jeeps" just like they did the old "C & R" car.

At Fort Benning we also got that strange-looking tank that had the cannon mounted on the side which was called the "General Grant." It mounted a 75mm gun that only had a seventeen-degree traverse. That tank was no match for a German panzer whose turret could swing all the way around. After firing a shot, this poor thing had to back up to get another bearing in order to fire again if its target had moved at all. We knew at the time that it wouldn't work and would be of limited value, but it was better than anything we'd had up until then. In the 14th Field Artillery Regiment we trained with several different types of weapons, all 75mm. Most of them were World War I-vintage French 75mms or the modified French 75mm with a panoramic sight. We had an M-283 antitank gun that was the sorriest antitank weapon that I have ever seen. Then we began to get newer adaptations of the old French 75mm, and finally they came out with the 105mm howitzers.

The 105mm howitzers we received were initially mounted on half-tracks. Later on they were mounted on a full-tracked vehicle officially called an M-7. We called it the "Priest" because it had a ring-mounted .50 caliber machine gun on the right front that looked like a pulpit. It had no overhead armor and the armor around the gun crew was like that on the half-track, but it was sufficient to protect you from small arms and the "splash" of artillery shells landing in the area. They could not survive direct fire from a heavy machine gun let alone a light antitank weapon like a panzerfaust. We went from no equipment to very inadequate equipment to borrowed equipment to better equipment to the self-propelled artillery, the M-7 "Priest" that we went to war with.

When I joined the 14th Field Artillery Regiment I was only there a few days before I was ordered to special duty with the 82nd Reconnaissance Squadron, as it was called then, that was being organized. It was supposed to be a cavalry outfit. The reason that an artilleryman was sent to help organize it was because the chief of cavalry was still very reluctant to assign any cavalry officers to what he considered

Courtesy U.S. Signal Corps

A 105mm howitzer carriage M-7. "We called it the 'Priest' because it had a ring-mounted .50 caliber machine gun on the right front that looked like a pulpit."

a bastard organization like an armored-car outfit. In his opinion, if it didn't have four legs and stirrups it couldn't be cavalry. So the assignment of genuine cavalrymen to the 2nd Armored Division was very slow in coming. As it turned out, my assignment there was to organize two troops of armored cavalry. This particular assignment was sort of déjà vu for me because it mimicked what I had done in the early days of the activation of the 21st Field Artillery Regiment at Fort Knox. I was with the 82nd Reconnaissance Squadron, under the command of an irascible old major by the name of I.D. White, for about a month or six weeks until they got enough assigned officers to take over. I later got to serve again under I.D. White in Europe. I had hardly gotten back to the 14th Field Artillery Regiment when I was ordered to the 78th Field Artillery Battalion that was just being activated.

When I reported to the 78th's headquarters there was no one there but the battalion commander. I asked him where everyone was. "Lieutenant, when you walked in here the strength of this battalion just doubled. As of this moment we're it." He and I continued to be the only officers in the battalion for a period of two or three weeks. The battalion commander was Lieutenant Colonel Thomas T. Handy, who later became deputy chief of operations under General Dwight D. Eisenhower. After the war when Ike became president, he brought Tom Handy in as one of his deputies. Colonel Handy was one of the finest people I have ever known, the salt of the earth. He was a quiet, soft-spoken Virginian, and at meals he would tell me about his Mexican border and World War I experiences. For those two or three weeks Colonel Handy was like a father to me, and it was a real pleasure to serve under him.

The most challenging task I had in organizing these new units was to draw all of the clothing needed for the draftees that were being added. I would drive over to the reception center in my own car—no Army transport had been assigned—to find out which soldiers were going to be sent to my unit the next day. Most of these kids were from Alabama, Georgia, Tennessee, Kentucky, and Florida, and a great many of them would literally arrive with only the clothes they were wearing. Some of them didn't even have socks on! So I would get their clothing and shoe size and go over to the quartermaster and draw clothing for them so that they had something to wear once they were turned over to us.

A very capable cadre of enlisted men had been assigned from regular Army units to process the new arrivals. The reception centers were well organized but there just weren't enough officers to go around. I was not the only officer who was temporarily transferred for this kind of duty. Many of my associates were utilized in the same manner. However, I don't think any were transferred as often as I was during this initial buildup of the Army.

After Colonel Handy received some additional officers from other regular Army units as well as the Reserves, I returned to the 14th Field Artillery Regiment. I suppose we were the best-equipped organization in the 2nd Armored Division at the time because the old 68th Field Artillery Regiment at Fort Knox had been split down the middle, so that the units that were sent to Fort Benning were completely operational. It was only necessary for it to expand from within. By the end of 1940 we had our full complement of officers and men. From then on the soldiers we received were not raw recruits but had already been through basic training. When we first began the buildup we had to train them from scratch, from absolutely cold civilians to competent soldiers. But by 1941 training centers or boot camps had been established around the country, and the men we got from that point on came to us with basic soldiering skills.

These men were all young, of course. Most were high-school graduates, though some had had very little schooling. All of them passed the basic Army test but some were not the most brilliant in the world. But I always believed that it would be detrimental to have a unit made up of intellectuals anyway. You always need some people whose minds are not very sharp to do some of the mundane tasks that have to be done. The real intelligent guys were not satisfied to do some of the repetitive kinds of tasks like digging latrines or doing KP duty. They would do it for a short period but would get bored quickly and wouldn't function well in those capacities in the long run. In any unit you had to have some privates who could do some tasks without becoming overly bored or detached.

1941

When I finally was sent to Artillery School at Fort Sill, Oklahoma, in January 1941, I was already a pretty experienced artilleryman. There were a lot of theoretical things I had to learn, but the artillery course there was a breeze. The things I learned came easily for me and reinforced the knowledge I had already acquired at Fort Knox and Fort Benning. I'd already done reconnaissance and selection and occupation of position, which is really the basic maneuver for an artillery unit when it went into the field to support either armor or infantry. The artillery had to select a position, occupy it, and then develop it and continue to supply supporting fire. I'd laid batteries and fired problems and done all the things required to command a battery—and made my own quota of mistakes. But at Fort Sill I learned the scientific principles and philosophy behind the employment of field artillery. I learned a lot about fire direction and the way that various types of artillery pieces such as rifles and howitzers operated.

We studied the two basic types of cannon, the rifle and the howitzer. The rifle was and is a flat-trajectory weapon. The French 75mm was a rifle because it had a flatter trajectory than the 105mm howitzer that the Army used during World War II. The howitzer was a short-barreled weapon with a high angle of fire. The advantage of a high angle of fire was that you could fire over obstacles such as hills, buildings, or other obstructions. The disadvantage of howitzers is that they are not as accurate as rifles, do not have the velocity of a rifle, and therefore were rarely used for direct fire. The 155mm GPF was a long-barreled weapon that was very accurate. All of our direct-fire weapons, such as our antitank cannons, were rifles.

At Fort Sill I learned the science of surveying. This was important because to hit a target you must know your exact location as well as that of the target. I learned all about the different types of ammunition that we were required to use, the types of powder, the way that the ammunition was assembled and loaded.

The basic types of ammunition we used during World War II were armor-piercing, high-explosive, white phosphorous, and the time and proximity fuse. The armor-piercing shell had a steel nose and was used chiefly for direct fire and was almost never used by howitzers. Howitzers generally used the "HE" or high-explosive ammunition. It was simply a projectile that was loaded with a considerable amount of TNT and did its damage not only by the explosion itself, but also by the fragmentation of the shell case that was designed to break up into small fragments to inflict casualties. We also had white phosphorous shells that were used to mark a target or to screen an area with smoke. The warhead contained large amounts of a white phosphorous preparation that generated a cloud of heavy white smoke.

Some of our earlier projectiles had time fuses, but you had to estimate the time of flight and cut the fuse so that it would go off just before it landed. That was a pretty difficult thing to do. We did that up until the proximity fused shells called "Pozit" were developed during the war. Time fuses were very effective but it took a great deal of expertise in order to adjust the fire so it would produce the desired effect. The disadvantage of using time fuses was the arming process would take a little extra time, but we could fire three rounds a minute without any trouble. We usually didn't want to fire any faster than that anyway. Normally the entire battalion fired three volleys when attacking a target, and if that didn't produce the desired result, then we fired another three-round volley.

With an experienced gun crew, time really was not a problem. A 105mm howitzer crew, for example, had six members, and each member of the crew had a specific duty. The gunner was the chief and was the one who set the range and the deviation. The Number One crewman was the one who loaded the shell, and the Number Two crewman was the man who pulled the lanyard to fire the gun. And Numbers Three, Four, Five, and Six all had ammunition duty. One set the fuse and another made sure that the powder was loaded in the canister and that the shell was assembled properly. Two men helped load the shell and another man went back and picked up the next round and brought it up for preparation. We could fire as many as eight or ten rounds in a minute if we just shoved them in there. One of the disadvantages in firing like that, though, was the heat from the shell casings made the inside of the vehicle awfully hot. Getting them out of the vehicle was another problem. Self-propelled artillery vehicles like the "Priest" were not made for rapid fire, but in situations that required direct fire we could fire pretty fast. I don't think that we had any 105mms at the time I was at Fort Sill. We still used modified French 75mms or on occasion a 155mm GPF. The equipment that we worked with and learned on was not the equipment that we later went to war with because it just hadn't been developed at that time.

At Fort Sill we also did a lot of actual fieldwork where we were taken to an observation point to direct fire on a prearranged target. We were required to calculate the data to send to the guns that gave them the information they needed to hit the target. We provided them the direction of fire, the type of target, the powder charge that they needed to use, and finally the order to fire. Generally the order to fire was the announcement of the range because that was the final thing that the gun crews needed to know. It only took about three sentences, really. It was during these field exercises that I learned that it was damned near impossible to hit the target with the first volley, and I quickly learned how to adjust fire. Adjustment of fire was very important, a very calculated and methodical procedure for bringing your fire onto the target. It's much simpler nowadays where computers do most of the mathematical calculations, but at that time we literally fired out of our hip pocket.

Utilizing artillery in those days was really just a mathematical problem. You had to figure in a lot of factors like windage and the distance that the earth would rotate during the projectile's period of flight. One of the most important units in our Corps Artillery was the meteorological section that periodically sent a balloon aloft with a device that measured air density, temperature, and wind speed and direction. We also had to take the temperature of the gunpowder. Gunpowder burns at a different rate when it's warm than when it's cold. We kept a thermometer with us that we'd put in the powder bag periodically.

Artillery was a very complex science. Now computers do so much of it that it's taken a lot of the fun out of it. A modern rocket launcher has a computer in it that's linked to a satellite, so when it moves into position the computer tells it exactly where it is. You can tap in the coordinates of the target, input the meteorological factors, and when that first round goes off you have a reasonable chance of hitting the target. That was something that was all done by human calculation during World War II.

I have a lot of memories of Artillery School at Fort Sill, including the terrible weather. It was almost always very windy there. They classified the weather by the number of maps that would blow away when you went on a field exercise. Some days the weather was a "two-mapper," others could be "four-mappers." Fort Sill, like most Army posts, was located on wasteland. They generally didn't establish Army posts and artillery ranges in highly developed agricultural or populated areas for obvious reasons, so it was pretty rugged country and generally treeless. And the temperature, at least at the time that I was there, was anything but pleasant. I was there about ninety days, from January till the latter part of April.

After I returned from Artillery School I stayed with the 14th Field Artillery Regiment until January 1942, when the 92nd Armored Field Artillery Battalion was organized in the 2nd Armored Division. During this eight-month interval there was continuous development of new weapons and new equipment. We would get new equipment all the time and that increased our training problems because with new equipment we had to develop new techniques. One of the particularly difficult problems we encountered was the necessity for using radio in armored units. Because of their speed and mobility, the armor didn't have time to string telephone line between the forward areas and the command posts, so we had to develop another means of communication. New radios had to be developed along with new systems of communication and new tactics.

As an example, when suddenly we were told that an artillery battalion would consist of six guns instead of the usual four, we knew that there was going to be a communication problem. Until that time the battery executive officer could stand behind the guns and shout the commands. The employment of six guns had to be different from the employment of four. It was no longer possible to put them in a straight line because our front would be too long. We'd usually put them into a position that looked like a human hand because we wanted our fire to cover as much territory as possible. If we put them into a handlike formation, and they all fired using the same range, that's the way the shells would land.

Before, when we had only four guns, we'd put them in a straight or staggered row and the executive officer could stand behind them and shout the commands because the men were all close enough to hear him. But with the different arrangement, it became necessary to utilize a different formation. We knew that we had to have a new means of communication so we invented our own system by using field telephones and field wire and a central switchboard that was connected to all six guns. The executive officer was able then to call each gun and give them the commands, usually simultaneously.

Another problem we encountered was communicating with one another while we were on the move. Idling armored-vehicle engines made a lot of noise even when the vehicles were not moving. Add to that the road noise when they were moving and communication became next to impossible. So we began to experiment with the first FM radios. It was a challenge to keep those things operating when they were first installed because they operated on crystals and large glass tubes, and half-tracks and jeeps were not known for their smooth ride. The M-7s did not carry a radio. We also found that if a vehicle had an FM radio mounted in it you had to park the vehicle a certain way if you wanted to contact people in a particular direction because of the receiving limitations of those early radios. We used fish-pole antennas on our vehicles. We found that we had to tie the tip of the antenna to the front of the vehicle to keep it from getting hung up on a tree branch or some other overhead obstacle. The crystals inside the radio required delicate handling. We also learned to lay telephone wire immediately upon reaching our position. Each gun section was required to have a soldier monitoring the communication headset at all times. Only through experience did we learn all of these things.

The problems we encountered required initiative and forethought by the small-unit commanders because they were the ones who had to deal with them. We didn't expect the battalion commander to solve our problems for us. He was sympathetic but relied on us to work these problems out. All of the officers and the top enlisted men worked together on solutions, and the enlisted men came up with some fantastic ideas throughout the war. One of the great things about the American soldier was his initiative and his knack for innovation. The enlisted men would come up with unbelievable solutions because they were the ones experiencing the problem and, in many cases, they quickly arrived at a solution. They would be able to adapt themselves to a situation or do what was necessary to overcome it. Many of them had no formal technical training. They came from all walks of life: factories, farms, Main Street businesses, and coal mines. They had good old American initiative and intelligence. They hadn't been paralyzed by discipline like German soldiers. We found in many German units that the lower ranks had not been given the opportunity to develop their own initiative. If something happened to their immediate superior, they would often just sit and wait until a replacement arrived. That didn't happen often with American troops, who always seemed to have a natural leader in their midst.

The first maneuver that the 2nd Armored Division went on was called the "Tennessee Maneuver." It was held in the vicinity south of Murfreesboro and Shelbyville and was a fairly extensive maneuver. We had two maneuvers in North Carolina as well as almost daily maneuvers on the military reservation at Fort Benning. They were designed, as nearly as possible, to simulate conditions that we would meet in combat. These were controlled maneuvers. Umpires would referee and assess losses and impose obstacles that had to be surmounted. Even though in the early days we had to attack these obstacles with imaginary weapons, we still had to deploy and utilize what we had just as if it was the real thing. Just going through a maneuver in

Louisiana was the best survival training in the world because we experienced just about all the discomfort that you'd find outside of the jungles of the South Pacific. Louisiana had every insect and reptile ever classified, I think. I never had as many chiggers in my life as I had in Louisiana.

I participated in the second Louisiana maneuver with the 14th Field Artillery Regiment. The 14th was initially organized as a regiment. Back in those days an armored artillery regiment consisted of a headquarters battery, a service battery, and four firing batteries. There was no intermediate battalion headquarters. It was an unwieldy organization. Very early on during the second Louisiana maneuver it became obvious that some sort of a battalion organization would be more flexible, so on this particular maneuver the regiment was divided into two battalions. The provisional battalion headquarters were organized out of the regimental headquarters, and two batteries were put in the 1st Battalion and two batteries in the 2nd Battalion. Then they created two provisional batteries, "X" Battery and "Y" Battery, and I was put in command of "Y" Battery. So in the 1st Battalion there were Batteries "A, B, X" and in the 2nd Battalion there were Batteries "C, D, Y." It was an experimental arrangement and we learned a lot from it. Upon our return to Fort Benning the 14th Field Artillery became a battalion instead of a regiment. The 92nd Armored Field Artillery Battalion was created from the 14th, and the 78th Armored Field Artillery Battalion was organized to replace the experimental one.

In the meantime the organization of the entire 2nd Armored Division had changed. The division originally started out as a brigade under the command of Brigadier General George Patton. The brigade was intended to be a fast-hitting, three-tank battalion force with one artillery battalion, which was the 14th Field Artillery Regiment. The rest of the division consisted of a regiment of infantry, a medium tank battalion, a battalion of artillery, and various support units, which was a bastard arrangement no matter how you looked at it. We discovered on various maneuvers that some sort of a triangular organization was necessary, and we moved very rapidly into a combat command or task force-type of arrangement. It was during these maneuvers that the 2nd Armored Division received its official nickname as the "Hell On Wheels" Division. The commanders were constantly revising their thoughts on organization and tactics throughout the 1940-41 period.

To be in the 2nd Armored Division and not have contact with George Patton was impossible. He was a very active commander who wanted to be where the action was. I remember several interesting incidents at the Officers' School, which was conducted at Fort Benning. Members of Patton's staff conducted the training most of the time, but he was always present. At the end of an evening's presentation he would get up and have some choice remarks for the troops. His talks were very effective. On several occasions he recited epic poetry that he had written. I remember one called "The Bayonet." Though I don't remember exactly how it went, it pertained to the fact that the bayonet was created in the fiery heat of a furnace and was destined to quench its thirst in the guts of the enemy, or something to that effect. And it was during one of these sessions that he made a famous statement that got him the nickname of "Blood and Guts" because he talked about lubricating the tracks of our tanks with the enemy's blood and guts.

We called these sessions "General Patton's School for Boys," and we made up a little song about it.

"High above the Chattahoochie,
High above the Upatoi,
Stands our grand old alma mater,

General Patton's School for Boys."

The troops called him "Georgie" and were very fond of him in spite of his many idiosyncratic ways and silly dictums. For instance, every man was required to wear a tie at all times unless he was assigned to KP or latrine duty. His uniform code was unreasonable at times. Wearing a tie while on maneuvers in the August heat was pretty unreasonable, we felt. Military courtesy was also very important to him. He was famous for gathering all the troops in one location to deliver a rousing address. In fact, his wife wrote the Division March that began with two or three pistol shots and a siren. It was a very rousing song composed of familiar passages from other Army songs. The 2nd Armored Division band would play various marches, but when the general walked on the stage they would play "Ruffles and Flourishes," the cannon would fire the appropriate salute, and then they would break into the "2nd Armored Division March." It was a very inspiring spectacle. He lived for the limelight.

I don't think anyone questioned Patton's abilities, but he was also very fortunate in his choice of staff officers. Patton had such rigid standards that if a guy didn't produce, he didn't stay long. Patton had very little patience, which I found out firsthand during the Tennessee Maneuvers in 1941. I was acting as a forward observer, and my mission was to be up front with the tanks to direct the artillery's supporting fire. I happened to be in a half-track in the middle of the tank column that was in the process of fording a small river. It was a pretty tricky situation. The drivers had to know what they were doing because if one of them got stuck the whole column would be held up. As far as that particular tactical maneuver was concerned it was a serious obstacle. As I pulled up to the river I saw General Patton standing out in the middle of it, with the water up to his ass, waving the tanks into the river and shouting, "Come on! Come on!"

As my half-track nosed up to the river he saw it and screamed, "Get that damn thing out of here!" and ran me off into the woods, where I had to stay until he left because he was afraid that my half-track was going to bog the column down. He didn't realize that I was the forward observer for the supporting artillery, and the delay deprived his column of artillery support. Those were the kinds of things Patton was famous for, which made for colorful stories around the Officers' Mess.

Pearl Harbor

On 7 December 1941 I was at Fort Benning in the mess hall having lunch when someone from the barracks area came running in and said that Pearl Harbor had been attacked. We all rushed out to the nearest radio to find out what the situation was. It was a complete surprise to us all, and to say that we were shocked is putting it mildly.

I was certainly aware of the fall and occupation of France and all the other things that had taken place in Europe and felt that our involvement there was inevitable. Of course, by December 1941 the buildup of American forces was in full swing, and the 2nd Armored Division was one of the new divisions that had been created to cope with the panzer threat. We had been briefed on the Germans' blitzkrieg tactics and knew that it was going to be a tank war this time. Tactics never change. It's the application of them that changes. The tactics that the Germans used were simply a more rapid version of cavalry tactics that had been developed long before. The tactics that we developed to combat them really were based on increasing our mobility so that we could be there "fustest with the mostest," which is the way Confederate General Nathan Bedford Forrest put it during the Civil War.

"Know Your Enemy" was the by-word at Fort Benning, and demonstrations that utilized captured German war material were held periodically, especially when the British seized a new piece of equipment. Until Pearl Harbor we didn't take the Japanese threat seriously. Most of us were focused on what was going on in Europe—not in the Far East. Although we assumed that we would eventually become involved in that war, we didn't know that the Japanese would be the ones to initiate hostilities. We spent our time planning for the war against Germany.

We, of course, knew nothing about the global strategy planned in Washington. At my level we felt that there was still a war in Europe that needed to be fought, so we didn't give a great deal of thought to the Japanese even after Pearl Harbor. We knew that forces had been designated to move to the Pacific in case of trouble there, but the 2nd Armored Division wasn't part of that plan. However, there's no question that Pearl Harbor put an urgent edge to our training. After 7 December we weren't playing any longer. We knew this was for real, and our training and attitude became deadly serious.

Rather then affecting morale negatively, the news of the Pearl Harbor disaster had a galvanizing effect on everybody. Prior to 7 December 1941 we all thought that the United States was invincible. For us the worst part about the disaster at Pearl Harbor was that it was a sneak attack and that the Japanese had gotten away with it while sustaining minimal losses. But it never entered our heads that we would lose the war. That was the feeling among all the people I knew from 7 December through the end of 1942. Sure, we had personal friends in Hawaii and in the Philippines. Some had been classmates or childhood friends. I knew most all of the members of the 192nd Tank Battalion from Harrodsburg, Kentucky. I'd grown up with them. Most of them were a little older than I was, but there were many who were my age and had been my friends. I knew that they shipped out for the Philippines and my family kept me informed as to what happened to them. As a matter of fact, that unit was training at Fort Knox at the same time that I was posted there, and I visited with them several times. I had known "Skip" Rue, who was the commander of the unit, as long as I could remember. He ran a photographic shop in Harrodsburg. Two of his brothers were also in the same unit. I knew them all very well. Fortunately, details about what had happened there were sketchy and the fall of the Philippines was not dwelled upon.

The American soldier has always been a pretty optimistic individual. Keeping up my unit's morale at this time was not a problem. We kept them so busy training that they didn't have time to think about anything else. As officers we acted as if it were business as usual, except with more intensity. The day after the Pearl Harbor attack we went right on out in the field and carried on our training schedule as we had before. Certainly Pearl Harbor and the Philippine campaign were the topic of conversation among the officers for the next several months, but there was no great anxiety and very little talk of revenge. There was intense disappointment that we had been clobbered, but in some ways it was a relief that we were finally in the war. We were just eager to get at the enemy.

The attitude of the American people made the initial reverses we suffered easier to take. They let us know that they were completely behind us. Unlike Korea and Vietnam, there was very little dissension among the American people regarding the steps that were taken by the president and the War Department to prosecute the war. There was no equivocation on the part of anybody. Before the war most of the soldiers in the regular Army were not people of means by any degree and their level of education was not great. Consequently, the general population scorned the soldier. But in the months after 7 December the soldier became a hero. We knew that "Rosie the Riveter" was going to work in the factories to free up men to fight, and that gave us the feeling that everybody was behind the war effort. The full energy of the country was being devoted to the single purpose of defeating the Axis powers. In the ranks we knew that American industry was behind us because we saw the results that arrived by truck or rail at the front gate to Fort Benning every day. World War II was going to be all-out war, and we knew it.

The result of Pearl Harbor for those of us in the regular Army who had been previously promoted temporarily but without monetary reward was that we did receive our pay increase, effective the day the Japanese attacked. As a first lieutenant I started drawing first lieutenant's pay on 7 December. That was one of the things that entered our minds after the shock of the attack had worn off, that we'd finally get pay for rank. That meant about a $65-a-month increase for me.

On 9 January 1942 I was transferred to the 92nd Armored Field Artillery Battalion, first as a battery commander and then shortly thereafter as the S-3, the Operations Officer. The 92nd became my home for the remainder of the war. A number of my associates in the 14th Field Artillery Regiment were transferred with me. Two batteries of the 14th were transferred to the 92nd, and one battery from the 78th Armored Field Artillery Battalion was brought over, so we started out with a number of experienced artillerymen.

After war had been declared the new armored divisions were rapidly organized, and we got down to the "nitty gritty" as far as training was concerned. We began to wear our steel pot helmets and dig foxholes when we went on protracted maneuvers to learn how to utilize the terrain, and we got down to the type of training that was absolutely essential if we were going to survive on the battlefield. We all felt that the more training we had the better off we were because it became increasingly complex and the field problems became increasingly difficult. Had the 2nd Armored Division gone to war immediately after Pearl Harbor, we would have been completely annihilated by the superior forces we would have faced. We certainly didn't have weaponry equal to that of the Germans. There were many, many things that we had to devise and improvise because there were no field manuals that detailed the proper utilization and employment of armor on the battlefield. No such manuals existed. Up to this time our training was the typical cavalry tactic of "harass, bypass, and haul ass."

Because of this lack of standardized doctrine regarding the employment of armor, I was sent to a conference at Fort Knox early in 1942, the purpose of which was to write the field manual for the employment of armored artillery, including the reconnaissance, selection, and occupation of position. I think there were four armored divisions in existence at the time, and I believe that there were five or six officers from each division there. Some were tank experts and artillery experts, as well as communication experts. We were divided into committees. The committee I was assigned to was to standardize liaison between the artillery and the supported units, the tanks and the infantry. We were there about two weeks, and the manuals were published as "Green Books." They served as the standard training manuals through the entire war.

I also got married in 1942. I had met my future wife in the summer of 1941 when I was home on leave from Fort Benning. A friend of mine was driving down the street with his date and spotted me. They were going to the Mercer County Fair and to a dance later that evening and invited me to go along. By the end of the evening I had decided that I liked my friend's date very much, and so for the next ten months I came back to Harrodsburg at every opportunity so that I could see Mildred. I would leave Fort Benning Friday after drill, which was about five o'clock in the afternoon, and drive all night to Harrodsburg. I'd sleep a little while after I arrived and then would spend as much time with her as I could. Then I would drive back to Fort Benning in time for reveille on Monday morning. Mildred and I were married on 24 June 1942. She was twenty-two and was doing social work and selling war bonds, folding bandages and things like that for the Red Cross at the time we were married. Her mother was initially against

"Mildred and I were married on 24 June 1942. She was twenty-two and was doing social work and selling war bonds and folding bandages for the Red Cross at the time we were married."

our marrying, not because of me but because it was such a short courtship and the fact that I would probably be going off to war very soon.

Unbeknownst to us on our wedding day, that "very soon" was more imminent than we had imagined. We began our invasion training shortly thereafter, when we moved to Fort Bragg, North Carolina, in August 1942. The Division was bivouacked in an isolated area twenty-five miles off the main post on the western side of the military reservation. This was to be our "staging area." We did amphibious assault training on Mott Lake. We had to learn the proper way to enter landing craft and how to position ourselves in them, as well as tactics for hitting the beach. All of our training during that period was based on a landing operation. We took part in a maneuver off Hampton Roads and simulated a landing there.

In planning an amphibious invasion our first problem was to neutralize the beach defenses by naval gunfire and air support so the troops attacking the beach would sustain a minimal number of casualties. Getting the assault troops to the beach was the second problem. Generally, some kind of landing craft had to be utilized because the ships couldn't just dump their troops on the beach. Getting those assault troops to the beach in landing craft required a lot of planning and training because men and equipment had to disembark and be unloaded in a particular way. Most of the ships that we used before the advent of the LST (Landing Ship Tank) were simply cargo ships. All the equipment that they carried had to be loaded in the holds, and a plan had to be made so that the equipment came out in the proper sequence. The equipment that belonged to the assault troops had to be loaded in the ships properly so that it was ready when those men hit the beach.

It was during these amphibious invasion training exercises at Fort Bragg that I was assigned to special duty from the Division to learn the art of being a transport quartermaster, which was new not only to the 2nd Armored Division but to the Army. The Army established a transport quartermaster school at the Army base in Norfolk, Virginia, and I was one of the first students in that school. I just happened to be chosen. I don't know that I had any particular

Grabbing some chow on maneuvers.

characteristics which suited me for the job, and it was a surprise to me when I was selected. We helped develop the entire organization and course of instruction there. Marines taught the school. No one had done this before except the Marines. They had had some experience in the South Pacific by the time we were ready to go into North Africa. I actually lived on a ship in Norfolk Harbor. I learned the technique of combat loading, which was a rather complicated process.

Each ship was assigned a transport quartermaster whose responsibility was to load the ship in accordance with the assault commander's wishes so that when the equipment was unloaded at sea onto landing craft, the various vehicles and equipment would come off in the order in which it was needed. Put simply, everything was loaded backwards so that the least-needed equipment would be unloaded last at sea, and the most-needed equipment would be unloaded first and was ready to go into combat when the troops hit the beach. The assault wave of infantry needed their supporting weapons such as mortars, light artillery, and light armor. The combat engineers were also very important in an amphibious assault. They would hit the beach with the assault troops in case there were any obstacles or barriers on the beach that would have to be blown up. Medium and heavy armor and artillery wouldn't go ashore until the troops had advanced far enough inland where they could be used more effectively.

I had to take the plan of each ship, go down in each hold, measure the area, measure the headroom, and make a template for each vehicle or munitions to make certain that everything would fit into the hold of the ship. I would number these templates with a priority number. I also had to figure in the size of the hatch to make sure every piece of equipment would fit through it. The cranes on the ship were used to load and unload everything. It was very tricky but lots of fun, and I was proud that I had helped develop that technique. As a matter of fact the War Department sent a camera crew and a director to Norfolk to make a training film of combat loading, and they happened to pick the ship that I was loading for the North African invasion. They filmed me talking with the captain, going down in the hold of the ship, going through the process of measuring, and then putting the equipment on and taking it off. I never saw the film but a number of people told me that they saw it and recognized me. It turned out to be a Marine Corps training film on combat loading. The film crew were Marines. The director was Louis Hayward, a movie star at the time, and the cameraman was the husband of Penny Singleton, who played Blondie in the movies.

I loaded two ships for what we knew was to be an invasion. After the invasion ships were loaded, they moved the rest of the division equipment up to Fort Dix, and from there it was loaded on ships that made up a convoy called the "Sea Train." While the initial assault troops sailed for an unknown destination, I was loading the rest of the division's equipment on ships for the "Sea Train" in New York Harbor. I finally boarded the *Thomas H. Barry*, a troop transport that departed from New York Harbor about twenty days after the assault fleet sailed. I thought we had been well trained and the men were eager. We didn't realize that we still had a few lessons to learn in North Africa.

Major Buster (far left) and fellow officers aboard the Thomas H. Barry en route to North Africa, December 1942. "The U-boat threat was never far from our minds. We were required to have our life preserver nearby at all times—even when we were sleeping."

CHAPTER FOUR: NORTH AFRICA

The idea of invading North Africa (Operation Torch) appealed to President Roosevelt because it would satisfy British and Russian insistence for a second front, and it would introduce American soldiers to combat without great risks. The landings were designed to threaten German General Erwin Rommel's rear by seizing Algeria and Tunisia, which were under the control of Vichy France. Only two weeks before the landings, Rommel's forces were defeated at El Alamein, Eygpt, and were in retreat. The immediate strategy behind the landings, which took place on 8 November 1942, failed when British Field Marshal Bernard Montgomery allowed a large portion of Rommel's forces to escape his grasp in the east and the retreating Axis troops beat the Allies to Tunisia.

After staying behind in New York to combat load the Sea Train (supply ships) of the American invasion force, William Buster, now a major, joined the 92nd Armored Field Artillery Battalion on the outskirts of Casablanca. Shortly thereafter, his unit moved to the Cork Forest near Rabat, where the 2nd Armored Division served as a strategic deterrent preventing Spanish Morocco from entering the war on the side of the Axis and hitting the American forces from the rear. While the 2nd Armored Division sat in reserve, the 1st Armored Division battled Rommel's Afrika Corps veterans to the east. Hard lessons learned by the 1st Armored Division at El Guettar and Kasserine Pass in February 1943 proved the inferiority of American armor compared to that of the Germans, and new, more effective tactics were developed that served the American forces well throughout the remainder of the war.

Following the defeat of the Axis forces in North Africa, the Allies invaded Sicily (Operation Husky) utilizing one of the greatest aggregations of seapower ever witnessed. Although the 2nd Armored Division played a major role in the Invasion, Buster's unit was held in reserve and was not needed. In November 1943 the 2nd Armored Division was sent to England to prepare for the invasion of France. On 27 March 1944 Buster was promoted to lieutenant colonel and given command of the 92nd Armored Field Artillery Battalion. From December 1943 through May 1944, the 2nd Armored Division participated in continuous training for the invasion of France.

Operation Torch

When I left Fort Bragg to prepare for embarkation, Mildred went home to her family's farm near Midway, Kentucky. We had lived in Southern Pines while I was stationed at Fort Bragg. When the Division left Fort Bragg for the port of embarkation I didn't know how long it would be before we sailed. So it seemed best for Mildred to go back home. However, once I arrived there and began loading the Division's equipment aboard the "Sea Train," I realized that it would be weeks before we would sail. So I sent for Mildred, she joined me, and we were able to spend several more weeks together before the convoy sailed. We stayed at several different hotels in New York, including the old Henry Hudson. We had to move three or four times because New York was pretty crowded in those days. John Mettler, a good Army buddy, was familiar with the New York City area and took us to all the famous nightclub spots like the Twenty-One Club. Money would go a long way in those days, and we had a good time.

Before I boarded ship to sail with the invasion fleet I had to report several times to the dispensary, where I was given just about every vaccination in the Medical Corps inventory. They'd give me two shots in both arms and then I'd have to go back a few days later and get some more. They inoculated us against just about everything. Putting two and two together we began to conclude that the invasion was probably going to take place in a tropical climate because there wasn't much chance of contracting malaria or yellow fever in Norway or France.

While I waited for my orders I took time to get all of my personal affairs in order. I knew I didn't have to worry about Mildred's well-being if my luck ran out overseas because I had signed up for a government life insurance policy when I first reported for duty at Fort Knox in September 1939. The policy I took out was similar to a tontine and wasn't offered by the Army after the mobilization effort began in the fall of 1940. Each soldier covered by that policy was not only insured if something happened, but was guaranteed a minimal dividend after the premium was paid up and the policy matured. As you out-survived other owners of the policy your share increased and so did your dividend.

I also made sure that while I was overseas the majority of my pay would be sent home to Mildred. I set aside a small amount for my own use but knew that I wouldn't have much need for money where I was going. I wanted to make sure Mildred was taken care of every month. And, finally, I wrote out a Last Will and Testament in case the worst happened.

The day finally arrived when I received my orders to report onboard the *Thomas H. Barry*, which was a luxury passenger liner that had been converted to a troopship. It probably is never easy for a soldier to say goodbye to his or her spouse in wartime. Mildred and I had already said goodbye once in North Carolina, so we managed to keep a stiff upper lip and parted at the hotel. Civilians weren't allowed down on the docks, and the departure times for convoys were kept secret. There were German sympathizers in New York watching the harbor who would contact German submarines by short-wave radio. The Navy didn't want to give the U-boat commanders any advance warning regarding convoy movements.

By the time the *Thomas H. Barry* sailed from New York Harbor the afternoon of 11 December 1942, the invasion of North Africa was well underway. The assault troops, whose ships I had helped load in Norfolk, had hit the beaches on 8 November at Port Lyautey, Fadala, and Mostaganem, and by 11 November the French Vichy forces had surrendered and Casablanca had been secured. The 14th and 78th Field Artillery battalions of the 2nd Armored Division took part in the actual invasion. The tactical arrangement for the invasion called for one-third of the Division to be held in reserve so that those forces could be moved to wherever they were needed. My unit, the 92nd Armored Field Artillery Battalion, was part of the reserve force. The invasion went so well that there was no need for us to be committed any sooner.

As we left New York Harbor and the Statue of Liberty slipped behind us, I never doubted for a moment that I would return. I viewed the war as a great adventure and felt that my training would enable me to react in the proper manner when I entered actual combat. Shortly after leaving the harbor we joined numerous other ships to form a large convoy. Our escort consisted of several cruisers and destroyers. The *Thomas H. Barry* still had very plush accommodations even though it had been refitted as a troopship. In the holds of the ship, steel bunks had been installed, and the ship was pretty well packed full of troops from the 2nd Armored Division. The officers were assigned cabins and staterooms, and I shared one with two other officers. The officers also ate in the dining room of the ship. Our dining tables were covered with white tablecloths, and we ate our meals using the ship's expensive silverware. Except for the danger of being sunk by a German U-boat, we were very comfortable.

The U-boat threat was never far from our minds. Each soldier was assigned a specific lifeboat station, and we had many lifeboat drills. We were required to have our life preserver nearby at all times—even when we were sleeping. Even though I knew how to swim, I realized that if a U-boat slipped a "fish" or two into us, the best I could hope for would be to keep afloat for a couple of hours and pray that I'd be picked up by an escort vessel before the elements incapacitated me. Many times on the voyage we heard the destroyers letting go with their depth charges or "K" guns. We never knew whether they actually detected a submarine or just suspected one was in the area. Nevertheless, the sound of depth charges exploding, especially at night, always increased our apprehension, and I expected to see the wake of a steel "fish" coming toward our ship at any moment.

During the two-week voyage, we tried our best to keep the men's minds off the danger by giving them plenty of things to do. We held calisthenics regularly during the day, ordered inspections of their quarters, held classes for them on various subjects, and had them clean their weapons frequently. When I had loaded the assault troops' ships in Norfolk, at the last moment I had been told to find room for about two dozen wooden crates that arrived at the dock in Army deuce and a halfs. At the time I had no idea what was in the crates. I found out aboard the *Thomas H. Barry* because we had several of the same size crates stowed in the hold of the ship. The crates contained a weapon none of us had ever seen before, the bazooka. We uncrated them after the ship had put to sea and practiced firing them on the way over to North Africa. The bazooka was a recoilless antitank weapon that fired a small bomblike projectile. The exhaust from the charge that propelled the projectile blew out the back end of the weapon. Before our men knew any better, some bystanders got hit in the face with the hot exhaust and suffered painful, but not permanent, burns.

Our convoy zigzagged all the way across the ocean and took a very circuitous route to Casablanca. We traveled south initially, almost to South America, and then back north out of the usual shipping lanes. The voyage took almost two weeks. After I arrived in Casablanca I discovered that a torpedo fired by a French submarine outside the harbor had indeed hit one of the cargo ships I had loaded for the assault forces. In addition to combat vehicles, I had loaded a tremendous amount of ordnance and equipment on that ship, including tanks, 300-pound bombs, small arms ammunition, and high-octane gasoline. Fortunately, the torpedo struck amidships and opened a thirty-foot hole in the hold where I had loaded the tanks and armored vehicles. I had loaded the bombs in the front hold of the ship and the gasoline in the hold aft. The ship was able to limp into port after Casablanca had capitulated, and the shore detachment was able to unload and repair it. The ship eventually was able to put back to sea. By the time I arrived, the docks in Casablanca were working very efficiently, and we were able to disembark in port and did not have to use landing craft.

When I rejoined the 92nd Armored Field Artillery Battalion on the outskirts of Casablanca, I did so as a major and as the battalion operations officer. I had been promoted while I was in Norfolk at Transport Quartermaster School. I found the 92nd bivouacked on a hillside across from a small cemetery named Pax. It was there where I experienced my first air raid. One cold, clear night—it could get pretty chilly in North Africa that time of the year—I was awakened out of a sound sleep by the scream of air-raid sirens. I jumped into my pants and jacket and stumbled out of my tent just as searchlights began to light up the skies in search of a flight of German bombers that were attacking the docks. I never saw such a display in my life. Searchlights crisscrossed the sky everywhere. Antiaircraft battery fire and tracer rounds made it seem like one huge Fourth of July celebration. It lasted close to an hour. I stood in front of my tent and watched for awhile, and then turned and looked around and saw that everyone in the entire battalion was doing the same thing without the least bit of concern or fear. It was the first time we'd ever experienced anything like that, and, being green troops, we still felt invincible. It wasn't until later on, after I had experienced a near-miss or two, that I discovered that a little fear could be a healthy emotion.

We stayed in Casablanca only a short time before we moved about a hundred miles north to an area called the Cork Forest, located just outside of Rabat. The Cork Forest was inland about two or three miles and was an enormous forest of cork trees that provided excellent conceal-ment from enemy planes. Our mission there, just south of the Spanish Moroccan border, was strategic in nature. General Francisco Franco, the Caudillo of Spain, was still an unknown quantity at this time but had definite pro-Nazi leanings. While the 1st Armored Division battled General Rommel's Afrika Corps farther east in Tunisia, the 2nd Armored Division acted as a deterrent to keep Spanish forces from entering the war on the side of the Axis and hitting the 1st Armored Division from the rear.

Rabat, the capital of French Morocco and the home of the Sultan, was a lovely town. The Hotel Belima was the major hotel there and was the main attraction because it had an excellent dining room and a nice bar. Rabat had another part of town called the Medina, which was off-limits to American personnel because it was considered dangerous and a base for subversive activities. Of course, that immediately made it even more attractive to those soldiers with per-haps more grit than sense. So, to accommodate the baser instincts of the soldiers more safely, General Patton sanctioned the operation of an unofficial bordello, complete with qualified doc-tors and MPs, for the enlisted personnel. Each unit in the 2nd Armored Division, on a rotating basis, got a chance to visit the facility, but they had to provide their own security force. When the troops in my unit were assigned to the security detail, some of the stories they told after-ward were right interesting.

Patton's thinking on the subject didn't shock me. I certainly agreed with the purpose, which was simply an attempt to control the spread of disease and to keep the soldiers out of any other trouble that might accompany this type of activity in unsavory parts of town. Frankly, this practice is either officially or unofficially established in most theatres of war by every army when its troops are in a static situation for an extended period, the theory being that a controlled situation is better than rampant venereal disease. The Japanese went a step further by provid-ing their troops with so-called "comfort women," mostly Koreans. But these women were noth-ing more than sex slaves, and the Japanese are only now admitting their guilt and attempting to pay reparations to the women who were forced into this.

When we moved to the Cork Forest we resumed our training, and with the Afrika Corps only a few hundred miles away we did so in earnest. The ocean breezes moderated the climate, and the area surrounding the Cork Forest was perfect tank and armored vehicle country. The really arid country was ten or fifteen miles inland. We trained intensively for many weeks and for the first time used live artillery fire in coordination with tank maneuvers. During training exercises in the United States we were forbidden to fire live artillery rounds during maneuvers to avoid the bad publicity accidental casualties would generate. But in the area outside of the Cork Forest we fired live shells to within fifty yards of our infantry and tanks in support of their simulated assaults. I was up with the assaulting troops on a couple of occasions during these exercises, and it got scary at times. The tankers would sometimes come back with stories about shrapnel clanging off the sides and tops of their tanks. A short round or a defective round could have caused numerous casualties, but I don't recall that we had any serious accidents.

There were some accidental Arab casualties, however. We would send out patrols to clear the firing range prior to the start of the exercise, but frequently an Arab on horseback or camel would appear on the horizon right in the middle of the assault. If we saw him in time we would stop firing until he ambled his way out of range. We were amused when we were told that if we accidentally killed an Arab we would have to pay the deceased's family fifty dollars as com-pensation. However, if the Arab survived but we killed his horse or camel, we had to pay the

Major Buster's accommodations by the sea in Morocco, February 1943. "The ocean breezes moderated the climate, and the area was perfect tank and armored vehicle country. We trained intensively for many weeks and for the first time used live artillery fire in coodination with tank maneuvers."

owner one hundred dollars. The animal was more valuable than the human being!

Initially, the commander of the 2nd Armored Division while we were in the Cork Forest was General Ernest Harmon, who had taken over the Division while we were at Fort Bragg. He was an old spit-and-polish cavalryman and was an aggressive leader like General Patton. I always felt he was a better commander than Patton because he was not interested in personal glory or making the front page of a newspaper. His only goal was to get the job done as efficiently and effectively as possible. He was a practical soldier, one who listened to the opinions of his staff and advisors.

While we were in the Cork Forest, General Harmon left the 2nd Armored Division to take over the 1st Armored Division after it had gotten the hell kicked out of it by the Germans in February 1943 at El Guettar and Kasserine Pass. General Rommel, the "Desert Fox," led the Afrika Corps. At Kasserine Pass Major General Lloyd Fredendall had commanded the American II Corps and Major General Orlando Ward the 1st Armored Division. I think that what happened at those two battles probably would have happened to any American commander at that time because our troops were green and under-strength. However, Patton replaced Fredendall shortly thereafter and in turn requested General Harmon to take over the 1st Armored Division. Before he left us General Harmon drafted two thousand men from the 2nd Armored as replacements for the 1st Armored Division. Legend has it that when he reached the 1st Armored Division he immediately called a meeting of all the officers. He held the meeting on the slope of the highest ground in the area and just chewed them out right in front of God and the enemy over their performance. After that the 1st Armored was never defeated again. They went back into combat and won back all the territory they had lost. I won't say it was all due to Ernie Harmon's leadership because the tide of the German offensive had begun to turn by the time he arrived, but his influence undoubtedly helped. The 1st Armored Division officers hated his guts, and to this day you won't find anybody from the 1st Armored Division who has anything good to say about General Harmon.

Unlike the other commanders, Ernie also would not take any guff from Patton, his superior officer. On one occasion stiff German resistance was holding up the 1st Armored Division, and Ernie had gone up to find out what the situation was. Patton called him on the field telephone and said, "Get moving! Get moving! You're a damn coward!" or words to that effect. General Harmon allegedly replied, "Georgie, I'm here at the front and I know what's going on. Why don't you come on up here? If you can get the advance moving faster, I'll go along with you!" He never heard anymore from Patton after that.

As the battle raged in Tunisia, we certainly got antsy back in the Cork Forest. We couldn't understand why we were held in reserve, especially after the way Rommel had clobbered the 1st Armored Division. We were training hard, but the biggest battle we'd had was against the bees that always showed up when we were trying to eat. We knew that there was a real war going on not far away and that the 1st Armored Division obviously needed our help. We wanted to get in the fight. At first we were embarrassed by the 1st Armored Division's performance and denigrated their fighting ability, but later on we came to understand that they were put into a very difficult situation. Rommel's Afrika Corps units were veterans of the desert and had better leadership, equipment, tactics, and esprit de corps. Our troops had had no desert training and were basically out-maneuvered, out-gunned, and poorly led. Defensively, mine fields had not been laid and the troops had been scattered piecemeal along the line, which made the defensive positions extremely thin. In addition, General Fredendall's headquarters were eighty miles behind the mountains his troops were defending. Given those circumstances the outcome of this first encounter against Rommel was not surprising. Rommel was tough and so were his troops.

The 2nd Armored Division just waited in the Cork Forest and trained during the daytime and tried to keep warm in our tents at night. I lived in a small wall tent, and the enlisted personnel slept in pup tents. We learned to make small charcoal stoves out of empty Spam cans to warm up our tents at night. At first we subsisted on C-rations until our supply line got straightened out. Later on we got good, hot meals once our cooks learned how to prepare powdered eggs, dehydrated potatoes, and Spam. We would supplement these rations with whatever local produce was available, like chickens or fresh eggs. We would buy or barter whatever we could from the natives. The local wine was a favorite refreshment among the troops, and forage details would come back with five-gallon water cans full of it. Amazingly, I don't recall any incidents of drunkenness or poisoning.

Of course, our training incorporated many of the things that were being learned the hard way by the 1st Armored Division over in Tunisia. After El Guettar, Sidi Bou Sid, and Kasserine Pass it was clear that our light and medium tanks—the Stuart, General Grant, and Sherman—would not be able to slug it out with the German tanks, which had more powerful guns with greater muzzle velocity. However, through experience the 1st Armored Division found that the German tanks were heavier, less maneuverable, and guzzled fuel. So we adapted our tactics to fit the situation, which meant taking as much advantage of the terrain as possible. As a result of the mauling the 1st Armored Division took, we taught our tank crews to hide behind hills or in depressions until the German panzer came in range. Our tank crews were then instructed to pop up over the hill and fire two or three rounds at the enemy, and then pull back and maneuver to another location. This tactic minimized our tanks' exposure to the superior German firepower. The North African campaign was a testing ground not only for our equipment but also our tactics.

The Cork Forest was not all work and no play, however. Martha Raye came to entertain us as part of a USO show and gave a marvelous performance, and the French liaison people once arranged a boar hunt for General Allen F. Kingman, who had taken over temporarily as the

Division commander when General Harmon left for the 1st Armored Division. The arrangements for the boar hunt were made by one of the local Moroccan leaders. As I recall this particular Moroccan was the Sheik of Kheufera. There were about thirty of us in this party of boar hunters. We mounted up in Jeeps and drove about seventy-five miles to the Atlas Mountains, where we exchanged our Jeeps for horses.

The gear worn by the horses fascinated me. There were saddles and stirrups that surely dated back to the early French wars and appeared to be of solid silver. The saddles had very deep seats and were very uncomfortable but were safe because you couldn't fall out of them. We rode a short while to an area where we were told to dismount and wait. After about an hour we heard shouting and clanging and banging coming from the top of the hill in front of us. A long line of natives on horses and foot called "beaters" were driving the wild game down the mountain in front of our position. Our group was armed with rifles, shotguns, pistols, and Thompson submachine guns. We managed to kill a number of wild boar and rabbits that afternoon.

Afterward we were led to a plateau where enormous tents had been erected. We were informed that we would be served lunch there. The floor of each tent was covered with an intricately woven Oriental carpet. Low tables surrounded by soft cushions were arranged around the inside. The French interpreter explained the seating arrangements, with the old chief and General Kingman at the main table. We couldn't speak the native language and they couldn't speak English, so we just sat there and ate. The food was brought in periodically in different courses. The first course was roast sheep—the whole sheep, head and all! We had been told that according to local etiquette, if you were offered something to eat, it was an insult to refuse it. The custom there is to take food with the right hand, never the left. We found out then that a local delicacy is the sheep's eye. The old sheik at our table took out his pocketknife and extruded one of the eyes from the sheep and held it out in front of him. We all looked at each other and wondered which one of us was going to be the lucky one who would be offered the "delicacy." I wondered what I would do if he offered it to me. But after what seemed an eternity he placed the eye on a little dish, looked around at us with a little smirk, and then proceeded to eat it himself. Then he pulled off chunks of meat with his hand and placed it on our plates. Another round of food followed. This went on for two and a half hours!

Another dish was called cous-cous, which was half-cooked grain pressed into little balls. We were told not to eat too much cous-cous because, once moistened, it would swell up inside of you. After the meal was finally over we sat around the tent with our legs crossed and drank a very sweet mint tea. We had been instructed on the voyage to North Africa not to eat the local food for fear it would be contaminated, and here we were in a position where we had to eat it or else! Although not all the dishes were to my liking, I don't recall that I became ill or that anyone else did, for that matter. Part of the experience of any soldier who went overseas during World War II was contact with different peoples and cultures, which served to broaden our horizons. We couldn't possibly have been the same person after the war that we were before because of what we did and saw.

In May 1943 General Hugh Gaffey took over command of the Division from General Kingman. I knew General Gaffey very well. He was an artilleryman, too. He had been a major in the 7th Mechanized Cavalry Brigade at Fort Knox when I was with that unit briefly. Unfortunately, I didn't think much of him as a soldier. I didn't consider him a terribly intelligent man and think he had been given command of the 2nd Armored Division because he had some friends in high places. I felt that he had built his entire military career on his associations rather than on his ability to command. He was not a commander that I admired. I liked him as an individual and he was always very nice to me, but as a commander I thought he left a lot to be desired. I'm sure his staff carried him.

During the Allied drive on Tunis in March and April 1943 the 2nd Armored Division was finally given orders to make a road march to Algeria and occupy the small town of Port-aux-Poules, just east of Oran on the Gulf of Arzew. With the German surrender of Tunis on 13 May, the North African campaign came to a close and we started to prepare for another invasion, although we did not know where. A lot of us speculated that Italy was the target, but that information was kept on a need-to-know level, and battalion S-3 officers certainly weren't on that list.

While at Port-aux-Poules we trained extensively for an amphibious invasion and were introduced to two new types of naval vessels, the LST, or Landing Ship Tank, and the LCT, or Landing Craft Tank. We had trained exclusively with the LCM, or Landing Craft Medium, and the LCVP, or Landing Craft Vehicle and Personnel, which were relatively small vessels that had to be off-loaded from mother ships off the coast. The LST, on the other hand, was a big, flat-bottomed ship designed to transport tanks and armored vehicles across the ocean and land them right on the beach through two large bow doors and a lowered ramp. We would drive our M-7s off the ramp into the surf and right up onto the beach, ready for action. Some GIs derisively referred to the LST as the "Large, Slow Target," and several were hit and set on fire during the invasion of Sicily.

Prior to our arrival at Port-aux-Poules I had never seen an LST or LCT. The LCT was a bargelike landing craft with a bow ramp, much smaller than the LST. We practiced our invasion tactics several times on the LCTs and even had some live firing exercises from the decks of the LCTs utilizing the 105mm howitzers mounted on our M-7s to help soften up the beach defenses as the assault forces moved in. There was also a large wasteland about six or seven miles from our bivouac area called the La Macta Marsh that we often used for artillery practice. Since the Army Air Corps had complete control of the air in North Africa, we were not in any danger during this period. We were able to conduct our invasion exercises and artillery practice without any disruptions. It was good practice and a lot of fun.

By the time Operation Husky, or the invasion of Sicily, was launched on 10 July 1943, the 2nd Armored Division had become a very flexible organization and was organized into three different combat commands: Combat Command A or CCA, Combat Command B or CCB, and Combat Command Reserve or CCR. Each combat command was self-sufficient and could operate independently of the others. The advent of the combat command organization was a result of what had been learned during the Tunisian campaign. Improved antitank weapons necessitated closer cooperation between the armor and the infantry. Under the new arrangement tanks and artillery would still be used to punch holes in the enemy's defensive line, but infantry was still needed to hold the ground once a breakthrough had been achieved.

Prior to the North African campaign the 2nd Armored Division had consisted of two tank regiments of three battalions each, one armored infantry regiment of three battalions, and three artillery battalions. After the Tunisian campaign, however, the Division was remodeled to comprise a mix of infantry and tank battalions: three of infantry, six of armor, plus the three artillery battalions. With no fixed regimental formations, the combat battalions could be utilized depending on the force structure needed for a specific task to form the three combat commands, which made the Division much more flexible.

For the invasion of Sicily, Combat Command A was selected as the initial strike force around the area of Licata, and Combat Command B was used as the immediate reinforcement force. CCR, or the reserve force, including the 92nd Armored Field Artillery Battalion, was left behind in North Africa in a state of readiness in case we were needed. There weren't enough ships available to transport the entire Division to Sicily anyway, and because of the Division's flexibility CCA and CCB had been tailored for the job. Because of the nature of Sicily's terrain and topographical features, they were designed as fast-moving units with very little support forces to slow them down.

To put in perspective how far down the chain of command I was, I found out that Sicily was the target of the invasion the day Operation Husky was launched—listening to a BBC broadcast. Up until the day of the invasion, information regarding the destination of the fleet was kept very secret and the commanders who did know were very tight-lipped about it. In fact, I know that a Corps commander, who was a major general, was relieved of command and sent back to the United States as a colonel because of a breach of security at his headquarters located at Port-aux-Poules. When his headquarters moved out of Port-aux-Poules to board the ships headed for the invasion of Sicily, some important papers were left behind in a wastebasket and were discovered, fortunately, by some MPs. That was a major violation of security, and the Army always dealt very swiftly and severely with the commander of a unit which was responsible for this kind of incident. In the Army the buck always stopped at the top, and in this case the Corps commander was held accountable. It ruined his military career and was a tragic thing. I knew him personally.

Enough went wrong during the early hours of the invasion that we sure didn't need to give the Germans and Italians any advance warning that we were coming. For instance, a flight of about twenty-six transport planes full of paratroopers from the 82nd Airborne Division was shot down by mistake by the warships that escorted the invasion fleet. Apparently, the planes were off course and flew directly over the invasion fleet, or the IFF—Identification, Friend or Foe—device on the lead plane malfunctioned. The escort vessels opened fire when they mistook the aircraft for enemy bombers. Whenever I reflect on the Sicilian operation I always think of those poor paratroopers who had trained so hard, only to be shot down by mistake by their own guys.

Once the invasion began I expected units of CCR including the 92nd Armored Field Artillery Battalion to be committed rather quickly as reinforcements for CCA and CCB. However, the invasion went so well during the initial days that we weren't needed. In twelve days CCA had swept west and north and captured Palermo, and the entire island of Sicily was secured in only thirty-eight days. I just sat on the beach at Port-aux-Poules with the rest of my unit and gritted my teeth. We all felt that we were far too good a unit to be constantly held in reserve. We were afraid the war would pass us by before we had a chance to prove ourselves. I was certainly pleased that CCA and CCB had been successful in Sicily because I had many friends who were in those combat commands, and I knew also it demonstrated that our hard training had paid off. I wasn't jealous over their success. The object was to beat the enemy and win the war. Whoever did it really didn't make a hell of a lot of difference. I just knew that the 92nd was highly trained and motivated and was afraid that unless we saw combat soon that we would eventually lose our sharpness.

It was during the Sicilian campaign that General Patton got himself in trouble in early August for slapping on two separate occasions two soldiers who were hospitalized for combat fatigue. My colleagues and I were appalled when we heard of the incidents because Patton had been a hero to the troops of the 2nd Armored Division since our days at Fort Benning. We all had a tremendous amount of respect for his aggressiveness and felt that under his command we were invincible. We also couldn't understand the ruckus the media created over the incidents. After all, Patton was delivering morale-building victories in Sicily. I'm sure if General

Hobart Gay, Patton's close friend and his chief of staff, had been with him at that hospital the incidents wouldn't have happened. "Hap" Gay was the one person who kept Patton under control when he dealt with superior officers like General Eisenhower or General Montgomery. After the incidents in Sicily, Patton was sent to England and did practically nothing for the next eleven months but keep the Germans on tenterhooks trying to predict where he would appear next.

Shortly after the Sicily campaign got underway I received a confusing EFM message from the United States. The message read, "Parcels received. Many thanks. Family all well," signed by my mother-in-law. At first it didn't make sense. On the back of the EFM form there were a series of numbers which corresponded to designated phrases, and when the message was transmitted only the numbers were sent, not the phrase. So I put two and two together and realized that some of the numbers must have been transposed by mistake and the "parcels received" part of the message could have meant "Son born." After several months' concern I was a father! Several days later I received a visit from a representative of the Red Cross who confirmed the fact that I was indeed a father. I knew Mildred was pregnant before I left New York and was relieved that everything had gone well. She wrote me a letter just about every day I was overseas, so I was always pretty busy at mail call. I wasn't as good a correspondent but managed to write her at least once a week. Since I was an officer I acted as my own censor. I was pretty careful about what I said but was able to give a few hints as to my location. Mildred also was good at the game. I remember one time cutting into a loaf of bread she had sent me, only to discover a bottle of my favorite Kentucky bourbon hidden inside.

After Sicily was secured in mid-August 1943 we were ordered to turn in all of our equipment and hardware and to pack up our personal belongings. We knew we were about to move but once again we didn't know where. When we turned in our vehicles and equipment we knew we were not going to participate in the invasion of Italy. We weren't even allowed to keep our trucks, and come November another unit had to take us down to the ships for embarkation. The ship we boarded was a British liner that had been converted to a troopship. The crew was all British. Once again our escort consisted of about a dozen destroyers and several cruisers. When we left port in convoy they finally told us our destination was England. Our mission was twofold: we were a strategic reserve so British troops could be sent elsewhere, and we were to train for the invasion of France.

During the voyage we practiced boat drills again and occasionally we'd hear depth charges going off in the distance, but this trip was not nearly so frightening as the one to North Africa. By the spring of 1943 the battle of the Atlantic had basically been won against the German U-boats. There were still many U-boats operating in the North Atlantic, but technological advancements and better weaponry such as radar and the hedgehog ship's mortar and more sophisticated convoy tactics had negated much of the effectiveness of the U-boats. Many were sunk in the spring and summer of 1943. In fact, the diminishing threat of the U-boats was a major factor in the Army's decision for us to leave our vehicles and equipment behind when we left North Africa. As more and more convoys arrived safely in England, the Quartermaster Corps was able to stockpile enough clothing and equipment to outfit an entire army. Instead of wasting valuable cargo vessels to transport our old equipment across the ocean, the Army decided it was much easier to transport just the 2nd Armored Division's personnel and to equip us with new equipment once we arrived in England. The equipment we left behind was used to help rearm eleven French divisions in North Africa.

On that voyage we sailed west for a long time and came to within approximately eight hundred miles of North America before the ship turned north and east and headed for En-

Division Artillery Field Officers' Quarters, Tidworth Barracks, approximately sixty miles southwest of London.

gland. Instead of in steel bunks, in the British tradition the troops slept in hammocks slung across the interior decks in the evening, and in the morning the hammocks were ratted up and stowed out of the way. The British crew then swabbed down the decks as we watched. The British captain ran a taut ship.

The British officers and seamen treated us royally. Our officers were permitted to eat in the salon, and we utilized the liner's shipboard linen, china, and silverware. Unfortunately, the only food available, for the most part, was customary English fare. Eating kippers for breakfast was a new experience. Our insistence in Oran to load some typical American food aboard ship had initially been met with some resistance by the British authorities. For example, the British used unrefined, brown sugar which our troops found unpalatable, and we had difficulty obtaining permission from the captain to load some of our own sugar aboard the vessel.

We also attempted, with only limited success, to get permission to load some American-style rations to supplement the ship's stores. The troops complained about the quality of the food for the entire voyage, but American soldiers always complain about food anyway. I really couldn't complain, though, because the food was wholesome, if not exactly to our liking.

"Splicing the main brace," which was the daily issuance of spirits or rum, was one of the nice traditions aboard British ships. In the days of the wooden ships the sailors were issued a daily ration of "grog" for medicinal and morale-building purposes, and the tradition was carried on during the Second World War. Every morning during our voyage to England I had the best-tasting Bloody Marys that I have ever had, so life aboard a British ship did have its advantages. This practice was foreign to the U.S. Navy, where no liquor is allowed onboard ship.

We finally arrived at Liverpool, England, on 24 November 1943. Liverpool, located on the Mersey River, is the most important seaport in the northwest section of England. Most of the convoys that originated in the United States unloaded there or at Bristol, which was approximately 120 miles south. We were immediately loaded into trucks and transported about 160 miles south to Tidworth, which is at the southeastern edge of the Salisbury Plain and approximately sixty miles southwest of London. It was a small town with good rail and highway connections, and it also had a couple of nice pubs that we patronized. We moved into Tidworth Barracks, which for generations had been a British Army base, and Salisbury Plain, only a twenty-minute march from our barracks, had traditionally served as the main peacetime maneuver area of the British Army. The British troops had been moved out to make room for us. The barracks consisted of twelve brick buildings plus the mess halls and various other outbuildings. Each barracks building had been named for a battle or campaign in India in which the British Army had participated. During World War II India, of course, was still a part of the British Empire. The barracks were named alphabetically, the last one being Mooltan, which was the barracks that my troops occupied.

The barracks buildings were not centrally heated. The squad rooms, which could accommodate perhaps thirty men, had coal-burning fireplaces at each end of the room and provided the only heat. This was the first time we had been quartered inside a real building since we left Fort Benning in June 1942. Interestingly, my unit had experienced very little respiratory or intestinal illness since Fort Benning even though we had been living in tents. But once we moved indoors at Tidworth Barracks the men began to contract colds and "flu" symptoms in abundance because they were housed together in close quarters. The utilization of the same shower, toilet, bunk, and mess facilities spread a virus pretty rapidly. When we were out in the field in North Africa, or later on the European continent, we had very little illness of this type.

[handwritten margin note: the fireplace didn't give much heat]

The mess halls at Tidworth were enormous buildings. Ours was so large that the entire Division Artillery was able to eat together. Our own cooks prepared the food and the menus were Americanized. The first day we were served an enormous Thanksgiving dinner. During our stay there we had lots of red meat and poultry that had been shipped over frozen from the United States. But a lot of the vegetables were procured locally from the natives. For example, we ate a lot of Brussels sprouts and potatoes. I got tired of Brussels sprouts pretty quickly. But the food was definitely better than field rations.

The troops were very closely monitored at mealtime to insure that food was not wasted. The Division Artillery mess hall alone served approximately 2500 men, so a great deal of food was required to feed all of us. The men were allowed to eat as much as they wanted, but they weren't allowed to take more than they could eat. They were allowed to go back for seconds if they were still hungry but weren't permitted to pile too much on their plate the first time through the chow line. Many times I inspected the garbage after a meal and found that the entire garbage from our mess hall fit into several No. 10 cans, unless we had eaten fried chicken or some other food which produced more waste. Our Division was taught to be very economical when it came to food.

All the artillery officers ate at the same mess table at the Officers' Mess, so for a period of three or four months we saw each other at every meal. During the meals there was every opportunity for everyone to take part in the discussions, and we were able to tell the Division Artillery commander, Colonel Thomas Roberts, how we felt about different situations and he would listen as well as teach. We got to know each other very well which, I'm sure, helped us operate as a team during the liberation of Europe.

One of the first things we did at Tidworth was draw new equipment, including new vehicles from the Tidworth Ordnance Depot (which became one of the U.S. Army's primary ordnance installations along with Rushden and Ashchurch). The 92nd Armored Field Artillery Battalion received brand-new M-7s with new 105mm howitzers. We also were given new half-tracks with improved radios mounted in them, and the 66th and 67th Tank Regiments received brand-new M-4 Sherman tanks. All of our support vehicles were also new. We were like kids on Christmas morning when we received the new vehicles. We had to check each vehicle thoroughly to make sure it was put together properly. Most of the vehicles shipped over from the United States required some assembly, and many of the workers were British civilians who were unfamiliar with the equipment. Pilferage of the tools, which came with every vehicle, was an early problem that the Army had with the British civilians. Early on there weren't enough tools or spare parts to go around. Substituting British Army tools didn't work because their nuts and bolts were a different size than ours.

The Salisbury Plain is a beautiful part of England. The gently rolling countryside reminded me of central Kentucky. Everywhere you went in England some historic landmark was nearby. The Salisbury Plain figured in the Arthurian legend, and Stonehenge was right in the middle of the area where we conducted maneuvers. We would drive by the large rock formation every day on our way to the range. Some of us were aware of the historic significance of Stonehenge, but I'm sure that to most of the GIs they were just large boulders sticking up in the air.

We were kept busy most every day of the week, especially when weekend maneuvers were scheduled. Generally, however, the troops were given Saturday afternoon and all of Sunday off for morale purposes. All work and no play made for a very grouchy Joe. On the weekends our troops had the opportunity to visit nearby communities and patronize the local pubs. London was only about sixty miles away, and you could catch the train at the Tidworth station and be there in an hour or so. I experienced several air raids when I was in London. Once I was staying at the American Forces Hotel when the German bombers came in the middle of the night. I was able to watch all of the fireworks from my hotel window, not thinking that the prudent action would have been to find a bomb shelter or at least to stay under cover. Fortunately, the bombers had concentrated their attack on another part of the city that night.

I didn't get to see the sights in England too much, but I did visit a friend of mine who was with the 82nd Airborne stationed at Oxford. We made friends with a very nice English couple who lived in Andover, and they frequently invited us over to their home for tea. In fact, there were a number of Royal Air Force personnel who lived in the Tidworth area, and they would invite us over when they were home on a weekend.

Great Britain was in a state of total war, and there were constant reminders everywhere. For example, all of the road signs had been taken down to confuse the enemy in case of an invasion, which also made it kind of difficult for us to get around. Rural intersections had no signs to indicate where you were, which way to turn, or distances. Usually the only signs had a number on them, like 0472, which meant that there was an ordnance installation with code number 472 in that particular direction.

Blackout conditions were in effect at all times to make it harder for the German bombers to locate their targets. Blackout curtains were used on the windows at night and, of course, there were no streetlights. You became quite adept at driving in the dark. The headlights and taillights on all vehicles were affixed with blackout covers, which emitted only a half-moon glow that looked like a cat's eye as the vehicle came toward you.

Of course, the devastation wrought by German bombers in London was horrific, and directions to the nearest bomb shelter were posted all over the city. In all of the wooded rural areas the sides of the roads were lined with corrugated steel-covered shelters which housed stacked artillery shells, and the open grounds of large estates owned by the landed gentry were used as massive artillery and armored vehicle parks. In spite of it all, the English people I came into contact with never complained about the living conditions or the shortages. In fact, I think they took pride in their ability to withstand whatever the Germans threw at them.

While at Tidworth some of our men were sent to different parts of the country for specialized training. For example, some of our men from the 92nd were sent to an antiaircraft school run by the British Army. Fortunately, as an artillery commander I was sent to Bournemouth to a Canadian field artillery regiment for two weeks as an observer. While I was there the unit participated in a mock invasion of the Isle of Wight. I was able to observe their landingcraft loading procedures, their invasion tactics, and their field maneuvers. The experience was very educational.

This Canadian unit was not an armored unit but a traditional line

Lt. Col. William R. Buster as the new CO of the 92nd Armored Artillery Battalion. "I became, by far, the youngest battalion commander in the 2nd Armored Division at the time."

artillery regiment. They were equipped with lighter guns than we had in the 92nd, which they towed behind trucks, and their communication system was more complicated than ours. Their organizational structure was, of course, based on the British system that wasn't as flexible as ours, but I admired many of the things they were able to accomplish. We learned from one another and became very good friends.

I was given command of the 92nd Armored Field Artillery Battalion on 27 March 1944 and did not relinquish command until after the war in Europe was over. Carl Hutton, the battalion commander of the 92nd prior to my taking over, was the senior lieutenant colonel in the Division Artillery. I had tremendous respect for him. He was quiet and uncommunicative in a personal sense, but once I got to know him I had full confidence in him as a commander. He was a good artilleryman and a bit of a daredevil. His soul, I think, was really in aviation. After the war he was assigned to Army aviation and helped establish the Army Aviation School at Fort Sill, then was responsible for its being moved to Fort Rucker, Alabama, where he was its first commandant.

What brought about my promotion to lieutenant colonel and command of the 92nd was the reassignment of the commander of the 14th Field Artillery Battalion. At that time the 14th really had some staffing and morale problems, and they were not functioning well as a team. Small factions or cliques had developed among the officers, and a few who had gained the ear of the commander were consistently given the choice assignments.

I was surprised that I was not the one sent to take command of that unit. I was delighted when Colonel Hutton told me, "Bill, you stay here and take over the 92nd. I'll go over and straighten out the 14th," which he proceeded to do. That was one of the finest things anybody ever did for me. I became, by far, the youngest battalion commander in the 2nd Armored Division at the time.

As the battalion commander I was responsible for the training, administration, and general operation of the 92nd. If we were not out in the field on maneuvers, I would do things like make unannounced visits to the motor park to check on the equipment and make sure they were being maintained properly, and I would visit the kitchens occasionally to inspect the facilities there. I would also order routine barracks inspections to keep the troops mentally sharp as well as looking like well-disciplined soldiers. The 92nd was a sharp outfit when I took over command, and I intended to keep it that way.

We spent 80 percent of our time out in the field when we were in Tidworth, either on maneuvers, road marches, overnight bivouacs, or the target range. On Salisbury Plain we repeatedly practiced the new tactics and techniques that we had learned from the British and through fighting the Germans in North Africa and Sicily. For example, we learned that General Forrest's maxim "fustus with the mostus" was a truism that often decided the outcome of battles. In particular, we worked on our occupation of position so we would be combat ready and prepared to fire our first volley very quickly. We became so adept that we could occupy a position and fire our first volley in less than three minutes. I don't mean that in three minutes the entire unit was in position and the men were in foxholes and the camouflage netting was set up, but that was damn fast in those days!

We also practiced the receipt of "march order," which was the term used to "hit the road" for movement to a new position. Everything was dismantled or taken off, packed up, and loaded on trucks such as tents, camouflage netting, radios, tables, maps, ammunition, and provisions. We became skilled at this as well and were able to have the first vehicle of the column on the road one minute after receiving a "march order." This was really quite an accomplishment because my battalion had three batteries of six M-7s each, and each battery had about fifty vehicles. In addition to each M-7's ammunition carrier there were reconnaissance vehicles, vehicles for the forward observers, an additional ammunition train, kitchen trucks, and the battery commander's and executive officer's vehicles, which were either half-tracks or "Peeps." "Shoot and scoot" became our slogan in England, and when we had to, we could really move. We knew speed and flexibility would be our only advantage when we faced the more heavily armored and bigger-gunned Tiger and Panther tanks in France.

I remember one embarrassing episode, though, that happened to us just after I assumed command of the 92nd. General Omar Bradley came down to Tidworth to inspect the 2nd Armored Division, and my battalion was chosen as one of the demonstration units. I was, of course, very proud and thought Colonel Hutton and I had trained the battalion to where we could accomplish anything. When General Bradley arrived he inspected my best battery, and we decided to give him a demonstration of our prowess by issuing a "march order." The battery got packed up and the first vehicle was on the road in less than a minute. I was just beaming. General Harmon, who had returned as our division commander, motioned for me to come over to General Bradley's staff car, and I was invited to ride with them. General Bradley was suitably impressed. He said, "Colonel, that was an outstanding performance. I would now like to see them go *into* position." Well, my jaw must have dropped because I didn't have my radio and had no way of contacting the battery to tell them to deploy. Even worse, General Bradley had been about an hour late, and I knew that when my guys had received the "march order" they assumed the demonstration was over and that they were to head for the motor park. I had no way to stop them. As General Bradley and General Harmon looked at me, after what seemed like an eternity, I finally stammered, "Well, I beg your pardon, sir, but I'm afraid the battery is headed for home for supper and I don't have any way to stop them!" Fortunately, he and General Harmon laughed and said they understood. I was able to get out of the car with no more than a red face. That was the last time I ever personally spoke with General Bradley until after the war was over.

The 2nd Armored Division required over 650,000 gallons of gasoline to "gas up," and if all of the Division's vehicles were put in a column it would have stretched for fifty miles. I know those figures are hard to believe, but a heavyweight armored division like the 2nd Armored was an awesome war machine. The M-4 Sherman tanks were medium tanks with five crewmen and were initially equipped with a 75mm short-barreled rifle. This gun proved inadequate for penetrating the thick German tank armor, and later models of the M-4 were equipped with a longer-barreled, high-velocity 76mm rifle. During World War II the U.S. Army never did develop a workable heavy tank comparable to the German Tiger or Panther. Our tactics relied on overwhelming numbers, speed, maneuverability, and artillery support. Our tanks could go places, like muddy fields or narrow bridges, where the monstrous Tigers and Panthers couldn't dream of going.

The "Peeps" were equipped with a 508 FM radio and used extensively for reconnaissance and liaison between the batteries and the forward supported units. Each battery had several 2 1/2-ton trucks to carry extra ammunition, provisions, and a field kitchen. In those days we had to make our own kitchen truck. The Army nowadays has a specially designed, prefabricated kitchen truck for each unit, but during World War II we had to improvise and use our ingenuity. In the 92nd we took ordinary "deuce and a halfs" and converted them into portable field kitchens by enclosing them and mounting stoves inside each one. I don't know if we invented the idea or not because in the Army one unit would come up with an idea that worked and then before you knew it other units would be doing the same thing.

The most important artillery technique we practiced in England was one that we learned from the English in North Africa: the advantage of massed artillery fire. It was an axiom that artillery was never held in reserve but was to be utilized at every opportunity. When an artillery unit was not being used to support tanks or infantry directly in its front, the unit could be used to reinforce the fires of other artillery units. Every available unengaged artillery unit that could reach a selected target was brought to bear on it.

Artillery at that time was given three different assignments: direct support, general support, and reinforcement missions. Direct support meant that you were assigned a unit to support directly, and you responded to their needs primarily. This meant you furnished them forward observers and established liaison with the supported unit's headquarters. General support meant your assignment was to reinforce the fires of several other battalions that were in direct support of tanks or infantry directly in front of those units. A reinforcement mission meant your primary assignment was to furnish direct support to the tank or infantry unit to which you were assigned, but you also reinforced the fire of other artillery units in your area.

We also learned how to coordinate the fire from all the participating artillery units in a massed artillery attack. The objective was to have all the shells from the first volley land on the target at approximately the same moment to maximize the destructive force of the concentration and to maximize the casualties caused by the explosions, shell fragments, concussion, and shock. The technique was called a "stonk" by the British and "Time On Target" or "TOT" by us, and it had a tremendous effect on the enemy's morale. Whenever we were positioned near a

British artillery unit and heard "Stonk! Stonk!" over the radio, or were given a "serenade" order, which was our code name for "Time On Target," we knew that the Germans were in for one hell of a pounding.

The British also found that the "Stonk" technique was quite deadly on German armor. The panzers had thinner armor on top than around the sides because they were designed to engage the enemy at ground level. The British found that the M-7 "Priests" they had bought or borrowed from the United States made excellent antitank weapons in North Africa because the high angle of incoming 105mm howitzer shells hit the German tanks on the top and could either destroy the engine or penetrate the turret. Massed artillery fire increased the chances of knocking out a significant number of enemy tanks.

In the latter days of April and early May our training schedule changed, and we practiced loading our equipment on LCTs that were to be the craft we were to use in the invasion of Normandy. From the time we reached England in November 1943 we knew that we were being trained for an invasion of France. What we didn't know was where or when, although we assumed that General Eisenhower would wait until spring when the weather in the English Channel was better. I attended a number of conferences where we were given the order of battle and the plan of maneuver. I was even shown a mockup of the area where we were to land and how it would look on the horizon from the invasion fleet. However, I was not able to identify exactly where the location was because that particular type of terrain was common along much of the coast of France.

Of course, I was never told the date that the invasion would take place. There were many factors that had to be considered, but the weather was really *the* critical criterion. Not only did the weather have to be good the day of the invasion, but it had to hold for several days afterward so that supplies and reinforcements could be brought ashore to keep the invasion from being thrown back into the sea. I was only told that my unit was scheduled to leave Tidworth Barracks for the marshalling area on D-Day. I was informed that when I received the order to move my unit to Southampton, I could assume that the assault forces were hitting the beaches in France.

When I received the momentous march order, I ordered my subordinates to make all preparations to evacuate Tidworth, and the barracks and motor parks became hives of activity. Then, inexplicably, the order was cancelled a few hours later. The weather in Tidworth was lousy, so I figured that the invasion had been postponed for that reason. The following morning, 6 June 1944, I received another march order to proceed to Southampton. This time no cancellation order came and we moved out. That was when I knew that the invasion had really begun. By the time we reached the marshalling area in the vicinity of Winchester, the BBC was broadcasting the news about the invasion of Normandy to the entire world.

We were scheduled to load our equipment and vehicles on the LCTs on 7 June and proceed across the Channel, but because of the fierce resistance our assault troops met on Omaha Beach, which was our invasion destination, our departure was delayed. The Germans had mounted 88mm multipurpose guns on top of the cliffs that commanded Omaha Beach, and these wreaked havoc among the assault troops and invasion craft. We learned later that for awhile it appeared as if the assault force would be thrown back into the sea and that the invasion at Omaha Beach would fail. It wasn't until 8 June that our assault forces were able to break through the German defenses and take the commanding cliffs. We finally received our orders the next day to board the invasion craft. I boarded a LCT in Southampton Harbor at 1430 on 10 June. After several hours of waiting the ship left the pier and headed out of the harbor and into the English Channel bound for Omaha Beach. For me and the 92nd Armored Field Artillery Battalion, it was really the beginning of the war.

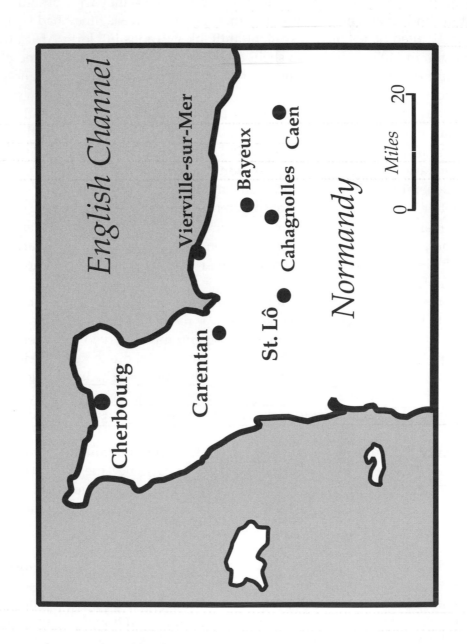

CHAPTER FIVE: INVASION

Operation Overlord, conducted by the American, British, and Canadian forces, was the largest amphibious operation in the history of modern warfare. Though it was a consummate military and political risk, it followed successful operations in North Africa, Sicily, and Salerno. This time the Allies faced what Hitler boasted was an impregnable Atlantic Wall defense line.

The initial objective of the invasion was to surprise Hitler by establishing a beachhead farther down the French coastline at Normandy, not the Pas de Calais, as the Germans expected. Once enough reinforcements and supplies were landed, a breakout from the beachhead would then be effected and the Allied armor could pour into the interior of France—blitzkrieg in reverse. Once the Allies broke out of Normandy and into open terrain, a second invasion force would land in southern France to prevent the German commanders there from sending reinforcements north to contain the American armor. The strategy then was to utilize the American advantage in men and material to overpower the Germans on the western front while the Russians sapped the enemy's strength in the east.

As a logistical operation, the invasion was extremely complicated and its success was due to the Allies' cooperative spirit, planning, and creative ingenuity. William Buster disembarked from his landing craft on Omaha Beach on 11 June 1944 (D + 5) amidst the wreckage of destroyed landing craft, vehicles, and beach obstacles. Once in the interior away from the coast, his unit stood in reserve while other units battled the Germans in the adjacent fields. By 2 July Buster's unit had been pressed into service on the line to provide artillery support for British operations. On 17 July they were relieved to prepare for a "break-out" action. Three days later Adolf Hitler survived an assassination attempt by several of his own generals.

Operation Overlord

Anyone who claims not to have experienced fear or apprehension before entering a combat situation is either lying or stupid. When I crossed the Channel I was most certainly apprehensive, although I always had great confidence that I was going to make it through the war alive. But some of the enlisted men in my battalion were superstitious and carried some kind of good-luck charm such as rabbits feet or four-leaf clovers. The only thing I did that might be considered superstitious came the day we landed. I began to grow a mustache and vowed not to shave it off until we captured Paris. Unbeknownst to me at the time, my mustache would become quite bushy before we ever saw the Seine River.

The only personal belongings I took with me were pictures of my wife and son. We were encouraged to leave most of our personal items back in England because there wasn't room to carry a lot of excess baggage. In addition, you didn't want to give the enemy any additional information they could use against you in case you were captured.

The commander of the 2nd Armored Division for the Normandy invasion was General Robert "Balls of Fire" Brooks. He acquired his unofficial nickname because of his penchant for saying "Great balls of fire!" whenever he got excited. He would not expose his troops to any unnecessary danger, but he was an aggressive commander. He was a good man to follow into Normandy.

I had been briefed on the trouble our assault troops had experienced on Omaha Beach, which is why my unit's crossing had been delayed several days, and I knew that the German defenses were going to be a tough nut to crack. But I can say in all honesty that my own safety was not a primary concern for me. I had too many other things to worry about.

For instance, one of the LSTs in our convoy across the Channel was carrying part of the 66th Armored Regiment over to Omaha Beach. It hit a mine and sank. Some of the troops aboard drowned, and all of the armored vehicles, of course, went down with the ship. So on the short voyage over to France I was more concerned about whether the other LCTs carrying the rest of my battalion would get there without incident and what the situation would be like once we landed.

We arrived off Omaha Easy Red Beach right about dusk the evening of 10 June. Division Artillery Headquarters and the 14th Armored Field Artillery Battalion had disembarked earlier that day and were in position a few miles inland. I wasn't prepared for the tremendous amount of confusion we encountered offshore. There were ships of all sizes—destroyers, LSTs, LCTs, LCVPs—all over the place discharging troops and equipment or just waiting their turn. When we arrived it was beginning to get too dark for us to unload so we just sat offshore aboard our LCTs all night. And what a night it was! As soon as it became totally dark the Luftwaffe showed up and made bombing and strafing runs up and down the beach throughout the night. The noise from exploding bombs, screaming aircraft, and our own antiaircraft fire made for a real interesting night. A ship not fifty yards from my LCT was hit by a bomb and sank, but because of all the noise and confusion we didn't realize it until the next morning. I finally succumbed to nervous exhaustion and actually fell asleep for a couple of hours while all of this was going on.

As soon as the first signs of dawn broke above the horizon, the German planes turned tail and headed back east, and I could see waves of American fighters and fighter-bombers appear over the northern horizon flying from their bases in England to cover the beachhead area. As we quickly found out, the Army Air Corps controlled the skies during the day but the Luftwaffe had more sophisticated night fighters and would come out to play after our fighters went home in the evening.

Because of the large number of ships waiting offshore to unload their troops and equipment, we didn't get to disembark from our LCT until two o'clock on the afternoon of the eleventh. Just before we disembarked the commander of our landing craft, a Lieutenant Seymour of the Royal Navy Volunteer Reserve, paid us a kindness I have never forgotten. He offered all of us a ration of rum and wished us good luck and Godspeed.

As we drove down the ramp of the LCT into the surf about fifty yards off the beach, I saw that our assigned portion of the beach (300 yards wide at low tide) itself was littered with the vestiges of the hard fight that the assault troops had experienced in establishing a foothold. There was a ten-foot-deep line of heavy wooden stakes angled toward the sea the length of the beach to prevent landing craft from approaching, and iron tetrahedral obstacles were scattered everywhere to tear the bottom out of landing craft or hang up tanks. There were many destroyed American landing craft and vehicles along the beach front, but by the time we landed, the beach parties had cleared channels through the obstacles so that the newly arriving ships had safe avenues of approach.

My battalion got onto the beach with relatively little difficulty. Some of the LCTs could not pull up right onto the beach itself so some of the men and equipment were unloaded into the surf. Even though we had waterproofed the vehicles prior to embarking at Southampton we had some vehicles drown out. With the exception of the intake and exhaust openings, we had sealed up all openings to each vehicle's engine. To the intake and exhaust openings we had attached long pipes so that they extended well above the top of the vehicles. Theoretically, the vehicles should have been able to run underwater. Even the "Peeps" were sealed so they would operate in two or three feet of water without drowning out. However, we did have some vehicles drown out in the surf, and as soon as the vehicles reached the beach the waterproofing equipment was taken off so the engines would not overheat.

We landed just below Vierville-sur-Mer, which was located on a cliff overlooking the beach, and we had to cross a flat shelf of sand to get to the road that led from the beach to the top of the hill. Right at the base of the cliff was a destroyed German 88mm multipurpose gun emplacement that had commanded the whole length of the beach. Although the Germans had been cleared out of their defensive positions on top of the cliffs, someone in the beach party warned us that there were snipers in Vierville and that some of the roads had been mined. I don't know if that

My command post at La Mine. "I remember that first night on French soil very vividly. My battalion had never been in combat before, and with reports and rumors circulating that there were snipers and infiltrators in the area the atmosphere was tense."

was true or if they were just trying to scare us, but we proceeded very cautiously on the way to our bivouac area. At the top of the hill we were met by a guide who took us through Vierville and Bayeux to our designated position, La Mine, which was just south of La Poterie, about eight or nine miles inland from the beach.

On the way there we passed the bodies of several GIs who had been killed opening up the very road we were traveling on and had not yet been picked up by the Graves Registration people. It was a very sobering sight. I don't recall my first encounter with a dead German. I might have seen a few in some of the gun emplacements or pillboxes we passed on the hill overlooking the beach at Vierville. But I remember vividly one of the most gruesome scenes I ever saw during the war. We were moving through the little town of Canisy at night after it had been captured that day following a severe battle. A German soldier who had been killed was lying in the middle of the street. Our half-tracks and tanks had run over him until he was flat as a pancake. I mean he was as thin as a piece of paper.

The sight of enemy dead didn't disturb me but seeing the bodies of American soldiers did. You try not to dwell on the dead and dying in a war zone because, ironically, it's just a fact of life. It's something that is to be expected and nothing to be too concerned about because when you encounter dead people, the event has already taken place and there's nothing you can do about it. You can get pretty callous, and the longer you're exposed to it the more callous you become.

I suppose that's the reason atrocities occur during wartime. Soldiers get to the point where human life is not nearly so important as it seemed before. Your mission becomes paramount. Not that, as a commander, you deliberately expose your men or civilians to unnecessary danger, but if it's necessary to the accomplishment of your mission, you can't hold back for that reason. For example, if a bridge has to be crossed and the enemy has it covered with machine guns and mortars, just because whoever goes across it is likely to get killed or wounded doesn't keep a commander from ordering his people across. The same applies to you as an individual. In France, Belgium, and Germany there were lots of places I certainly didn't want to go, but I did go because I had to accomplish my mission.

We arrived at our bivouac area near La Mine about 1530. I remember that first night on French soil very vividly. My battalion had never been in combat before, and with reports and rumors circulating that there were snipers and infiltrators in the area the atmosphere was tense. We posted our own security, set up listening posts, and implemented a system whereby each listening post had to report in at scheduled times during the night. Despite these precautions, nervous, sporadic shooting happened throughout our bivouac area all night, and I wasn't about to go out and find out who was doing it. As jumpy and tense as my men were, I realized that I could just as easily have been shot by one of them as by the enemy. After what they had seen on the beach they were in the mood to shoot first and issue a challenge later. However, we all settled down very quickly after the first night, and there were few repeat performances the remainder of the war.

We stayed at La Mine for ten days because the invasion was going well and there was no need to commit the 2nd Armored Division to combat. Our division was intended to be the reinforcement for the initial invasion force. While we unloaded and assembled, the assault troops expanded the beachhead and the Air Corps pounded the German armor that was sent to reinforce their battered defenses. On 13 June the Germans did launch a strong counterattack led by Tiger tanks in the vicinity of Carentan, which was located at the juncture of Omaha and Utah Beaches and divided the V and VII Corps. Junctures like this are sometimes weak spots because coverage responsibilities between units are occasionally unclear. Rommel, who was in charge of the German defenses, gambled that that would be the case here. The counterattack was met by the 101st and 82nd Airborne. Combat Command A of the 2nd Armored Division was sent in to support them and, of course, the Germans were repulsed.

That battle was mostly a tank and infantry fight because it was fought in the area of France dominated by hedgerows. I don't think anyone in their wildest imagination visualized what a nightmare fighting in the hedgerows would be. The "bocage" area, as it was called, was a complete surprise to all of us. It was something for which the whole army was totally unprepared, not something that was peculiar to members of the 2nd Armored Division or our Corps. It created a tactical situation that didn't exist anywhere else except, perhaps, in the jungles of the South Pacific where the vegetation was so thick that the enemy couldn't be seen from a distance of ten feet.

We knew about the existence of the hedgerows from aerial photographs, but the photographs did not do justice to the actual terrain we encountered on the ground. The hedgerows were not just rows of trees but were mounds of earth eight to ten feet high. The tree line on top of each hedgerow had formed an interlocking root system that made an almost impenetrable barrier. The hedgerows were constructed by the French farmers to act as a barrier to the strong winds that came off the Normandy coast. The only connections between the fields were gateways that the inhabitants long ago had cut into the hedgerows.

This area presented us with a great many problems. In order for the tanks and infantry to attack through this terrain they either had to use the existing openings or blast new holes through the hedgerows. Using the existing openings was very hazardous because the Germans had those covered with tanks, 88mm multipurpose rifles, and machine guns. Blasting a new hole only served to inform the enemy of your intentions, and by the time the first troops emerged through it the Germans had shifted some of their guns to cover that area as well. It was a very difficult situation and one that produced a high number of casualties. This was not tank country at all, especially for the attackers.

It was not good artillery country either. Ground observation was difficult because even on high ground it was almost impossible to get any field of vision other than of the small area or field directly in front of you. Each field in the hedgerow country was no larger than ten acres, and most were smaller than that. Each field had to be fought for individually. Ladders became a scarce commodity because they were used to put observers up in the trees or on top of hedgerows so they could see two or three fields ahead. It was here in the hedgerow country that the value of the flying OP (Observation Post) was proven because by flying back and forth over the area you could adjust artillery fire to render support to the attacking troops ahead of you. It was impossible to do this from the ground.

The aircraft we used for the flying OP were Piper Cubs or L-4s, which were not very powerful or expensive. These little two-seat planes only had a 65 horsepower Continental engine in them and reached a top speed of less than 100 miles per hour. We called them "Grasshoppers" for obvious reasons. The pilot would ride in the front seat and the observer would sit behind him. The aircraft was equipped with an FM radio so that the observer could contact individual artillery battalions and tank or infantry units they were supporting. Aerial observation really proved its value in the hedgerow country, and we utilized it whenever we could throughout the remainder of the war. Our observers became so adept by the end of the war that they could identify a target and bring fire down on it almost immediately without any need for fire adjustment. The accuracy of our maps and meteorological data was so good that directing artillery fire from the L-4s became almost an exact science.

The hedgerows created other problems of observation for us as well, as we found out the first few days at La Mine. As the Luftwaffe pilots headed home at dawn after a night of attacking the beach area, they would fly low and strafe targets of opportunity. They would come in so quickly over the hedgerows that they were on top of us and gone before we could even put up any antiaircraft fire. Occasionally a German pilot would linger too long over the beach and would be caught by American fighters at daybreak. The American-built P-51 Mustangs and P-47 Thunderbolts were superior aircraft to the mainstay of the Luftwaffe, the Messerschmitt-109F, and a match for the Focke-Wulf 190. When caught by the American planes the only hope of survival the German pilot had was to stay low to the ground and take his chances running the gauntlet of our antiaircraft batteries. We knew the American pilots were forbidden to fly that low because of the possibility of their being shot down by our own ground forces, so we realized that anything flying low was the enemy. Several mornings in a row fleeing German aircraft buzzed us.

One particular morning my unit decided they had had enough and were waiting for the German aircraft to appear. Out of seemingly nowhere one came over and "Zoom!" was gone before we could even get off a shot. Almost immediately another plane came over, and this time the antiaircraft boys really let him have it. The plane began smoking and eventually crashed in the distance. Unfortunately, it turned out to be an American who had been in pursuit of the Messerschmitt. The pilot had either disregarded the order to stay at a higher altitude or had become so engrossed in the dogfight that he forgot where he was. On 22 June General Bradley issued an order stating that unless directly under attack, no units other than regular antiaircraft units were to fire at enemy aircraft. I don't know if the order came as a result of the incident involving my unit because it happened more than once to other units as well. But the 92nd's first inflicted battle damage of the war happened to be one of our own planes. It was really due to the nature of the bocage country, where there was no field of fire and you couldn't see a whole lot.

Lt. Col. Buster with mustache and red scarf. "Someone discovered that the silk from the parachutes made a comfortable barrier between the collar of the uniform and the skin."

The hedgerow country wasn't suited for attacking infantry either. You had to fight hedgerow by hedgerow, and murderous machine gun, antitank, and rifle fire covered each hedgerow by the entrenched enemy. As the infantry negotiated their way over or through the hedgerows they were in great peril. When a tank attempted to go over a hedgerow and reared up to clear it, the lightly armored underbelly was exposed to the antitank fire of the German 88mm rifles. If a bulldozer was used to plow a new hole, it was immediately shot up as well. The 67th Tank Battalion experimented with mounting a platform containing approximately sixty 4-inch rockets on one of their tanks. They fired the rockets directly at one of the hedgerows to blow a hole through it but found that the dispersement of the exploding rockets was too great to be of any use. There was simply no way to get through the hedgerows without taking heavy casualties.

The German 88mm rifle was a splendid weapon, much feared by our tankers. The Germans had developed their artillery rifles to a far greater extent than we had. The 88mm rifle had been developed initially as an antiaircraft weapon. It had a long barrel to increase the muzzle velocity needed to propel shells a couple of miles into the air and sophisticated muzzle brakes that controlled the recoil when it was fired. In North Africa the Germans discovered that it also made a fine antitank weapon. The projectile itself was not that large but it was delivered with such speed and accuracy that it put the fear of God into our tankers. An 88mm shell could penetrate our Sherman tanks like a hot knife through butter. The smell of a burning tank is one that few veterans who have had the experience will ever forget, and we saw plenty of them in Normandy.

The Germans also utilized a rocket launcher technically called a Nebelwerfer but which we nicknamed the "screaming meemie" because the rockets produced a nerve-wracking screeching sound. The Nebelwerfers were six-barreled weapons that fired either 150mm or 210 mm rockets that shook the earth when they exploded. The rockets had a range of over 7,000 yards but, fortunately, were not very accurate. I think they were used more for their psychological effect on the Allied troops than for their ability to produce casualties, although the rockets did possess a lot of destructive power. We got hit several times by "screaming meemies" while battling our way out of Normandy and, believe me, they scared the hell out of us.

The existing roads in Normandy were actually just channels running between the hedgerows and these were ideally suited for German ambushes. The Germans covered them with antitank fire as well as intensive machine gun fire. Tactically, the bocage area was very difficult terrain to work in. We paid a terrible price punching holes in the German defenses. It basically came down to individual American soldiers devising their own means of penetrating the hedgerows, clearing out the enemy, and then moving on to the next hedgerow.

The soldiers came up with some marvelous innovations. I remember some of the experimentation that occurred in the 2nd Armored Division, and I'm sure each tank unit was trying to think of some way to even the odds. The most effective invention was a sickle-like blade made from scrap metal from the German beach obstructions and welded like teeth onto the front of the tanks. We called these tanks "Rhinos." As the tank would hit a hedgerow, the teeth would sever the roots of the trees and allow the tank to move through the hedgerow instead of having to go up and over, thereby exposing the underbelly of the tank. The employment of tanks in the hedgerows became much more effective after this invention, but it took a while to develop.

Communication between the infantry and the supporting armor was also an early problem. It's difficult for ground troops to support a tank or vice versa if they can't communicate with each other and discuss where to go or what to do. In order to overcome that, the tankers attached a telephone on the outside of the tank that was connected with the tank's communication system so that an infantryman could tell the tankers the location of machine-gun emplacements or snipers or mine fields. However, tanks attracted a lot of enemy fire, and being near one was not the safest spot on the battlefield.

We developed all sorts of different techniques and tactics, none of which we had practiced in England because we didn't expect this kind of terrain. The Ordnance Department also did what they could to help us deal with the situation, including outfitting replacement tanks with larger-caliber guns. Our M-4 Shermans were initially equipped with short-barreled 75mm rifles. On 21 and 22 June we tested the armor-piercing capabilities of the 2nd Armored Division's weapons against a German Mark V "Panther" tank which had been captured by the British 7th Armored Division. The results showed that the Sherman's 75mm rifle and the 3-inch gun on a tank destroyer could penetrate only the sides of the tank at close range. Only the 155mm howitzer and the 90mm towed gun were able to penetrate the frontal armor of the Panther.

On 18 July the 2nd Armored Division began to obtain some Shermans which mounted a long 76mm rifle. In addition to having a slightly larger projectile with more explosive power, the longer barrel on the 76mm rifles increased the muzzle velocity that made them more effective against German armor and fortified machine-gun emplacements.

While the struggle for control over the hedgerow area was being contested, the 2nd Armored Division was kept in reserve. The Normandy campaign became a typical beachhead operation. The first objective of an amphibious operation is to establish a foothold. Then, while the assault troops wear down the enemy's resistance and expand the beachhead, reserve forces are landed until they're strong enough to effect a breakout. We remained in our bivouac area near La Mine during this period, and the Quartermaster and Ordnance Corps were able to supply us with our full complement of ammunition and supplies. We weren't hard to find.

All of the units in the Division had code names that we used on road signs or in the telephone directory for the remainder of the war. The code names all began with the letter "P." The 92nd went by the code name of "Projectile," the 14th was "Powder," and the 78th was "Primer." Division Artillery was "Polygon," the supply battalion was "Produce," and Division Headquarters was known as "Powerhouse." For security reasons they would never put "Headquarters, 2nd Armored Division" on a road sign. Instead they painted the word "Powerhouse," and everyone understood that that meant the 2nd Armored Division Headquarters. You identified yourself on the telephone or radio the same way. Anyone who came to visit the 92nd at our bivouac area near La Mine had only to look for the word "Projectile" on the road signs to find his way.

I remember that while we were at La Mine, we were issued new clothing. When we went into France we wore poison gas-protective clothing because we didn't know how the Germans would react to the invasion. The protective clothing was hot and heavy and had a terrible odor to it. It was also roughly textured; the collar would rub your neck raw after a few days. This led to a clothing innovation among the artillery troops which after the war became a traditional part of an artilleryman's uniform. There were many parachutes left behind by the 82nd and 101st Airborne divisions in the areas we went through. Someone discovered that the silk from the parachutes made a comfortable barrier between the collar of the uniform and the skin. Soon practically every officer and enlisted man in the 92nd, as well as other division units, was sporting a scarf of parachute silk around his neck. After the war the artillery adopted a red scarf as part of their uniform. Thus, what began as a practical solution to a problem developed into a tradition for artillery units.

We wore the gas-protective clothing for about two weeks until the beachhead was well established and the fear of gas warfare abated, and then we were issued new clothing. The new clothing was a dark-olive, drab color. The Army had not yet developed the more comfortable combat fatigues that were worn in Vietnam and are generally worn in the Army now. Our wool clothing got itchy when you were hot and perspired. As an officer I had to purchase my own clothing. (Officers were not given their uniforms.) Most officers in the 2nd Armored Division wore the dark armored force jacket that was shorter and fit more snugly than the standard-issue M1943 jacket. The armored force jacket had a smooth exterior facing, perfect for crawling in and out of armored vehicles. Loose-fitting clothing would catch on hatch openings. I had extra clothing in the baggage train that followed along behind us in the rear areas wherever we went. Although it wasn't accessible while we were on the move, once we settled down someplace for a while the baggage train would eventually catch up with us and I could go back and take what I needed from my footlocker.

I wore basically the same clothing as the enlisted men because it was safer to blend in and not stand out as an officer. In close combat our infantrymen were told to pick out officers as targets, and we assumed the German foot soldier had been told the same thing. Because of that our officers wore blackened-metal rank insignia instead of the shiny silver or gold. I also wore a steel pot helmet equipped with camouflage netting, and my blackened rank insignia was on the front and I had a white stripe down the back of the helmet. The white stripe was there to alert friendly troops that I was an officer. Most front-line American officers wore helmets like this.

I wore standard combat boots that were very comfortable and lasted a long time, and a three-inch-wide webbed belt around my waist. From my belt I attached various equipment such as my first-aid kit, canteen, and .45 pistol. Infantrymen usually carried additional things such as extra ammunition clips, a bayonet, ration bars, and sometimes a small container of lubricating oil for their rifle. In the artillery we usually wore the least amount of gear possible because we were constantly hopping in and out of our vehicles. We left most of our other equipment in the half-tracks or support vehicles.

During the initial days of the invasion we were also issued gas masks. Everyone was supposed to have his gas mask attached to his webbed belt for quick access in case of a sudden poison-gas attack. The masks were bulky and were considered a nuisance. As time went on we all became more and more careless about keeping our gas masks handy. I recall one night in July, just before Operation Cobra began, a machine gun cut loose in the distance and then followed voices yelling "Gas! Gas!" I don't know how it got started; perhaps someone mistook an exploding canister of white phosphorous for mustard gas. All I know is that the alarm spread like wildfire up and down the front-line for miles. Naturally, everybody started scrambling for their gas masks. My executive officer, Bill Bowers, a fairly big man, had left his mask in his trailer along with his other equipment when he climbed into his pup tent for the night. At the sound of the word "Gas!" I saw him dash across the bivouac area in his underwear headed for that trailer. He dived in the back of it and things began flying out until he finally emerged wearing only his underwear and his gas mask. By that time the alarm had been over for several minutes and his fellow officers with some good-natured derision greeted him! Bill had acquired a reputation in the States as a ladies' man and was a real character.

On 1 July we received orders to move from La Mine over to the left flank of the American line where it joined the British right flank at Cahagnolles. The purpose was to increase the artillery capability of the American V Corps and the British 50th (Northumberland) Division. Field Marshal Bernard Montgomery had assured Generals Eisenhower and Bradley that the British Second Army would breach the German defense at Caen, which would lead to an Allied breakout from the Normandy beachhead.

When we arrived at our position we established liaison with the adjoining British Second Army, specifically the 2nd Gloucester Regiment and the 3rd Royal Highlander Artillery. I got to know Lieutenant Colonel William Norman of the 3rd RHA quite well. It was common practice to establish contact with any neighboring units in your area, and in doing so we offered them our support and requested their support when it was needed.

That day we fired our first artillery mission of the war. At 0100 on 2 July the Division fired its first "serenade" or "Time On Target" attack of the war on the village of Anctoville, where our aerial observers had reported a concentration of German infantry. From that day forward we were firing counterbattery, harassing, interdiction, or propaganda missions practically every day until the end of the war. At 1200 on 4 July the Division fired an "Independence Day Salute" again on Anctoville, and even the British artillery joined in. Two hundred and eighty guns participated in this attack, the target being a large concentration of German troops and a heavy tank battalion of the 101st SS Regiment. The next day the Germans returned the favor and shelled us. The 987th Field Artillery got hit the hardest, but we also took quite a few rounds in our area.

On the sixth we were called upon to reinforce the artillery fire of the British in their attack against St. Germain d'Ectot. The battle lasted for three days and was a series of attacks and counterattacks by both sides. At 1100 on 8 July we fired a preparation barrage in support of the British 2nd Essex Brigade which finally routed the enemy from St. Germain. We were located west of Hottot on some high ground that overlooked a valley. At 1230 British "Sound Rangers" located a column of thirty Mark IV "Tiger" tanks and three companies of enemy infantry advancing down the valley in an attempt to retake St. Germain. The British requested through our headquarters that we fire a "stonk" against the advancing German column. The request was immediately approved, and we later found out from a captured enemy officer that we had caught the Germans in an orchard as the unit commanders were getting their orders at their command post. Our attack resulted in the destruction of four "Tiger" tanks, heavy casualties among the infantry, and the destruction of the command post with most of the officers and staff. We fired almost eighteen hundred rounds that day. The following day we broke up another counterattack before it ever got started and destroyed two more tanks.

We were really in a fortunate position on the left flank of the American line. An extensive wire communication system linked us with the British units and also our own headquarters, so we became a relay station for information. The British artillery headquarters would give us the location of targets that their "Sound Rangers" had spotted, and we would give them the location of targets that our aerial OP had observed. On one occasion the 2nd Gloucester Regiment launched a small attack in order to gain some information about the German positions and units which were in front of them. They gave us the mission of firing a box around the area. When the attack began we fired on both sides of the box and then fired across the ends so the enemy would be discouraged from bringing up reinforcements. The British troops were able to go in, capture several prisoners, and withdraw without any casualties on their part. The coordination between our unit and the supported British unit worked quite well on that particular occasion.

I was very impressed by the bravery of the British soldiers. British tactics were somewhat different than ours. On many occasions they declined to take advantage of any natural cover when advancing. Our troops were taught to "advance by infiltration." This meant that they were instructed to hit the ground and crawl on their bellies when under fire, and then get up and run again when the opportunity presented itself. When the British went into combat they just fired from the hip and kept walking forward. There would be guys falling all over the place but the line would keep advancing. It must have been terrifying, I think, to an enemy to see that kind of courage. Psychologically, it was a good tactic, but it was rather costly.

I remember one of the British attacks in early July on St. Germain that we supported with artillery fire. The next day I went over to see the British infantry battalion commander to find out how the attack had gone. All he said was "Poor show." I think they had suffered about 40 percent casualties that day, but he didn't make a big deal out of it. I found that to be typical British stoicism.

On 10 and 11 July we fired three propaganda "serenades" against the enemy's front line. These attacks began with a broadcast from our Division G-2 across the front line trying to persuade the German soldiers to surrender. To emphasize the futility of their situation, we then fired a "stonk" on their positions. I never knew the results of these propaganda efforts, but it had to have exerted some effect on the enemy's will to fight. We knocked out another German Mark IV tank with precision fire on 13 July, but two days later we got a taste of our own medicine when the Germans shelled us again. During this attack the 92nd suffered its first casualties of the war, with two dead and two wounded.

On 17 July we were pulled out of the line. Our position was taken over by the British 8th Armored Brigade and the British 50th Division. Despite Field Marshal Montgomery's promise to General Eisenhower that he would achieve a breakthrough at Caen, the British attack had stalled. Only that part of the town that lay west of the Orne River was in Allied hands.

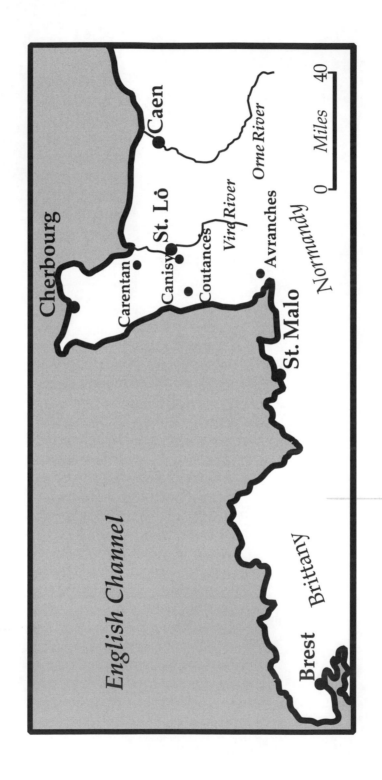

CHAPTER SIX: OPERATION COBRA - THE ST. LO BREAKOUT

Seven weeks after D-Day, the Allies launched Operation Cobra, an offensive designed to break through the German defenses in Normandy. The ground assault was preceded by a massive aerial bombing attack in order to open a narrow corridor through the German lines through which the American armored forces could drive and effect a breakout from France's Cotentin Peninsula. The attack began tragically on 24 July when supporting bombers unleashed thousands of bombs which fell short and into the American lines. After providing artillery fire to support the first day's attack, the 92nd Armored Field Artillery Battalion moved out and for the next six days followed the 2nd Armored Division's attacking tanks and infantry through the remaining hedgerows and into open country. Engaging the enemy in several pitched battles, Buster's unit assisted in outflanking retreating German units caught in several pockets by the hard-charging American forces. The 92nd Armored Field Artillery Battalion distinguished itself near St. Denis le Gast while destroying a retreating German column. Following the successful breakout from Normandy, the 2nd Armored Division and other Allied forces were poised to exploit the interior of France.

On 18 July Montgomery launched "Operation Goodwood," one final attempt to breach the German defenses in the vicinity of Caen. Unfortunately, the attack advanced only six miles before it, too, was stopped. In the meantime the American VII Corps, which held the right flank of the beachhead, had been trying to advance out of the marshy ground where the Douve and Taute Rivers converge near the Carentan area. But they had met with little success because of the hedgerow terrain and stiff German resistance. This lack of success on both Allied flanks caused General Bradley to propose a powerful thrust, code named "Cobra," that would break through the German defensive line around the area of St. Lo and allow our armored forces to advance farther inland out of the hedgerow country. Once beyond the hedgerows we could better utilize our mobility, speed, and firepower.

The 2nd Armored Division was given the job of spearheading this American breakout from the Normandy beachhead. After we were pulled off the line on 17 July, we were sent to a rear area where we rejoined the rest of the Division. For the next several days we prepared for the attack. All units that were going to participate were pulled back and shielded from contact with the enemy so that our whereabouts would not be known. New units that would ordinarily have been thrown in as reinforcements against probing attacks by the Germans on the right flank also were not committed in order to keep the Germans in the dark as to our total strength and intentions. We knew that our biggest advantage would be the element of surprise. On 22 July I was personally surprised to learn that I had been awarded a Bronze Star for my participation in the British attacks on St. Germain. That same day we heard rumors that Hitler had survived an assassination attempt by some of his own generals. Things were beginning to look up.

The first time I heard the word "Cobra" used was the day after we were withdrawn from the front and moved back. As the plan was explained, it appeared very similar to an off-tackle play in football where the offensive line opens up a hole and the running back goes through and exploits the territory behind the line. In reality that's the way the plan worked out. General Bradley's plan called for saturation bombing by Army Air Corps light and heavy bombers of a two-mile-by-four-mile rectangle just west of the town of St. Lo to soften up the enemy. The infantry could move forward and roll back the enemy's flanks, and then the armor could go plunging through the hole much like the halfback carrying the football.

There was a great deal of rain during that preparation period, and no one at my level knew exactly when the attack would begin. I was told that when the 92nd received orders to move to a position right behind the front-line infantry, the attack was imminent. I was informed that after the 92nd was in position, the attacking tanks would pass through our position if necessary to make the breakthrough. I had the understanding that "Cobra" was going to take place on 21 July, but because of the bad weather conditions it was postponed several times.

We were told that there would be a massive preparatory carpet bombing of an area nine thousand yards wide and twenty-five hundred yards deep in the St. Lo area prior to the ground assault. It was an excellent plan but, unfortunately, at this point in the war coordination between ground forces and the Air Corps was not all that good and this led to early disaster at the outset of the attack. As a matter of fact, during the Normandy campaign some ground commanders asked the Air Corps *not* to provide close ground support because there had been several occasions where the aircraft had missed the intended target and a serious number of American casualties had resulted.

General Elwood Quesada was instrumental in bringing about the necessary coordination. He commanded the 9th Tactical Air Command and established an advance headquarters in Normandy on D+1. It was the 9th Tactical Air Command that developed the technique of assigning pilots, equipped with Army Air Corps radios, to ground-troop units to act as ground liaison for the Air Corps. When this technique was refined, the coordination between ground forces and aircraft became much better and the admiration between the two services grew. But during the Normandy campaign close ground support was a technique that still had to be refined.

When the bombing began at 1100 on 24 July, we thought the attack was beginning and prepared to move the battalion to the vicinity of Pont Hebert just behind the front line. However, the bombing stopped very shortly after it began when the weather deteriorated again. Air Marshal Sir Trafford Leigh-Mallory himself had come over to watch the bombing effort. When he arrived and found overcast skies he decided to postpone the attack just minutes before the first planes were due to arrive over the target area. But about 20 percent of the aircraft didn't receive the word and released their bombs over what they thought was the target area, with disastrous results. Many of the bombs fell short, and there were over a hundred and fifty casualties inflicted on the American 30th Infantry Division.

The next day was a perfect one weather-wise. I was in a splendid position to observe the bombing attack because my battalion was in an assembly area on a high point overlooking the target area. At 1100 we saw what seemed to be an endless stream of bombers come in from the north. They came over perpendicular to our lines and dropped their bombs. The front-line infantry had been withdrawn about twelve hundred yards prior to the attack as a safety precaution. As it turned out that wasn't nearly far enough.

The bombing attack made a magnificent sight because the falling bombs looked like confetti, and then the ground in the target area would erupt as the bombs struck home. The bombers would fly on for a short distance, turn to the right 90 degrees, and then make another 90-degree turn to head back to England. Soon there was wave after wave of bombers going in both directions and the target area was just being torn to pieces. This went on for two and a half hours.

After the heavy bombers had dropped their payloads, and while the medium bombers and fighters were making their runs, I received orders to move my battalion to our pre-selected location just behind the infantry withdrawal line. The medium bombers and fighters flew over us the entire time that we were moving into our jump-off position near Pont Hebert. On one occasion I looked back and saw a flight of B-25 Mitchell bombers off in the distance behind us.

While I watched I suddenly saw them release their bombs five thousand yards behind us. I'm not sure what happened to that particular flight, but they obviously had mistaken their position and dropped their bombs prematurely.

As the bombing proceeded, the smoke and dust obliterated the target area. Then the wind shifted and started wafting the smoke and dust toward our lines so the bombardiers began releasing their bombs shorter and shorter, thinking that the smoke was the target area. Eventually the smoke drifted over our lines and the troops just ahead of us began to be bombed by our own planes. General Lesley J. McNair and his staff had selected a position on high ground about a thousand yards in front of my battalion as an observation point to watch the attack. As the smoke drifted over our lines they were bombed by our own aircraft. General McNair, along with several members of his staff, was killed. General McNair was one of the highest-ranking American officers killed in action during the war.

We were actually located in the middle of the 30th Infantry Division. Their soldiers occupied the field in front of our battalion assembly area. After the bombing was over we hurried into that field and found many casualties. It was a disastrous way to begin the breakout attack. I understand that the 30th Division had gotten clobbered the day before as well.

The result of the errant bombing was that infantry regiments that were supposed to open the attack for "Cobra" were so dazed and demoralized that they weren't able to coordinate the attack immediately after the bombing stopped. Their communication systems were disrupted, and many of the soldiers were in shock. These were the troops that were supposed to roll back the German defenses and "hold their block" until the armored units barreled through. During the day we fired missions in support of the infantry and two "Time on Target" attacks on enemy columns entering the battle area. Because of the effects of the bombing on our own troops, the attack bogged down and no breakthrough took place that day.

During the night it was decided that at 0900 the 2nd Armored Division would launch their attack with or without infantry support. The two infantry regiments committed for the attack still were in no condition to move. It was a dangerous tactic and a gamble. At 0900 Combat Command A (CCA) attacked south. We remained in our position behind the infantry's main line of defense and fired in support of CCA's attack. The plan was for CCA to launch the attack and continue south through the town of Canisy. They would then secure the Vire Ridge, including the village of Tessy Sur Vire on the Vire River. Combat Command B (CCB) was to follow CCA to Canisy and then make a right turn and launch an attack due south. The 92nd was given the task of providing direct support for CCB.

Consequently, when CCA began its attack, my battalion reinforced the artillery fire of the 14th Field Artillery Battalion and an unattached artillery battalion as long as we could. But since our main mission was to support Combat Command B, after CCA moved out of range we did no more firing until CCB began its advance.

We moved out at 0700 on 27 July and proceeded to a position that we had reconnoitered the day before which was south of a little place named Hebecrevon. While the main body of CCB was on the road we again moved into range of CCA and were able to help support their continuing attack. Hebecrevon is just north of Canisy, and there we saw the effects of the carpet-bombing effort. The damage was horrific. When CCA launched their attack they found the cratering effect from the bombing so bad that they were unable to use the roads for any appreciable distance. They finally had to take parallel routes through the fields and make their way around the bomb craters and debris.

When we took up our position near Hebrecrevon we saw the devastation firsthand. There didn't appear to be a green sprig of vegetation anywhere, and there were bomb craters all over the place. However, engineers from the 17th Armored Engineer Battalion were already working to fix the roads. On several occasions we discovered German soldiers crawling out of their hiding places or bomb craters. Some of them were so shell-shocked that they were unable to hear or speak. They went all to pieces when they saw us. I don't recall how many prisoners we took, but there were several hundred. We encountered complete and total devastation.

At 1600 on 27 July I again received orders to move the 92nd. By this time Combat Command B had moved through Canisy and begun their attack to the south. At dusk Colonel Thomas Roberts summoned me to the Division Artillery Command Post. He told me that in order to provide support for both CCA and CCB I was to reconnoiter and occupy a position on a transverse road between the two routes of advance. As I looked at my map I discovered that the road was really just a country lane, and since it was between the two columns, it had not been cleared of mines or the enemy. I brought this fact to the attention of Colonel Roberts, who said, "Oh, you can make it. Just go ahead and move in there."

So I climbed into my Jeep with my driver and one of my warrant officers, an enormous guy of American Indian descent and a great fighter, and off we went. We stopped to gather up the three reconnaissance parties from the 92nd's three batteries and then proceeded into the darkness. We entered an area that had not seen our Division reconnaissance forces or any other of our combat elements. It was the first time that I had ever been really scared, and I think everyone with me was, too. We didn't know what was in front of or beside us. I think we all expected to hear the stutter of burp guns or the crack of an 88mm rifle at any second. I certainly didn't feel like running smack into a "Tiger" tank in the middle of the night. I remember the fear that pervaded my whole being. My mouth became so dry I could have spit cotton the farther we went down that country lane.

We continued down the road and got about halfway to our destination when I decided that we had gone far enough. We made a fast reconnaissance of the area and found positions where we could put our three batteries and the headquarters. I radioed back to the assembled battalion and told them to get on the road, and then sent back a guide to meet them and guide them to our position. That might have been the longest hour of my life, just sitting quietly waiting for my battalion to arrive.

About the time the battalion began to move out, the German night-fighters arrived and dive-bombed our column and worked over the whole area that CCA had taken. I don't think the 92nd was their specific target, but they were intent on attacking anything that moved. Although the battalion had to pull off the road a time or two because of these attacks, they proceeded on and finally arrived around 0130 the next morning. Boy, was I glad to see them! And, after all that, we weren't called on to fire a single mission all night because Combat Command A had apparently settled in for the night. The attack had gone so well and we had advanced so much farther than anticipated that day that G-2 (Intelligence) hadn't had enough time to gather the information needed to prepare harassing or defensive fires. We just plain didn't know what was ahead, behind, or around us.

Being an armored battalion we didn't have any infantry attached to us to provide us with security. Certainly, we were not incapable of defending ourselves. Armored units were designed to be quite capable of fending off determined infantry attacks. When we stopped and went into position our security teams were immediately sent out. We set up listening posts and roadblocks. We were also well armed. All of the M-7s and half-tracks had either a .50 caliber or a .30 caliber machine gun mounted on them, and every soldier was armed with a carbine or submachine gun. We also had bazookas and antitank mines as well. However, because we were an armored artillery unit, the enemy was anxious to destroy us because we could inflict a lot of damage very quickly. We weren't eager to pick a fight, especially in the dark.

The next morning at daybreak we flushed over fifty Germans out of the hedgerow right next to my battalion headquarters. After that scary episode I ordered each of the artillery batteries to send out patrols to clean out the hedgerows in their areas, and they in turn captured a good number of Germans who apparently had been too demoralized or too frightened to offer much resistance. I don't recall what division they were from but I'm positive they weren't from Panzer or SS units. They certainly weren't Panzer Lehr troops, whom we would meet later on. Our S-2 interrogated them before we sent them to the rear area.

It was a ticklish situation, and it's the most frightened I've ever been. It was the kind of situation we experienced often during our drive across France and Belgium. I always had an uncertain feeling because I never knew the true nature of the situation we were in. Many times we had to move into areas that had not been cleared of the enemy. This was a different situation than that faced by the lead infantry and tank units who were looking for the enemy. In our case we had to keep one eye open for the enemy while still trying to concentrate on our mission, which was to support the attacking infantry and tank units. Sometimes it's difficult to do both, as we were to find out. I particularly didn't appreciate my senior commander, Thomas Roberts, putting my men and me in that position. But he was a fearless leader and bucking for a star. He was a colonel and wanted to be a general.

The next morning we received a march order, so we continued to follow the march route of Combat Command B. We moved south just behind the advance guard of CCB and took up a position just across a little bridge at a place called Pont Brocard. We were still in hedgerow country, though they were beginning to thin out and become a less imposing obstacle. These were more orchards than anything else. We were located on high ground and had a commanding position overlooking a valley. A road farther to our west was on the other side of the valley. Except for some cover that the orchard provided, we were in an exposed position. Before long the action really became hot because the advance elements of CCB that we were supporting began to come in contact with pockets of resistance around the area of Notre Dame de Cenilly.

At 1000 hours as CCB advanced down this road between hedgerows just east of Pont Brocard, we saw the battle begin to develop across the valley as the leading elements of CCB ran into German roadblocks. We prepared to fire our guns, and in minutes I had one battery firing direct support for the advancing tanks. Almost simultaneously, explosions rocked our area as the enemy began firing antitank weapons directly at us from the road on the other side of the valley, about eight hundred and fifty yards away. I ordered the guns of the battery firing in support of CCB to re-deploy and engage the Germans in counterbattery fire. About the same time, the 188th Field Artillery Group just in front of us was hit hard by a German infantry assault and was overrun. The 188th lost twenty-two men and two howitzers during the battle.

While we were still engaged with the enemy, Division Artillery Headquarters ordered me to send fifty of my men back along our line of march to help contain a German counterattack taking place there. So I assembled some men from the service and headquarters batteries and sent them to the rear as infantry to assist in suppressing that counterattack. As soon as they left the Luftwaffe showed up and got in a couple of bombing and strafing runs but, fortunately, caused little damage and few casualties. However, our antiaircraft support was quite busy for about ten minutes. Around 1500 hours we received tank and infantry reinforcements. They drove the enemy out of the valley, taking one hundred and seventy-five prisoners and capturing a four-gun howitzer battery. That was about the hottest action we were involved in at any one time during the war. We were firing in direct support of our attacking tanks, firing direct fire at enemy tanks on our right flank, repelling an air attack, and at the same time furnishing troops to blunt a German counterattack behind us. It was exciting, I'll say that!

The enemy troops across the valley who were firing at us were trying to escape the prongs of the Allied pincer movement attempting to encircle Coutances. We ran into these German troops again the next day. After the day's fighting we spent that night and most of the next day at Pont Brocard.

On 29 July the noose really tightened around the Germans. What began as a trickle of enemy forces attempting to break out of the trap became an avalanche. During that day all of the Division Artillery of the 2nd Armored Division fired on retreating German columns. The 78th Armored Field Artillery Battalion in particular had a series of sharp encounters with retreating German columns, often having to resort to direct fire at less than one hundred yards. Shortly after 2000 hours I received orders to move the 92nd just north of St. Denis le Gast, which was our objective for "Operation Cobra." Combat Command B's mission, after breaking through the German defensive line at St. Lo, was to block German units attempting to retreat south or units advancing north to reinforce their comrades. It wasn't long after we established our new position at St. Denis le Gast that all hell broke loose.

At 2330 a German column, remnants of the 353rd or 243rd Division retreating from the north, was detected coming down the road that went right through St. Denis. The Germans didn't know that they had already been cut off until they ran smack into us. As the battle developed it soon became the most confusing battle I was ever involved in, and I began to understand what soldiers meant when they used the term "the fog of war." It certainly is a very appropriate expression, and the farther down the chain of command one is, the foggier it generally gets regardless of the degree of sophistication of your equipment and communications.

Battle scene near St. Denis le Gast soon after breakthrough at St. Lo, July 1944.

You simply do not know what people are going to do under certain circumstances, and there's no way for a commander to know how well his orders or plan of action is understood by his subordinates in the field. Any plan is a great plan until the troops actually jump off, and then the people in the field make the decisions on the spot from then on.

At St. Denis le Gast we had forward observers from two different units in the same vicinity of the strategic crossroad. One observer would call for artillery support and as soon as the shells began to land the other observer would yell over the radio that friendly fire was falling on his position. The battlefront was very narrow, so our observers, although with different units, were close together and the enemy was in-between. The enemy eventually got so close that our observers called down fire on their own positions because they couldn't distinguish friend from foe. The splash from a 105mm howitzer shell was lethal to people lying on the ground within ten yards of the point of impact, or fifty yards to those caught standing up.

While this was going on, machine-gun tracers and small-arms fire were whipping through our battalion headquarters area. One of our battery commanders was wounded that night, but otherwise we sustained very few casualties.

Although my position was less than seven hundred and fifty yards away from the fighting, I couldn't see much of the battle except for the explosions caused by our artillery fire. But I sure could hear it. Combat is loud, especially in an armored artillery unit. At St. Denis our howitzers were firing, the M-7 engines were running, vehicles were moving, bullets were buzzing overhead, artillery shells were exploding, people were yelling and screaming, and the telephones and radios were crackling with activity. Under these circumstances you can become very energized no matter how tired you are. The battle continued until just before dawn, when the last of the Germans were either killed, surrendered, or retreated. When I surveyed the battlefield the next morning there were over ninety German vehicles of every description wrecked and burning, and several hundred dead and wounded German soldiers were scattered all over the area. We had annihilated that German column. It had been a hairy situation and a very exciting evening. The 92nd later received a Presidential Citation for our efforts that night at St. Denis le Gast.

On 30 July at 1400 hours we moved back to the vicinity of Notre Dame de Cenilly and spent the night there. The situation had stabilized, and the primary mission of the 2nd Armored Division, the successful breakout from the Normandy beachhead, had been accomplished. We now had to prevent enemy reinforcements from entering the area from the south.

As a battalion commander in support of Combat Command B, I was kept informed by Headquarters of the overall tactical situation in the Normandy area. I knew all of the staff officers very well. Some of us had known one another for three or four years and worked well together. For example, I knew that while we had been battering our way south from St. Lo, the 3rd Armored Division had come in behind us and cut to the right, where they began an attack across the Cotentin Peninsula. Their ultimate objective was to encircle Coutances. With the capture of Coutances, the way would be clear to break out of the hedgerow country into Brittany. A key objective in Brittany was the port of Brest with its well-developed dock facilities. The capture of Brest's port facilities intact was considered vital to the continuance of the Allied offensive in France. It turned out to be a tough assignment, however. The German garrison there held out until 18 September, and destroyed the docks before surrendering. As it happened, we didn't need those dock facilities anyway because by then the fighting was well to the east.

I also made sure that my own officers were kept informed of the latest developments. I called a series of what were known as "BC Calls" or Battery Commander meetings. Unless our

A French town "liberated" after the St. Lo breakout, July 1944.

unit was in actual combat, the battery commanders, chief of staff, and myself assembled and discussed the situation almost on a daily basis. They were all bright boys and made many fine suggestions, which I listened to and found very helpful. I felt very fortunate to have the confidence of all my battery commanders, and they were free to express their opinion. But when I made a decision they understood that that was the end of it. They never once refused to carry out an order or showed any bitterness if their idea had not been adopted. They were all good, sound individuals and did a wonderful job.

In fact, during the "Cobra" offensive morale couldn't have been higher among my troops. Even though our spirits were dampened somewhat after the aerial bombing fiasco at the start of the operation, we were all excited about the launching of "Cobra." For many of us, it was the first time we had seen American soldiers killed right beside us, although we had previously sustained some casualties when we were supporting the British during their attack on Caen. During that attack our headquarters area had been shelled rather severely, which killed two men and wounded several others. Those were the first casualties that we suffered in combat in Europe. But I never had any morale problems among my men. The American soldier has a wonderful resiliency, an ability to overcome hardship and to take care of himself and his friends, too. There wasn't much time for sitting around moping. They knew they had a job to do and prepared themselves to do it. It was an inspiration to have command of people like that.

On 31 July 1944, after the Normandy breakout had been solidified, an infantry unit relieved us. From the time we jumped off until the last day of July, a six-day period, practically no one had gotten any sleep. Even though we were pulled back to a so-called "rest area" for two days, we weren't that far from the front, so our guns were positioned and trained on different targets in case they were needed. We were prepared to respond to any calls for help from Headquarters. Fortunately, no concerted German counterattack developed at this time, and the breakout from the Normandy beachhead was a complete success. The drive across France towards Paris was about to begin. It had taken us almost two months to break through the German defenses at Normandy. Once the breakthrough was achieved, the enemy couldn't stop us. I was mighty eager to get rid of my mustache.

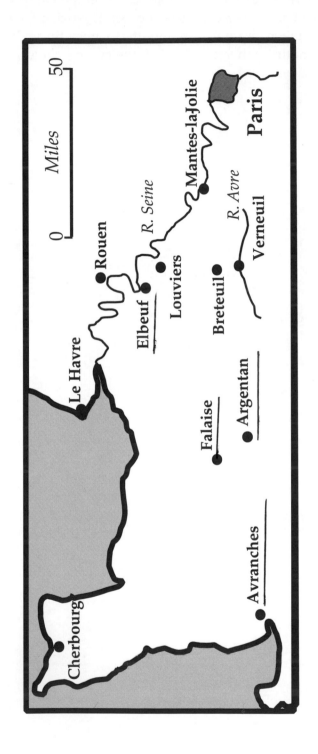

CHAPTER SEVEN: THE DRIVE ACROSS FRANCE

Hitler, recovering from wounds suffered during the unsuccessful assassination attempt, demanded that his generals stand their ground in Normandy and sent them several motorized divisions from the Pas de Calais area as reinforcements. The German generals were even ordered to mount a counterattack in the vicinity of Avranches as a delusional Hitler dreamed of driving the invaders into the sea, a second Dunkirk. The Allies had expected the German High Command to withdraw from Normandy to natural defensive positions along the Seine River once the Allied breakthrough had been achieved. Generals Eisenhower and Bradley and Field Marshal Montgomery immediately recognized Hitler's strategic blunder and moved to entrap German units in what became known as the Argentan-Falaise Pocket. Although not totally successful (more than 40,000 German troops escaped the trap), the Allies did prevent the enemy forces from establishing a line of defense at the Seine River. Instead, the Germans were forced to retreat all the way to the German border. On 15 August, the Allies landed another invasion force on the southern coast of France.

During the first two weeks of August, Buster and the 92nd Armored Field Artillery Battalion provided support during several engagements as the 2nd Armored Division pushed south of St. Lo toward Barenton to flank the German forces. On 18 August the 92nd joined the rest of the Division on a lightning armored strike east toward the Seine River. Encountering hastily erected roadblocks defended by enemy tanks, 88mm artillery guns, machine guns, and rifle fire, as well as enduring strafing enemy aircraft, the unit raced to prevent the Germans from reaching the Seine. On 24 August the 92nd reached the French city of Elbeuf located on the Seine. As part of the attack, the 92nd poured artillery fire into the German positions before the town capitulated, thus cutting off the Germans' last avenue of escape. On 25 August the Germans surrendered Paris to the Allies' French 2nd Armored Division. Three days later the American 2nd Armored Division was ordered to cross the Seine to pursue the retreating German forces all the way to the German border.

During the three-day period that the 92nd was pulled off the line and sent a few miles back, Combat Command A continued to push farther south and captured the town of Villebaudon. The 2nd Armored Division had by this time been assigned to XIXth Corps, and we stayed a part of it all the way to Germany. While my battalion rested I took the opportunity to make several reconnaissance tours of the front line area where I thought we might operate in the next few days to support both CCA and CCB's attack. One of these excursions turned into a very harrowing experience.

The circumstances surrounding that incident seem almost comical now but certainly didn't at the time. On 1 August just after dark my driver and I were returning from the front line in my Jeep and were headed back to headquarters. Having only been in the area a few days, I was still unfamiliar with the road system and had to refer to my map periodically. As darkness was approaching I had to use my flashlight to see the map clearly. To illustrate a little bit of American ingenuity, some GI had discovered that the red cellophane encasing the Lucky Strike cigarette packs made an excellent covering for the ends of our flashlights so that we wouldn't expose our position to the enemy with the harsh glare of white light. What I didn't realize at the time, however, was that when reading a map that had red indicators on it, such as roads, the red cellophane filter would cause those red lines to disappear! When my driver and I arrived at a crossroad on the way back to Canisy, I referred to my map using my flashlight with the ersatz filter and chose the wrong road because the road we were supposed to take was delineated in red. The road we mistakenly took led into Tessy-sur-Vire, which at the time was no-man's land. Tessy was right on the front line, and the 22nd Infantry Regiment of CCA had fought for it all day and had actually owned it at one time but had been driven out again after a strong German counterattack.

As we entered the town my driver and I suddenly looked at each other because we simultaneously got the eerie feeling that something wasn't right. Just as we passed under a railroad overpass the ear-splitting crack of an 88mm rifle round whistled very close overhead. Almost instantaneously, my driver took the first road to the left to get us out of the line of fire and to find us some cover. Once we were safely hidden I got my map out again, only this time I didn't need my flashlight because some of the town was still burning. This provided enough light for me to see, and it was then that I discovered my mistake. Not knowing the layout of the town or where the enemy was, I decided that the safest way out was the way we had come in. So my driver revved up the Jeep and we tore down that street, turned the corner almost on two wheels, and hightailed it back up the street where we had been shot at before and got the hell out of there. Fortunately, we must have startled the Germans because they never got off a shot. That was a close call, one of several I had in Europe.

The next day, 2 August, I received orders to move the 92nd seven miles to the vicinity of Villebaudon. After we had rejoined Combat Command B we began to push farther south to deepen our defenses against a German counterattack. On 3 August I was ordered to move the 92nd nine miles to a position near Courson. During this push south we met enemy resistance several times every day. Generally, the action amounted to hit-and-run ambushes or the elimination of fortified roadblocks which covered the main avenues of approach. When our tanks or infantry ran into a roadblock, rather than barrel right through it, they would outflank it and then attack after we had softened it up with artillery fire. From our position outside of Courson we fired more than twelve hundred rounds over a two-day period in support of these flanking operations. The 92nd was credited with destroying several Tiger tanks during these attacks.

On 4 August CCB reached the vicinity of Percy. Colonel Thomas Roberts, the division artillery commander who had sent me down that country lane without protection seven days earlier, was killed there. Colonel Roberts was a fine person and a good friend. He was an aggressive officer, but at times he was too hardheaded. He always rode out in front of the column looking for better positions for the artillery so that we could be employed more effectively. He taught us to be aggressive and to stay within range of the attacking units no matter what. In many cases, Colonel Roberts positioned us so close to the front line that, as in the case of the St. Lo breakout, our attacking tanks had to move through our position in order to reach the enemy's defensive line. As they moved forward and drove the enemy back, we followed right behind them.

Generally, we followed the "five thousand yard rule." As soon as the attacking force got five thousand yards in front of us, we would begin moving out. Our 105mm howitzers had a range of fifteen thousand yards, so we would leapfrog our batteries forward in order to give the attacking units constant artillery support. Colonel Roberts felt that these tactics were necessary for the proper utilization of armored artillery, and he insisted on close cooperation between the involved units.

On 4 August Colonel Roberts went to the front line near St. Sever Calvados to do some scouting, only to discover one of CCB's columns stopped. I know the following sequence of events because the company commander of that particular unit was at the head of the column with a forward observer from my battalion, and the commander later related to me what had happened. We had been providing artillery support for this particular column's attack. Colonel

Roberts sought out the commander to find out what was holding up the column. The company commander pointed ahead to one of our tanks which was on fire off to one side of the road and told Colonel Roberts that a Tiger tank was hidden somewhere up ahead. The commander explained that he had called for infantry support so that he could outflank the tank and take it from the rear where it was more vulnerable.

Unfortunately, this explanation didn't satisfy Colonel Roberts. He implied that they were cowards and ordered another tank to continue up the road. The tank commander, fully aware of the likely outcome if he took on a Tiger tank with his medium Sherman, refused. Whereupon Colonel Roberts ordered the tank commander out of the tank, climbed up on the tank himself, motioned to my forward observer to join him, and told the company commander that he would lead the way and the rest of the column was to follow. My forward observer, who was an experienced man, at first politely refused, but upon receiving a direct order from Colonel Roberts to mount the tank, did so. Colonel Roberts ordered the tank driver to advance up the road. Just as they reached the position of the other burning tank, the Tiger tank fired and Colonel Roberts' tank burst into flames, killing him and the entire crew, including my forward observer.

Colonel Carl Hutton, my old boss who had generously given up command of the 92nd in England, replaced Colonel Roberts as Division artillery commander. In my opinion a better choice could not have been made. Colonel Hutton was just as aggressive as Colonel Roberts but was not headstrong. I felt he did an excellent job and always had the utmost confidence in him.

On 5 August we moved to a position near Mesnil Benoit and fired more than six hundred rounds over the next two days in support of CCB's attack south. The Germans were desperately attempting to escape the Mt. Pincon-Roncey pocket while trying to stop our armored columns from exploiting the breakthrough. Both CCA and CCB had encountered fierce resistance and

Fire from the 92nd Armored Artillery Battalion knocked out this Panther tank near Mortain.

heavy fighting throughout this period, and CCA had suffered a large number of casualties. On 7 August the Germans launched a counterattack on Mortain as part of a larger counterattack in the direction of Avranches. We found out later that Hitler had ordered Field Marshal Guenther von Kluge, the overall German commander, to take the offensive. Hitler believed that this attack on our right flank, if successful, would allow von Kluge to drive directly to the beachhead and destroy the entire Normandy invasion. Hitler had no idea just how badly we had mauled his forces in Normandy and that to undertake this kind of operation was beyond von Kluge's ability. In fact, after getting as many of his forces out of the Argentan-Falaise Pocket as he could, von Kluge committed suicide by shooting himself in the head.

That day, as the German counterattack unfolded, I received orders to move the 92nd Battalion thirty-three miles to St. Hilaire du Harcouet. We fired over five hundred rounds that day in support of the 39th Infantry Regiment and the next day moved another fifteen miles to a position near Barenton. Combat Command B had swung around to the south and Combat Command A was attacking toward Mortain, which is northwest of Barenton and which had been captured by the Germans the day before. By the end of 8 August the momentum had swung back to our side and the Germans were once again on the defensive.

My battalion was supporting the 41st Infantry Regiment that was involved in a vicious battle trying to take the high ground in the vicinity of Barenton from the 275th and 2nd Panzer Divisions. These were not run-of-the-mill Wehrmacht soldiers who were good soldiers but knew when to give up. These were the elite of the German Army, especially the SS units. When we engaged SS units we knew it was going to be an all-out, winner-take-all affair. They were real sons of bitches who rarely gave up.

We were also under constant attack by enemy aircraft, and my battalion suffered a number of casualties. On one occasion an enemy aircraft dropped an antipersonnel bomb over the battery I was visiting. The bomb exploded in the air and scattered smaller bombs over the battery. These little bombs had propellers on them that served as arming devices. They were supposed to explode on impact but, fortunately, none of them did. Over fifty of these little bombs fell over the battery area. If they had exploded like they were designed to, the battery would have suffered many casualties. I called for the bomb-disposal experts, who came and disarmed them.

The only warning we had that we were about to be bombed or strafed by aircraft was when the plane or planes appeared on the horizon and we saw that they were headed toward us. We had no advanced radar warning system like they do today. Fighter planes carried out these dive-bombing attacks because by this time the 8th Air Force and the RAF had destroyed most of the Luftwaffe's high-altitude bombers and Stukas. I always found an air attack a strange experience. As the bomb was falling it always appeared to me like it was headed right for me even though it might end up landing a hundred yards away. Other people told me they had the same feeling. You only get this feeling after you've been in combat awhile. When you first experience combat and witness people getting killed or wounded, you sort of feel that "It can't happen to me," and you can watch it dispassionately. But after one or two artillery rounds land in your area, or you've been bombed or strafed several times or come under small-arms fire, you become increasingly concerned. It gets to the point that every time you hear artillery rounds exploding anywhere close by, you get very nervous. You realize that the direction of fire can change quickly and that the next round might land right in your back pocket.

During the next six days, from 8 to 13 August, we fired five thousand rounds from our position southwest of Barenton to help smash the German defenses. By the end of the day on the thirteenth, our forces had recaptured all of the ground we had lost during the initial hours of the German counterattack toward Avranches. On 14 August we were pulled off the line, and for the next four days we rested and cleaned our equipment. The next day we got the news that a combined American, British, and French invasion force had landed on the southern coast of France. The race to Paris was on.

Drive to the Seine

On 18 August I received orders to get the 92nd on the road. The Germans were retreating, and Headquarters told us that our mission was to pursue the enemy and, when possible, cut them off. We were attempting to execute a classic pincer movement in what became known as the Argentan-Falaise Pocket. Our job was to keep in contact with the German flank, push in when we could, back off when we met stiff resistance, and swing around to try to cut off the enemy from his line of retreat. We knew that the more Germans we could eliminate in France, the fewer we would have to face once we got to Germany.

The German field commanders like von Kluge knew that the battle for France was lost, and their strategy was to get as many of their troops and materiel across the Seine River and headed back to Germany for a last stand. We didn't know this at the time, however, at least at my level in the chain of command, so it was an exciting time for the 2nd Armored Division. We didn't really know the strength of the German forces in front of us or whether German reinforcements were on the way. It was at this time that Headquarters really turned the armored divisions loose and, boy, did we eat up some territory!

By 1130 on the morning of 18 August we were on the road. We didn't stop until we had

A destroyed roadblock near Domfront.

established a new position six miles south of Sees, which was an incredible road march of fifty-eight miles. An M-7 had a top rate of speed of about twenty miles an hour, so we could roll down the road at a pretty good clip when we had no opposition. The next day we traveled another thirty-seven miles to a position in the vicinity of Longny du Porche, and on 20 August we moved another twenty-three miles to Boissy-les-Perc, where we deployed and fired four hundred and fifty rounds in support of our tanks. The tanks had run into a series of roadblocks hastily erected by the Germans who were retreating south of Verneuil.

We ran into several different kinds of roadblocks during our drive across France. The enemy would fell trees or put some kind of obstacle in the road and then cover it with machine gun, tank, and mortar fire. Or they would fortify a building or a house and turn it into a pillbox with several machine guns inside and an 88mm rifle nearby. This tactic was pretty effective in stopping an armored advance. Our method of attacking these roadblocks was to engage the personnel defending the roadblock and then outflank it with tanks or infantry. As soon as the tanks would get behind the roadblock it would all be over very quickly. Then we'd move down the road again until we ran into another one three or four miles, or maybe just five hundred yards, farther down and then we would have to repeat the process. The deeper we went into France, however, the fewer and farther between these obstacles became. This had really become a road march. This was what armored divisions had been created for and what we did best. The Germans had used the tactic during the blitzkrieg of France in 1940 and now we had turned the tables on them. Most of the hard fighting at this time was occurring north of us. While we were rolling along, General Patton's XV Corps on our right flank to the south was doing exactly the same thing.

This drive was not conducted without losses, however. The 2nd Armored Division was getting pretty beaten up, and during this period the Division lost four armored battalion commanders, two or three infantry commanders, and a number of key staff officers. I knew all of them personally, having been with the Division from its inception. My old roommate at the Military Academy, Mart Bailey, was one of those killed during this drive. He was with Combat Command A as a staff officer and was killed in the vicinity of Verneuil while German aircraft was strafing his column.

Fifty years later, while on a tour commemorating the fiftieth anniversary of the war, I had a very eerie experience while attending a reception in Galeen, Holland. During the reception, a very nice looking couple introduced themselves and said that they were trying to find someone who might have known some of the people with whom their father, a Dutch Army lieutenant, might have served. It seems that, after the U.S. forces reached Belgium and Holland, there was a great need for interpreters and liaison officers who spoke the languages of the area and knew the habits of the people there as well as of the Germans. Their father, as a member of the Dutch Army, had volunteered and apparently was assigned to Combat Command A for that purpose. In our pleasant conversation they mentioned many names that they had obtained from their father's diary. Most of them were very familiar to me as either personal friends or staff officers with whom I came in daily contact as an artillery commander. One of the names, that of Colonel Bailey, really stunned me. I told them he had been a classmate and roommate of mine at West Point. They said that their father had not known him personally because Bailey had been killed in combat just prior to his joining, but that Bailey's name and reputation for bravery were highly revered by the officers and men of the CCA staff. This couple went on to inform me that they, in fact, had Colonel Bailey's helmet which had been lent to their father and which he wore for the rest of the war.

It seems that their father, Lieutenant Adrian Paulen, had reported for duty in his Dutch

Prisoners taken in a fight for a gun position during dash across northern France, August 1944.

Army uniform but without battle gear, including a steel helmet. Being a tactical headquarters in combat, CCA carried no supplies such as uniforms and personal equipment, so they lent him the only helmet they had on hand, Mart's, which had been left in his halftrack when he was evacuated. The insignia of rank had been removed, but otherwise it was intact with the name Benjamin M. Bailey written with a marker pencil on the headband. Lieutenant Paulen wore it until he was released from his assignment. By that time most of the original CCA headquarters personnel had scattered for various reasons and the issuing personnel were no longer with the unit, so he brought it home with him. It was among the items on display at the little museum there in the Galeen City Hall, especially set up for the occasion. They immediately fetched it and showed it to me. Mart's name was there on the headband. As soon as I got home I contacted Mart's family and told them the story, and they in turn contacted the Dutch couple. The helmet now is in the possession of Mart's son, Ben Bailey Jr., who resides in California.

Every time I received word that one of our officers had been killed, it was a personal loss for me because not only did I know them, but in many cases I also knew their families. Those were some of the toughest moments in the war for me.

On 21 August we crossed to the north side of the Avre River to bypass Verneuil, which was still in enemy hands, and traveled fifteen miles to a new position southeast of St. Quen d'Attez. During the day we fired close to eight hundred rounds to break up roadblocks and harass the enemy.

These rapid advances, particularly by our leading tank elements, required me to adjust my thinking as an artillery commander. I found that the only way I could provide support for our tanks, that were moving very rapidly, was to be up front with the commander of the unit that I was supporting. I had to find out what he was going to do and when he was going to do it. On several occasions our tanks had just taken off without telling us and were ten miles down the road and out of range of our supporting guns before we knew anything about it. When that happened we had to scramble like crazy to get on the road and follow them, all the while

A destroyed German half-track.

praying that no German unit in the meantime had slipped between us and the tanks and were waiting to ambush us. To avoid this situation I found that the best thing for me to do was to be up front with the tankers. As soon as they began to prepare to move I would radio back to my executive officer, Bill Bowers, to get the 92nd on the road to follow close behind.

On 22 August I received orders to move the 92nd to a new position near Breteuil. On the way there, just outside of Lignerolles, we ran headlong into a German machine-gun position, and a private in my battalion was killed before we could knock it out. This was a really scary time because the enemy was in full retreat and German stragglers were all over the place. Some were regular Wehrmacht soldiers who were tired of having the hell kicked out of them and consequently had no fight left in them and were just waiting to be captured. Others were conscripts from conquered countries like Yugoslavia or Czechoslovakia and weren't crazy about fighting for Hitler in the first place. But others, like the damned SS troops, were still willing to die for the Fuhrer, and we were more than happy to oblige them.

Our advance parties were always accompanied by elements of the 82nd Reconnaissance Battalion, a very mobile and well-armed unit. They had light tanks to protect themselves in case they got into minor difficulties. Their job was to scout ahead so that we would not be taken by surprise, and they generally did their job very well. But there were so many German stragglers around that it was impossible to account for them all.

Our little L-4 aircraft were really the eyes of the column and one of the reasons we were able to travel with such considerable speed after our breakout from the hedgerow country. Our spotter aircraft flew back and forth over our columns as we drove across the roads of France. The artillery observer in the aircraft would alert the 82nd Recon Battalion to any unusual activity or suspicious areas ahead, and the Recon people would check it out. The observer would radio the coordinates of an enemy position directly to our artillery battalion, and we would immediately go into position and fire on those coordinates. Our observers in those aircraft became so good at their jobs that they were able to pinpoint enemy artillery positions as soon as they fired. We noticed after just a short period of time during our drive across France that when our L-4 aircraft were in the air, enemy artillery activity dropped off considerably.

The L-4 was an ideal aircraft for the job because it was small, slow, and maneuverable. It was a two-seat aircraft in which the observer sat behind the pilot. Because it was slow the observer had plenty of opportunity to locate targets, and because it was so small and light it could land almost anywhere, from a road to a fairly level field to even tracks made by tank treads. But being so slow and light also had its obvious disadvantages. The planes were vulnerable to small-arms fire as well as the heavier stuff. We lost a few during the war. One of ours landed in a treetop after being chased by a Me-109F fighter plane. Both the pilot and the observer survived and were able to climb down the tree safely. Another one of our L-4s had an 88mm antiaircraft round pass through its tail without exploding. The L-4s were basically kites with 65-horsepower motors. I always admired the people who flew in them because it took guts.

We fired over six hundred rounds on the way to Breteuil to reinforce the fires of the 78th Armored Battalion. By the end of the day on 23 August we had just about closed the door on the Germans who were retreating from the Argentan-Falaise Pocket. American forces were astride all west-to-east roads from Verneuil to Louviers, and road-blocks had been set up to prevent the Germans from retreating across the Seine and escaping the trap. Only one way out remained, and that was through the city of Elbeuf. That day the 92nd traveled twenty-seven miles to a position near Le Neubourg. That

"With the crossing of the Seine in August, the outermost parameters of Operation Overlord, the invasion of France, had been met."

evening we fired close to five hundred rounds as the retreating Germans ran right into our roadblocks and ambushes, which resulted in the destruction of hundreds of enemy vehicles. Generally speaking, we bypassed any fair-sized towns because not only were they enemy strongpoints, but the narrow streets were also not conducive for moving tanks and heavy equipment. If there was a way to bypass those places, we did and left the infantry behind to go into the towns and pry the enemy out. This often involved bitter house-to-house fighting. The armor was the spearhead and the infantry was the mop-up force, so our advance continued unimpeded.

One of the advantages in the use of armor, in addition to packing a punch, is speed. Our mission was to "harass, bypass, and haul ass," so we tended to travel light and adapted our lifestyle to our mission. In France and Belgium we always utilized a tent for our battalion headquarters. It was not until we entered Germany that we began utilizing buildings for command posts. For one thing, in France most of the buildings we encountered had been pretty torn up during the fighting. In many cases just the shells of the buildings remained. Second, we were fighting during the summertime when it was warm, and we preferred a tent to being inside. And finally, the situation was so fluid and we were moving so rapidly that it didn't make sense to set up any kind of permanent residence anywhere. When we reached the Siegfried Line and the Germans were fighting for their homeland, advances were sometimes measured in yards, not miles, and our positions sometimes became more static. We were able to set up more permanent command posts.

Our command post tent was specially designed for rapid movement. It was made of a heavy dark-green material and had a little passageway, with flaps at both ends, that you had to walk through before you actually got into the main area of the tent. It was designed that way to ensure blackout conditions at night. Inside my battalion headquarters tent were two boards with crossed-leg supports set up. One of them was for my S-3 (Operations Officer), the other for my S-2 (Intelligence Officer). On one end of the room we had a large operations map mounted on an easel that we referred to twenty-four hours a day. We also had a radio and telephone operator monitoring the communications net inside the battalion headquarters tent. We usually had at least two telephones coming into that headquarters tent. Someone was assigned to monitor the communications network twenty-four hours a day as well.

Whenever we went into position for a few days I always preferred to use the telephone to communicate with my batteries or Division Headquarters because the telephone lines were more secure. Radio transmissions could be intercepted by the enemy and often were. Whenever we used the radio we had to communicate using code words. You had to be very careful with the information you put out on the radio. In many cases we would maintain radio silence to conceal what we were doing. During this drive across France I was rarely in my battalion headquarters because I spent most of my time up front with the unit we were supporting.

Early on the morning of 24 August we were relieved by the 28th Infantry Regiment, which freed us up to participate in the attack on Elbeuf, the last avenue of escape across the Seine for the retreating Germans. We moved to a new position close to Cesseville and fired over one hundred rounds at several roadblocks we encountered along the way. Elbeuf, on the Seine River southwest of Rouen, was actually located in the British zone of operations. But we got there first and so we attacked anyway. The next day CCB attacked the town, and we fired over thirteen hundred rounds to help demolish the enemy's defenses. By 1500 hours Elbeuf was ours, and the next day we fired an additional six hundred and fifty rounds at the retreating German columns. We then turned over the occupation of Elbeuf to the Canadians who finally arrived, albeit late. Because the British had a nasty tendency to take credit for things Americans had accomplished, General Brooks refused to turn over the town to the Canadians until a Canadian officer signed a receipt for it!

Early on 27 August I received orders to follow the 65th Armored Field Artillery Battalion to an assembly area near Longuemare on the west side of the Seine, a distance of forty-nine miles. The XV Corps had seized the bridgehead at Mantes intact. The retreating Germans had blown up all of the bridges between Mantes and Rouen. However, the XV Corps had run into very little resistance in their drive east and had surprised the German garrison at Mantes before they had a chance to set any demolition charges.

The following day the 2nd Armored Division reached a milestone. At 0600 hours CCB was ordered to attack across the Seine. The 92nd was ordered to reinforce the 78th Armored Field Artillery Battalion's artillery barrage, but resistance was light and we only fired one hundred and twenty rounds. At 1200 hours I received an order that made me a very happy man. The 92nd was to cross the Seine at 1500 hours that afternoon. As my Jeep rolled across the bridge spanning the Seine I knew that the growth on my upper lip was about to meet its own Waterloo. Frankly, I was glad to get rid of it, and not just because of its symbolism for the men and me. I guess some guys become attached to their mustache but I never did. That evening I took out my razor and without any ceremony became clean-shaven once again. Georgie Patton would have been proud!

With the crossing of the Seine, the outermost parameters of Operation Overlord, the invasion of France, had been met. It has been estimated that German losses in killed, wounded, and captured amounted to over half a million men during the campaign in northern France. However, there was no celebration. Our next objective was Germany, and once there we figured the Germans would fight like hell to keep us out. We were about to get a taste of that in Belgium and Holland.

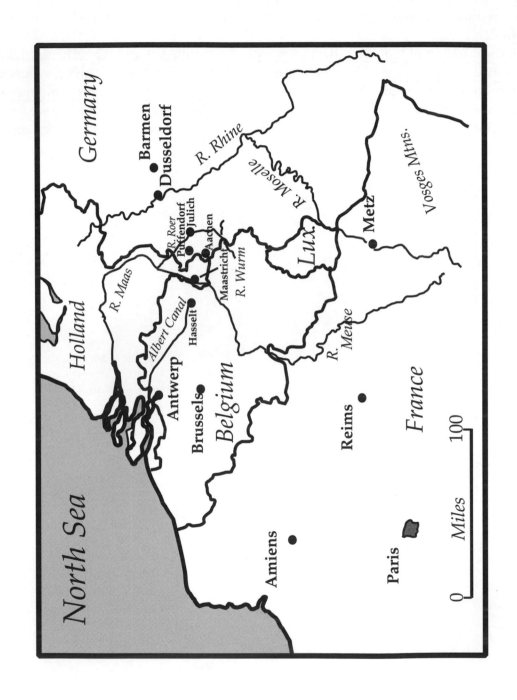

CHAPTER EIGHT: BATTLING TO GERMANY

By September, as Allied forces took aim on the German border in a four-pronged advance, they began to outrun their ability to supply themselves with gasoline and ammunition. Simultaneously, the Germans were forming a defensive line that ran along the Maas River in the Netherlands to the north, through the Siegfried Line, and to the Moselle River and Vosges Mountains to the south in northeastern France. British Field Marshal Bernard Montgomery attempted to end the war quickly by seizing a bridgehead over the Rhine River in Holland (Operation Market-Garden) in hopes of then driving straight through the Ruhr Valley to Berlin. Montgomery's audacious plan failed and resulted in many Allied casualties.

Following the drive across France, the 2nd Armored Division was ordered to proceed as far as its gasoline supply allowed. The 92nd Armored Field Artillery Battalion literally ran out of gas at the Belgian border. After waiting several days to be refueled, the 92nd supported the Allied attack on the Albert Canal. Throughout the remainder of September, German resistance continued to stiffen as the 2nd Armored Division drove across the German border to the Siegfried Line. By early October, the 92nd was located in the middle of the Siegfried Line, a position it held for thirty-three days.

By early November the Allies had brought up enough reinforcements and supplies to breach the vaunted Siegfried Line. The objective of the offensive was to drive to the Rhine River while surrounding the Ruhr Valley, Germany's industrial heartland. The offensive ground to a halt, however, because of resistance encountered by George Patton's Third Army at Metz and in the Saar River Valley to the south, and because of a strong German armored force opposing the 2nd Armored Division. As part of the Roer River offensive, the 2nd Armored Division was transferred from First Army to Ninth Army, under the command of General William Simpson. The 2nd Armored Division participated in the largest tank battle on the western front during the war at Puffendorf. During the two-week brawl (16 November-3 December) the 2nd Armored Division lost more than half of its 232 tanks. By the end of November, as the weather worsened, the Allied drive stalled, and by the end of the first week of December a static situation had developed.

On 28 August 1944, the day after crossing the Seine, I was ordered to move the 92nd about fifteen miles to a position northeast of Dennemont. We were told that we were headed for the Belgian border and our objective was to capture Brussels and Antwerp, important deep-water seaports. As we moved farther and farther away from Normandy, Cherbourg, and Le Havre, our supply lines were becoming longer and longer. General Eisenhower knew that to continue the offensive to the German heartland we were going to require seaports closer to the front lines. Our mission was to capture these seaports with their docks intact.

Once we crossed the Seine enemy resistance slackened noticeably. The French 2nd Armored Division, commanded by Major General Jacques Philippe LeClerc, had taken Paris. Earlier in the campaign LeClerc had cost our 5th Armored Division an opportunity to capture the town of Argentan before the German defenses were ready. By ignoring operational orders and launching the attack, LeClerc tied up roads that had been reserved for use by gasoline trucks attempting to refuel the 5th Armored. Because of the delay caused by LeClerc, the 5th Armored had to postpone its attack for a crucial six hours that allowed the Germans to prepare their defenses and ended up costing the 5th many casualties.

The French were good, experienced troops, though, and they were fighting to free their homeland. The 92nd had trained with them for a while in North Africa, so we were familiar

(Left) *"The French people would crowd the streets waving American flags and wearing anything red, white, and blue that they owned. I often wondered where in the world they got all this material in time for our arrival."* (Below) *Graaf family visiting Lt. Col. Buster soon after the liberation of Maastricht, Holland.*

with them. For political purposes the job of liberating Paris was given to them, and I think rightfully so. During our drive across France we had seen very little of the French population because the situation was still very fluid. Oftentimes we entered a town just as the Germans were leaving or were being driven out, and the local populace wasn't sure if the Germans were coming back. But once we crossed the Seine and the French people began to realize that the Germans were being driven back to Germany, all hell broke loose when we entered a town or village.

In many cases our advance was held up not by German resistance but by the indigenous French population! The people would crowd the streets waving American flags and wearing anything red, white, and blue that they owned. I often wondered where in the world they got all this material in time for our arrival. It was almost like a parade when we went through a town or village of any size. Church bells rang and the French people would choke the streets and stand on balconies waving, cheering, shouting, and tossing apples and cookies and all types of food at us. If you stopped, the people immediately swarmed all over you, kissing you and patting you on the back. Our steel helmets really came in handy in protecting us from the apples and other food that was being tossed out to the troops as we went through. I never could figure out where in the hell they got all of the American flags we encountered. It really brought out the goose bumps in everybody to see such unadulterated joy being expressed by the French people, and it certainly made us feel proud to be Americans and liberators. In other towns where we had to fight our way in against the Germans, oftentimes there wasn't much left standing, so no one felt like celebrating and we didn't feel much like liberators.

After we crossed the Seine and turned northeast, the only question that remained was whether those Germans still left in northern France could withdraw more quickly than we could advance. Our reconnaissance patrols and spotter planes reported that the enemy was retreating into Belgium with all available transport, and Wehrmacht soldiers we captured informed us that German officers were deserting their commands and had told their troops to find their way back to Germany as best they could. On 29 and 30 August we traveled a total of thirty-five miles and fired only two hundred and fifty rounds in support of the leading tank units.

At this point we were having a difficult time keeping up with the advance units because they were encountering very little resistance and were moving rapidly. Some have likened our drive across northern France to a stampede of wild horses, and I think that's a pretty accurate description. In fact, at one point, following on the heels of the advance of Combat Command A, Colonel Sidney Hinds and General Robert Brooks were standing in the middle of the crossroads town of Marchiennes when out of nowhere a German column came barreling down the road straight for them. General Brooks and Colonel Hinds personally operated machine guns and blazed away at the enemy until they were able to effect their escape. Once out of the enemy's range they quickly called for artillery fire and the entire German column of one hundred and twenty-three vehicles and over three hundred soldiers was annihilated.

Because of the speed with which we were moving, XIX Corps Headquarters exerted only limited control over troop movements and instead delegated a lot of responsibility to their subordinate commanders in the field, who could see the situation firsthand. This is where the time we spent together back in England training and hashing over problems over dinner in the officers' mess hall really proved useful. Thorough knowledge of our tactics and familiarity with one another, as well as our superior mobility, allowed us to operate as independent teams, something which the German Army could not emulate. In this dash across northern France we didn't have to ask XIX Corps Headquarters for instructions on what to do or where to go. Basically, Corps Headquarters told each division, "See you in Belgium," and how we got there was our business.

Travel sometimes became difficult. Refugees and military vehicles crowded the roads, and it also had rained like hell and the roads were rivers of mud. Additionally, many of the roads were littered with German equipment that our fighters, fighter-bombers, and tanks had located and chewed up during the German retreat, which made travel even more difficult. Sometimes we had to wait for bulldozers to clear a path through the wreckage. The Germans were still using a lot of horse-drawn equipment, and sometimes the roads would be chockfull of horribly maimed dead and dying horses, as well as destroyed equipment and dead Germans that our bombers or artillery had destroyed. The stench was overwhelming. Sometimes we would wait for hours until a bulldozer could be brought up to clear a path through the carnage. Some of the older officers told me the slaughter was far greater than anything they had seen during World War I.

Gasoline also became a major concern at this time. We were moving so far so fast that our supply lines were stretched to the breaking point. The 2nd Armored Division's operational orders the last two days of August and the first two days of September were very simple. They merely stated, "The Division will advance in zone as far as gasoline will permit." In the 92nd I issued an order to "deadline" some of our vehicles, which meant emptying the gas tank and leaving the vehicle on the side of the road. The gasoline was then transferred to the self-propelled guns and the ammunition carriers so that we could continue to support the leading tank units. By doing this we were able to travel a total of ninety-one additional miles until we were just southwest of Mouchin, France, just outside the Belgian border. My headquarters was located in Orchies. At that point we literally ran out of gas. We just sat and waited for three days and took a breather until our supply units, chiefly the "Red Ball Express," could catch up with us and give us some gasoline. There was no question in our minds that had we had enough gasoline we could have driven all the way to the Rhine, and maybe to Berlin, at that time.

Frankly, though, I was not unhappy at the delay. My men were beginning to show the strains of a month of uninterrupted combat. We were tired and needed a hot bath and some good, hot meals. On many days we lived on 10-in-1 rations, cigarettes, coffee, and little or no sleep. We had some soldiers who were evacuated because of combat exhaustion. They would acquire what was known in the Pacific Theater as the "Thousand Yard Stare," where they would withdraw from reality during the long road marches. Other units, especially in the infantry, had many cases of combat fatigue. Our vehicles would pass a company of infantry marching down the road and those men wouldn't even know we were there. They all had blank looks on their faces. They were just like zombies putting one foot in front of the other, asleep on their feet. That's how they were able to endure the grueling pace they were being forced to undertake. On 31 August I lost another good friend, Aquilla "Mike" Calhoun, who was killed during combat operations. I got to know Mike and his family at Fort Benning when the 2nd Armored was first organized. He was one of the many Auburn graduates we had in the Division.

Looking back on it now, what we accomplished in just over a month, from the breakout at St. Lo to the drive into Belgium, seems miraculous. But back then it seemed like time had stood still and the offensive seemed to go much slower. We began to think, "Will the war ever be over?" You know the old story about being in the Army, it's "hurry up and wait." This is especially true in combat. Here we were poised to strike into Germany before the enemy was ready for us, only to run out of gasoline.

One of the good things that did happen while we waited for fuel was that our mail caught up with us, and that really boosted morale. The importance of soldiers' receiving regular mail from home was one of the things that was thoroughly understood throughout the chain of

The wreckage of a destroyed German column, July 1944.

command in the American Army. Whenever we were in a static situation for even a few days, mail was given a priority.

The Red Cross and USO were also instrumental in keeping up morale. Whenever we stopped for just a few days, more often than not the Red Cross or USO "donut dollies" would show up in their trucks to hand out sandwiches or donuts and coffee. For our soldiers to be able to talk to these young women was a real treat and morale booster. I can't give these young women enough credit. We sometimes had the devil's own time keeping them out of the front lines! I remember we had a visit from three young starlets of the day who had arrived to visit the troops around Barenton, France. I forget now who they were. In the middle of one of our operations I turned around just in time to see three Jeeps barreling down the road toward the front line with these young women aboard dressed up in combat gear. We were able to stop the vehicles just in time to tell the women that our position was as far as they could go because we were attacking and there was in-coming artillery fire up ahead. I ordered the drivers to turn those Jeeps around and head back the way they had come so that my men could concentrate on winning the war, which the drivers did over the protests of those young women.

During this delay we were able to perform some much-needed maintenance on our equipment and go back and pick up the "deadlined" vehicles we had left behind. Each column had an ordnance battalion attached to it, and they took care of major repairs to equipment. They carried spare parts including whole new engines. However, because the 92nd was moving so far so rapidly, when one of our vehicles like an M-7 conked out, we were simply sent a brand-new one. The replacement system was very quick and effective.

By the time we were all gassed up and ready to roll again on 6 September, the Second British Army had stunningly swept forward and captured Brussels, Antwerp, and Ghent. The seaports having been secured, the XIX Corps was then given a new objective. I was ordered to move the 92nd Battalion across the Belgian border eighty-five miles to a position near Dion-le-vale. With nothing to shoot at we remained there through the next day. On 8 September I received a march order to move another forty miles to Herck la Ville, and we stayed there for the next three days with nothing to do. Our reconnaissance patrols and spotter planes reported that the enemy was digging in along the Albert Canal from near Antwerp all the way to Maastricht, Holland. This was to be their first line of defense before we actually hit the Siegfried Line. It was actually just a stalling tactic on their part. The Siegfried Line had fallen into disrepair, and the enemy needed time to repair and rearm the West Wall.

The Germans had destroyed all of the bridges over the Albert Canal and were defending them from pillboxes and trenches which had overlapping fields of small-arms, machine-gun, antitank, and artillery fire. On that day General Ernie Harmon retook command of the 2nd Armored Division. General Brooks had been promoted and had been given command of the V Corps. Since leaving the 1st Armored Division, General Harmon had been sent back to the States to take command of the XXIII Corps that was being organized at Camp Bowie, Texas. When Brooks was given V Corps, General George C. Marshall asked General Harmon if he wanted the 2nd Armored again, and Ernie jumped at the chance to get back into the fight with his old command. Losing General Brooks was a blow, but getting Harmon back was quite a tonic. In fact, one of the first things he did was to arrange for the men, on a rotating basis, to take hot showers that had been set up near Hasselt, Belgium. I can't be certain, but those may have been the first hot showers that we had had the opportunity to take since leaving England three months earlier.

The Albert Canal itself was a formidable obstacle. It was deep and unfordable, and intelligence told us that forces from at least twenty different German units were engaged to defend it, including battle groups from three Panzer divisions. Rather than assaulting the German positions directly, General Harmon sent Combat Command A on an end sweep to cross the canal at Beeringen, which had been secured by the British. CCA then rolled up the German flank toward Maastricht.

We remained in position near Herck la Ville for three days until I received orders to move the battalion twenty-nine miles to a position just north of Munsterbilsen, just opposite Maastricht near the Vaart Canal. Our mission was to combine fire with the 62nd and 65th Field Artillery Battalions to exert pressure on the enemy there and prevent them from reinforcing their flank. The 92nd fired close to three thousand rounds over the next three days in support of the attack on the Albert Canal defenses. We were given singular credit by Division Artillery Headquarters for the accuracy of our fire on dug-in positions east of the canal.

On 15 September we traveled twenty-two miles to a position just east of Maastricht, and the next day we fired over nine hundred rounds in support of CCB's attack on the city. On the seventeenth we crossed the Vaart Canal and traveled to a position northeast of St. Horlach, Holland. The Germans had successfully held up our advance by three days, which allowed them to fortify their defenses closer to Germany. Each line of resistance we began to meet became tougher and tougher to overcome. The going really got tough east of Maastricht, and some days our forward units couldn't advance a hundred yards, let alone a mile. Also, the closer we got to Germany the less enthusiastic the local population became about our arrival.

Crossing the Albert Canal in Belgium. "The 92nd fired close to three thousand rounds in support of the attack on the Albert Canal defenses. We were given singular credit by Division Artillery Headquarters for the accuracy of our fire on dug-in positions east of the canal."

Instead of the people giving us the V-for-Victory sign, flowers, cognac, hugs, and kisses, we began receiving sullen stares or outright signs of hatred. Occasional snipers fired into our columns as we moved through some of the border towns.

Our air observers began to report seeing more enemy artillery positions than they had ever seen before, and we subsequently began to receive more artillery fire in our area. To complicate the situation, we once again experienced a supply shortage. This time we had plenty of gasoline but were running low on—of all things at a time like this—ammunition. Corps Headquarters told us that only two hundred and twenty-five rounds of 105mm-howitzer ammunition would be available per day for the next ten days, which amounted to about eleven rounds per gun per day. This restricted our ability to reply to the shellings with effective counterbattery fire.

Being shelled is a bad experience because there's nothing you can do except hit the ground and pray. The shellings became more frequent and more severe the closer we got to Germany, and my fear increased proportionally. When we first got to France I would never duck when I heard a shell whistle overhead. And even during the drive across France the German artillery was more harassment than effective. They would shell a road or crossroads at timed intervals whether anyone was there or not. If you waited a while and timed the barrages, you could figure out their timing intervals and go through that area and be well out of range by the time of the next barrage. But by the time we got to Holland I was hitting the ground when I heard incoming rounds, as was everyone else around me. It becomes an instantaneous reaction that you can't control because you never know which round has your name on it.

On 18 September we traveled thirteen miles to a position close to Wintrask, Holland. Because of the ammunition shortage we fired less than two hundred rounds that day. One of the forward observers from my battalion actually established his position on German soil, and I found out later that he may have been the first American soldier, other than prisoners of war, to enter Germany. The next day we moved to a position southeast of Viel, Holland, and fired over three hundred rounds. The 92nd was put in charge of direct support of both the Division's reserves, who took over CCB's zone, and the 113th Cavalry Group on the left, whose front bordered the Meuse River. CCB was pulled back to assemble a task force to exploit a gap in the Siegfried Line that was to be opened up by the 30th Infantry Division.

However, the weather turned lousy and the attack kept getting postponed. We stayed at this location for the next four days, firing a total of four hundred rounds of high-explosive ammunition. The enemy fired back, of course, and they began throwing some heavy ordnance at us. On 22 September the 14th Armored Field Artillery Battalion received fifteen rounds of 240mm-mortar fire from the Germans that created craters fifteen feet across and seven feet deep, which is truly impressive.

On 24 September I shifted the 92nd about a mile to a new position just west of de Kling, Holland, and once we went into position we fired over three hundred rounds at the German defenses. We remained at this location for the next five days, firing over four thousand rounds at targets of opportunity including individual targets such as antitank guns, vehicles, and pillboxes located in and around the towns of Brehern and Gielenkirchen.

Occasionally during the drive across France and into Belgium we had deliberately fired on towns where the Germans had set up roadblocks or where retreating enemy columns were located. In those cases we didn't know for sure if there were any civilians still in the town at the time, but I'm sure there had to have been some. The presence of civilians didn't stop us from shelling a town. In combat you are often confronted with many unfortunate circumstances that as a commander you are forced to deal with. Several times in France and Belgium I found my options personally distasteful. I couldn't very well let the Germans escape or not provide our

A stern warning to American soldiers passing through Ubach, Germany.

troops with support. At the same time I knew there were probably innocent civilians in those towns. This just made me hate Hitler even more for putting my men and myself in this kind of situation. Once we got to Germany, however, we fired a considerable number of stonks and harassing fire into German cities and towns where there were military targets and also large civilian populations, and this didn't bother me a bit. This was Germany and they were the enemy, as far as I was concerned.

On 29 September the 92nd fired four hundred and fifty rounds to support an attack on the town of Nieustad by the 113th Cavalry Group, which resulted in the capture of the town and over one hundred prisoners. The next day at 1650 hours we crossed the border and entered Germany and took up a position one mile west of Grotenrath. The 30th Infantry Division's attack to breach the Siegfried Line was scheduled for the next day. As part of the attack General Harmon reorganized the Combat Commands of the 2nd Armored Division. The 92nd remained with Combat Command B, which was commanded by General I.D. White. CCA, commanded by Colonel John H. Collier, was the reserve force.

However, the next morning we awoke to a driving rainstorm that continued the whole day, and so the attack was postponed yet again. The attack was to be preceded by a carpet bombing attack by the combined Allied air forces similar to the one that had led the way for the St. Lo breakout at Normandy. "H-Hour," or the hour for the air attack, was scheduled for 0900 on 2 October.

The next day the air attack began on schedule and was supposed to continue until 1050 hours, when the 30th Infantry Division was supposed to jump off and begin their attack on the Siegfried Line. However, shortly after the bombing began a thick cover of low clouds moved in and blanketed the area and obscured visibility to the point where the bombing became ineffective. It was then decided that artillery support would be substituted for the aerial bombing.

Primarily, the 116th Panzer Division, the Adolf Hitler SS Division, and the 12th, 49th, 183rd, and 246th Infantry Divisions occupied the German defensive positions. Except for the SS units these were not first-rate soldiers. Most of the Wehrmacht infantry divisions were under-strength and were not homogeneous units. They were hastily assembled stragglers or remnants of previously decimated divisions and regiments. However, what they lacked in esprit de corps and cohesiveness was made up for by the strength of their defensive positions.

On 2 October the 30th Infantry Division began their attack across the Palenberg Bridge over the Wurm River at 1200 hours, but by 1330 the attack had ground to a halt due to severe enemy artillery fire on our bridgehead. There was only one bridge over the river, and that caused a lot of congestion and gave the German gunners a lot of easy targets. To support the attack the 92nd fired close to a thousand rounds that day, mainly on the town of Ubach. By the end of the day the 30th Infantry Division had penetrated one mile on the north end of the line. The next day CCB was given the mission of widening the crack opened by the infantry.

For the attack Combat Command B was split into two task forces, S-1 and S-2. The 92nd's mission was to support both task forces. The 3rd Battalion of the 67th Armored Tank Regiment was the spearhead of the S-1 Task Force. We fired six hundred and seventy-five rounds to support their attack, and one of my forward observers actually managed to advance to the edge of the Siegfried Line. However, the 3rd Battalion of the 67th lost over half of its tanks attempting to drive the Germans back from the bridgehead.

On 4 October we began the day with a stonk on a half-dozen dug-in Tiger tanks and an entrenched machine-gun position which one of my forward observers had discovered. The observer reported that the barrage destroyed one tank and badly damaged three others. The infantry and machine-gun positions had also been neutralized. Enemy resistance was fierce on this day. Every yard was now being contested. The 92nd fired over twenty-five hundred rounds that day to support the attack. By the end of the day the attack against the Siegfried Line had advanced only a few hundred yards and was spread out north and northwest of Ubach. Information gathered from prisoners of war indicated that the enemy intended to counterattack that night, but it never materialized.

The next day the attack continued, and we fired another fifteen hundred rounds. The advance was forming a distinct bulge in the line east, north, and south. By the end of the day I was able to get "C" Battery across the Palenberg Bridge. The forward elements of the attack were still running into murderous resistance including tanks, antitank guns, artillery, pillboxes, entrenched infantry positions, mortars, and mine fields. Many veterans of Morocco, Tunisia, Sicily, and St. Lo said it was the hardest fighting they had ever experienced. The pillboxes they encountered were constructed of reinforced concrete six to eight feet thick, impenetrable to all but our 240mm mortars and 8-inch guns. The pillboxes were built relatively close together and had mutually supporting fields of fire. They were located on ground that dominated the rolling terrain and were protected by double rows of dragon's teeth, which were concrete antitank pillars. Dug-in Tiger tanks and 88mm rifles supported these pillboxes. The attacking tanks and infantry ran into a virtual curtain of screaming steel. Each pillbox had to be singularly eliminated, which took time.

During the day we took part in ten serenades on enemy positions that were holding up the attack in the vicinity of Floverich and Immendorf. Many times we would provide covering fire to drive the Germans into the pillboxes while our tanks moved in on them. The tankers found that their 75mm guns could penetrate the steel doors located on the backside of the pillboxes, and that's how many of them were eliminated.

On 6 October I was ordered to move the 92nd to a position just southwest of Geilenkirchen. The attack against the Siegfried Line continued and a major breakthrough was achieved by "C"

Company of the 3rd Battalion of the 67th Armored Tank Regiment in what amounted to an old-fashioned cavalry charge. The battalion's medium tanks, the M-4 Shermans, had just been getting the hell beaten out of them the whole day. The ground was wet and muddy and the Shermans just couldn't maneuver fast enough to get out of the sights of the Tiger tanks and the antitank guns. Someone suggested that maybe the M-5 Sheridan light tanks of "C" Company might be able to surprise the German defenders with their greater speed, which was about thirty-five miles per hour. If the Sheridans could get in behind the German defensive positions and cause confusion, then perhaps the situation could be exploited by an attack of the heavier M-4 Shermans. This would either be a brilliant plan or turn into disaster because the lightly armored M-5s were equipped with only 37mm guns as their main armament.

As the M-5s attacked, the German gunners discovered that they couldn't keep the light tanks in their sights long enough to get off a shot, so they fled in terror. The 92nd fired over twelve hundred rounds in support of this attack. The Division Artillery as a whole fired 5470 rounds during the course of one hundred and fifty-five fire missions that day against enemy infantry and machine-gun positions, self-propelled guns, antitank guns, tanks, pillboxes, antiaircraft batteries, and artillery positions. By the end of the day our front lines extended just south of Gielenkirchen, Wansichen, Beggendorf, Floes, and Merkstein.

The next day at 0645 the 92nd, 14th, and 78th Artillery Battalions woke up the Germans with a stonk, and we got shelled in return. Our air observation aircraft were coming under increasingly thick antiaircraft fire from German batteries, and so it was increasingly difficult to get accurate fixes on enemy positions and troop movements. In addition, one of my forward observers had his vehicle knocked out by enemy artillery. We fired over five hundred rounds that day to break up a counterattack, and four hundred and fifty rounds on 8 October as we held our positions while the 30th Infantry Division attacked to the south in an effort to connect with the 1st Infantry Division to cut off Aachen. The German artillery fire began to slacken noticeably as our counterbattery fire began to take its toll, although we did get some harassing fire by a 210mm mortar.

On 9 October I was ordered to move my battalion to a position northwest of Ubach. We were located right in the middle of the Siegfried Line. At this point the mission of the 2nd Armored Division became defensive in nature, which thoroughly irritated General Harmon. We were to protect the flank of the 21st Army Group to the north and the First Army to the south. Throughout the month of October the weather was generally cloudy and wet except for maybe ten days. The weather really hampered our ability to see what the enemy was doing because our air OPs were grounded most of the time.

We were receiving sporadic artillery fire throughout this period, and on 13 October one round landed on one of our armored trailers and just demolished it. Occasionally we would also be bombed or strafed by Focke-Wulf 190s. On 16 October, after vicious street fighting which lasted four days, the 3rd Battalion of the 66th Armored Tank Regiment occupied Aachen. The 2nd Armored Division had successfully breached the vaunted Siegfried Line at the cost of over one thousand casualties. Out of the scores of tanks that had been knocked out of action by enemy fire, only twenty-eight could not be repaired and put back into action.

We remained in our position northwest of Ubach for the next thirty-three days. During that time we fired over twelve thousand rounds. Our fire missions were chiefly counterbattery, harassing, Time-On-Target, and propaganda missions, as well as strikes against enemy infantry, armor, antitank, antiaircraft, and other vehicular targets. Our main targets were located around the towns of Oidtweiler, Floverich, Geilenkirchen, and Bettendorf. We were supporting the 3rd Battalion of the 67th Armored Regiment and the 2nd Battalion of the 405th Infantry

Regiment.

We also were engaged in psychological warfare as well. Several times we were called upon to fire propaganda leaflet missions. The one we fired on 31 October contained leaflets that pictured one of our fearsome-looking bulldozer tanks with the appropriate language that called upon the German soldier to surrender. The Germans retaliated a couple of days later by setting up a public-address system on the front line and playing the song "Especially For You." At the end of the song a voice would say, "We are not afraid of your tank 'dozers. We have got a surprise for you, especially for you!" Of course, we showed our appreciation for their music by immediately firing a stonk on their position, which shut them up for awhile, but they would reappear from time to time at different points in the line to play their tune.

I recall that on 15 October one of my forward observers located an enemy command post that was set up in a tower in Geilenkirchen. This was a difficult target for our 105mm howitzers to hit, so I put in a call to Headquarters and requested the loan of a 155mm Long Tom, which was more of a direct-fire weapon than a howitzer. Headquarters sent me one from the 258th Field Artillery Battalion, and that gun destroyed the tower with five well-placed rounds. On 18 October I was ordered to put all of the Division's available reserve tanks in indirect-fire positions. The tanks were to be used for the interdiction and harassing fire missions because the Division's stockpile of 105mm ammunition was once again running low.

For over a month my headquarters was located near Palenberg. The houses that we occupied were about a hundred yards apart and were part of the Siegfried Line defenses. The house I was in sat on an embankment that overlooked the Wurm River. The basement was actually a pillbox. All of the houses in that area had pillboxes built into them, and the Germans had been very clever in concealing some of them. During one of the attacks on the Siegfried Line I recall watching one of the 67th Armored Regiment's tanks advance on an obvious pillbox. The tank was firing tracer rounds from its machine gun and accidentally sprayed what appeared to be a haystack with several rounds. After watching the tracer rounds bounce off the "haystack," we realized that it was another cleverly disguised pillbox.

Our quarters during the month of October were the most comfortable we had occupied since the invasion of France. Up until that time we had lived in our tents, and this was the first opportunity we had had to use any building or house for shelter for our headquarters as well as for the firing batteries. As the bad weather continued we sought shelter not only from enemy artillery fire but also from the elements. In this house we occupied near Palenberg we made use of the food the family who lived there had left behind. Once we got on German soil we began living off the land when we could, and we did so without guilty consciences because this was now enemy territory, not the land of our allies. In many of the towns in Germany the civilians would attempt to hide German deserters or troops that had been bypassed by our armor. Headquarters informed us on 17 October that civilians engaged in this kind of activity were to be taken prisoner and processed just like any other prisoner of war. We found the German civilians to be very hostile and arrogant.

During this time period, in addition to firing harassing, interdiction, and counterbattery missions, we were performing much needed maintenance work on our vehicles and equipment, which had suffered a lot of wear and tear during the drive across France and Belgium. We were also getting resupplied and had time for some rest and relaxation. I recall that on 4 November we listened as Army beat Villanova 83-6, and Navy beat Notre Dame 32-12, on Armed Forces Radio. Almost every section in my battalion, and probably the whole Army, was allowed to use one of their radios to tune in to the Armed Forces Network as long as we remained in a defensive posture. It was good for morale to let the men listen to the football games, music, and news from home.

I knew from my meeting at headquarters on 6 November that plans were being laid for another offensive. Everyone was optimistic that the Germans would capitulate very soon. In fact, everyone felt that had we not run out of gasoline and ammunition the war would have been over. I remember that I had a bet with my S-2, Captain William C. Knight, that the war wouldn't be over before 11 November. I won the bet, but if someone had told me that it wouldn't be over until May of the following year, I would have thought he was crazy. We absolutely believed the Germans were whipped and were ready to throw in the towel with just a little more encouragement. We were wrong by only seven months.

On 22 October XIX Corps, including the 2nd Armored Division, was reassigned from First Army to Ninth Army, under the command of Lieutenant General William H. Simpson. Ninth Army had been responsible for the capture of Brest and, with the Siegfried Line breached, was now poised to participate in Operation Queen, the Roer River Offensive. The mission of XIX Corps was to seize river crossings at Julich and then drive on to Dusseldorf and join up with XIII Corps, which would cross the Roer River at Linnich. From 28 to 30 October the 2nd Armored was pulled out of the front line to prepare for the new offensive.

The Roer Valley was ideal tank country. The large plain was dotted with small villages and cultivated fields that made the small hillocks strategically important. The Germans had been busy sowing minefields, digging antitank ditches, and flooding the Roer River, which reduced the number of fords. The German High Command moved in the 9th, 10th, and 15th Panzer Divisions, as well as the 183rd, 246th, 330th, and 340th Volks Grenadier Divisions, to oppose us. A company of the 330th Infantry Regiment, consisting of Hitler Youth armed with panzerfausts and Schmeisser machine pistols, was also on hand. On 11 November I was ordered to move the 92nd to a new position just southeast of Ubach in preparation for the attack. We fired one hundred and eighty-eight rounds that day. In a bit of irony, we fired ninety rounds specifically to commemorate Armistice Day.

The attack, which began 16 November, was preceded by an even larger aerial bombardment than the one that had preceded the attack on St. Lo. The 2nd Armored Division was given only a two-mile front from which to operate. Our immediate objectives were the capture of the towns of Loverich, Puffendorf, Floverich, Apweiler, and Immendorf. CCB was chosen to lead the attack. General White divided CCB into three task forces to secure the objectives. The 92nd was assigned to Combat Command A that General Collier had divided into two task forces. The 92nd was part of Task Force B and was to support the 1st Battalion of the 66th Armored Tank Regiment and the 2nd Battalion of the 119th Infantry Regiment. The weather that had held up the attack for several days had turned the fields into quagmires. Every tank carried a supply of logs or saplings which could be put down under the treads and used for traction in case a tank became bogged down in the mud.

"H-Hour" was 1245 hours. We fired a rolling barrage ahead of our leading tanks to keep the Germans pinned in their foxholes while our tanks and infantry overran them. The 92nd fired over nine hundred rounds that day to support the attack, and the operation progressed so smoothly that by 1515 hours the advancing elements had secured all of their initial objectives.

The next day the Germans launched a fierce counterattack that developed into the largest tank battle of the war on the western front. I call it the "Battle of Puffendorf" although no official histories written about the war refer to it as such. The 92nd was placed under Division Artillery control during the battle, and we fired over twelve hundred rounds in support of our units. I remained at my battalion command post throughout the battle. Although we couldn't see what was happening, the clash of the armor was certainly audible in the distance. At 1000 hours one of my forward observers spotted a column of four tanks advancing toward our lines, and we fired on them and destroyed one before the rest withdrew. After that German tanks and infantry seemed to materialize out of nowhere all over the front-line area, and it was common to hear forward observers from different artillery battalions reporting anywhere from ten to forty enemy tanks attacking at once. By the end of the day the Division had destroyed over eleven German tanks and had taken more than three hundred prisoners.

The next day as the 1st and 2nd Battalions of the 67th Armored Tank Regiment moved out into the open fields to commence the attack they were hit by a savage counterattack by at least twenty Tiger, Panther, and Royal Tiger tanks backed by infantry and artillery. Colonel Paul A. Disney, whom I knew quite well, commanded the 67th. Colonel Disney was a very fine man and later commanded the 2nd Armored Division after the war. The out-gunned Shermans were no match for the heavily armored Panzers, and after a one-sided battle what was left of the two battalions of the 67th withdrew to the town of Puffendorf, where they were reinforced by the timely arrival of Task Force A of Combat Command A. Rather than risk an attack against Puffendorf and make themselves targets for the 90mm guns of the 702nd Tank Destroyer Battalion (which was part of Combat Command A), the Germans decided to withdraw as well. The 67th, however, had been mauled, losing almost half of its tanks during the six-hour battle. Additionally, another good friend of mine, Lieutenant Colonel Charley Etter, a battalion commander with the 41st Armored Infantry Regiment, was killed while repelling the German counterattack. The 92nd fired a total of fifteen hundred rounds that day in general support of the 67th and 41st Regiments.

On 20 November the attack continued, and by the end of the day Gereonsweiler, one of the offensive's major objectives, had been secured. Two days later the Germans made a determined effort to hold Merzenhausen against an attack by CCA and constructed barricades anchored by Tiger tanks that were difficult to dislodge. We fired about eighteen hundred rounds on the town that day but we still couldn't capture it. It took five more days of hard fighting, culminating in an all-out attack by CCA on 27 November that we supported by firing eighteen hundred rounds, to finally drive the Germans out. That evening around 2000 hours one of my forward observers reported a column of eight enemy tanks with infantry support was nearing the crossroads north of Merzenhausen preparing to launch a counterattack into the town. I immediately ordered my batteries to bring the column under fire, and during the ensuing bombardment, in which we fired over twelve hundred rounds, we knocked out one tank, hit several others, and decimated the supporting infantry before the enemy dispersed. The next day CCA secured the town of Barmen and our air observers reported that the Germans had flooded the approaches to the bridges across the Roer River at Julich.

During the two-week period, 18 November to 3 December, we fired a lot of steel at the fierce German resistance. Progress was measured in yards, not miles. Over those fourteen days the 92nd fired over eighteen thousand rounds in support of our attacking units and moved just over eight miles. Our Headquarters G-2 was telling us that German prisoners were confirming the effectiveness of our Time On Target attacks. One prisoner, a veteran of the combat around Monte Cassino in Italy, stated that our artillery fire was the worst he had ever experienced and that we were exacting a terrible toll among their officer and enlisted personnel. The Germans also lost more than ninety of their best tanks during this period. We had an even greater number of tanks knocked out of action than the Germans did, losing over one hundred of the Division's two hundred and thirty-two tanks. The difference was we were able to recover and repair ours and put them back into action. Once the Germans lost a tank, it was no longer available to them.

On 3 December I received notification that I was to leave all of the 92nd's M-7s in position five hundred yards northwest of Durboslar while the men would be taken back to Ubach for a couple of days of well-deserved rest and relaxation. When we returned to our position in the line, the situation had become static. In fact, on 13 and 14 December we had time to provide an M-7 and crew to give a demonstration for Lt. General W. H. Simpson, Ninth Army Commander. We had accomplished our objectives for Operation Queen, and the 29th Infantry Division was moving in farther north to capture Linnich. Our fire missions at this time were mainly counterbattery fire, and we were shelled several times ourselves. Things remained so quiet that we were again relieved on 13 December and sent back to Baesweiler for three days of hot showers, good food, and lots of shuteye.

The month of November and early December was certainly the most intensive period of fighting that the 2nd Armored Division had undergone up to this point, and we began to realize that the war certainly wasn't over. We went from betting on the day the war would end to the stark realization that the Germans still had a lot of fight left in them. We were amazed that the enemy had been able to recover from the disaster in France and were able to put up such a fierce defense in such a short period of time. What we still didn't realize, however, was that not only were the Germans fanatically prepared to defend their homeland, but that they were still thinking of winning the war offensively.

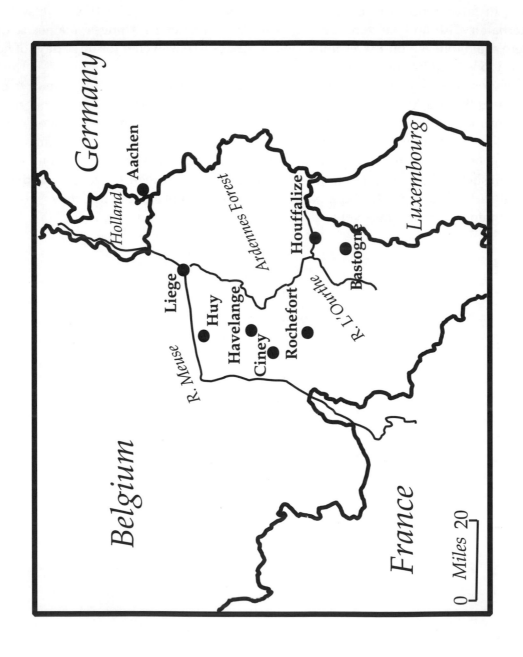

CHAPTER NINE: THE ARDENNES COUNTEROFFENSIVE

On 16 December 1944 the Germans launched their final offensive of the war—a thrust through the Ardennes Forest in Luxembourg and Belgium aimed at seizing the port of Antwerp. Hitler amassed twenty-five divisions from the eastern front and other areas in a gamble that he hoped would allow him a quick victory that would lead to a separate peace accord with the U.S., Britain, and France. Once accomplished, he could return his attention and the bulk of his forces to the Soviet armies in the east. The attack caught the Allies by complete surprise, with their forces thinly stretched along the Ardennes front, and bad weather grounded the Allies' ground support aircraft.

After achieving initial success, the German attack bogged down in the snow and cold of southern Belgium. As the weather began to clear, Allied air support savaged the attacking German columns. Moreover, pockets of stubborn Allied resistance in places like Bastogne, a town heroically defended by elements of the American 10th Armored and 101st Airborne Divisions, stuck like thorns in the German avenues of attack. News of the massacre of American prisoners of war by German SS troops at Malmedy further stiffened resistance.

The 2nd Armored Division, stationed north of the German attack, was reassigned to the Ninth Army under the command of British Field Marshal Montgomery. On 21 December 1944 the 2nd Armored Division was sent on an eighty-two-mile march south to stop the German spearhead. On Christmas Day William Buster's 92nd Armored Field Artillery Battalion found itself in the thick of the fighting in support of American armored units battling elements of the Panzer Lehr Division, one of Hitler's crack armored divisions, in the vicinity of Humain, Belgium. The ensuing clash was the second largest tank battle on the western front during the war. After being reinforced by additional Panzer divisions, the attackers came to within one hundred yards of the American lines before being driven back by murderous artillery fire. By 27 December the 2nd Armored Division had blunted the German spearhead and had prevented them from reaching the Meuse River, a key objective of their attack.

During the first two weeks of January 1945, in some of the harshest climatic conditions faced by American troops during the war, the 92nd Armored Field Artillery Battalion participated in several more battles that pushed the Germans out of the town of Houffalize, the last major bulge in the Allied line. On 19 January 1945, the 2nd Armored Division was ordered to Liege, where it was again placed under American command. The Battle of the Bulge was over, and so was Hitler's last chance for a decisive victory.

On 16 December I left the Baesweiler rest area and headed back to the 92nd's position near Durboslar. In the early morning hours the Germans had saturated the areas around Gereonsweiler and Linderen with heavy artillery bombardments followed by a strong counterattack by infantry. The attack was contained and thrown back by our own artillery fire, including almost three hundred rounds fired by the 92nd. Later that day we began to receive sporadic reports of isolated German counterattacks all along the line of the V and VIII Corps just to the south of us, but our commanders did not consider them to be anything serious.

The next day we began receiving weird reports from units in our sector. Two German planes, a Dornier 217 heavy bomber and Heinkel 111 medium bomber, were shot down by the 29th Infantry Division during the night, and the wreckage from both planes was said to have contained the bodies of paratroopers. Later that morning nine paratroopers landed near XIX Corps Headquarters, and ten more landed outside the town of Merkstein. At 2000 hours Headquarters issued orders to the field artillery battalions, including the 92nd, to mount patrols along the southern route to Engelsdorf and Durboslar to look for paratroopers. By the end of the day more paratroopers had been captured near Bradenberg, and intelligence learned from prisoners that the 2nd and 12th Panzer Divisions were forming to mount a strong attack in the vicinity of Eupen and Malmedy within thirty-eight hours. We heard that along a ninety-kilometer front German counterattacks had penetrated our lines to a depth of five to sixteen kilometers. At this time there was a growing concern in Division Headquarters about the turn of events, but the Intelligence people believed that the Germans were only stalling for time and that these were only limited counterattacks and not a large counteroffensive. However, the weather was very rainy and the skies so heavily overcast that air observation was impossible and it was difficult for anyone to tell what was happening.

On 18 December I attended a demonstration by Ninth Army on the new POZIT antipersonnel artillery shell. Until that time we had used timed fuses on our artillery shells to control the timing of the explosion. The new POZIT artillery shell was actually an adaptation of a naval antiaircraft round. It came equipped with a crude little radar device in the nose of the shell. When it got within a few feet of the ground or to a large enough object, the radar sent a signal which exploded the shell. This type of explosion was designed to send the shell fragments straight down and became a deadly weapon against dug-in infantry. We found them very effective during the ensuing days of the German counteroffensive through the Ardennes.

Throughout the day on 18 December news about continued German counterattacks kept filtering back to us through Headquarters, and it began to sound more and more ominous. By 1700 hours that day Intelligence had confirmed that the Sixth Panzer Army minus one division was on the offensive in the south against the V and VIII Corps. Around 1330 on 19 December we received the shocking news that a spearhead of seventy-five Tiger tanks supported by infantry had reached a point only twelve miles southeast of Liege, Belgium. Liege was behind us! Intelligence had concluded that Liege was the target of the attack by the I and II Panzer Corps. Historically, the road through Liege had been a favorite invasion route. The German Army had come through the Ardennes on a couple of other occasions in both world wars, and if they were attempting to split our forces, Liege was the logical place to do it. The Germans had now driven a wedge thirty-two miles deep into the American line. Headquarters believed that the situation was still under control and that this could be an opportunity to deliver a knockout blow to the Wehrmacht.

Late that night really ominous news began to reach Headquarters. It was reported that two hundred GIs who had been captured by SS troops had been herded together and shot outside of Malmedy. It was further reported that upwards of one hundred and fifty English-speaking Germans of the 150th Panzer Brigade were riding around in American Jeeps wearing American uniforms complete with dog tags and identification cards with the mission of destroying headquarters and communication centers. We spent the day of 20 December being relieved by other units as the 2nd Armored Division was transferred to Ninth Army Reserves and told to await orders to counterattack. By day's end V Corps reported that they had the German attack under control, and it began to look as if the situation was not as bad as it looked earlier.

The following morning we received orders to make ready to fire preparation barrages to support CCA's counterattack. However, at 1300 hours those orders were rescinded and we received a new one, one that drove home to me the seriousness of the situation we now faced. Something had gone terribly wrong to the south of us. The 2nd Armored Division was ordered to move south, south to the area that was now referred to as the German "offensive," not "counterattack," where we were to join up with the 3rd Armored Division. The 92nd was assigned to

Combat Command A under the command of General John H. Collier.

General Collier was a very short man. He was a "runt" at West Point, being only about 5' 3" tall, and was a fiery little man and very decisive. We nicknamed him "Peewee." We were all very fond of him, even though he often would get in a huff if things didn't go just exactly according to plan. During those times he could be a tough commander to work for. But we respected him, and he did an excellent job. I knew General Collier but had never really worked under him much, and I found that he was fierier than General I.D. White, who commanded Combat Command B, and perhaps more daring. It seemed that all through the European campaign General Collier's command was always given the tough jobs to do. CCA was always in the thick of things and, consequently, invariably seemed to be in trouble. The 92nd, of course, had forward observers with almost all the units in CCA. The flexibility of our armored artillery battalions was such that we never knew when our assignment was going to change or when some other unit not originally assigned to us needed our help. Consequently, we had forward observers not only with each attacking unit no matter what combat command they belonged to, but also with the reserve units in case they were called upon and needed help. So I was familiar with General Collier and knew what to expect from him.

At 2200 hours the 2nd Armored Division was officially released from Ninth Army control and reassigned to VII Corps of First Army. First Army was put under the control of Field Marshal Montgomery. When the lines of communication were ruptured by the German attack, General Eisenhower felt that the best course of action was to give Montgomery command of those forces north of the breakthrough and to assign General Bradley command of the forces south of the German spearhead. The 2nd Armored Division was north of the German attack so we were placed under the command of Monty. As far as we were concerned it didn't make any difference except for the fact that it appeared to us that Monty was quick to commit American troops to combat while withholding British forces. We were told that the situation south of our lines all the way to Bastogne was "extremely fluid," and small enemy units were reported in the rear of VIII Corps sector.

I don't think any of us in the 2nd Armored Division were surprised that we were called upon to stop the Germans. The 2nd was one of the oldest armored divisions in the European Theater, and as I've said before we were a heavyweight armored division. We had not been reorganized on the lighter armored division model, and we had plenty of combat experience against heavy Panzer units. Everyone I knew in the Division just figured that wherever the action was the hottest and heaviest, that's where we belonged. So at 0230 hours on the morning of 21 December, when I received the order to put the 92nd on the road, I was prepared.

By evening we had traveled an amazing eighty miles in one of the most miserable road marches that I have ever participated in. We drove through the burned-out town of Aachen and didn't stop until we arrived in an area southeast of Huy. We drove under blackout conditions in pouring rain and fog, which meant we had to drive within sight of the little cat's eye taillights of the vehicle ahead of us. Our "Peeps" and trucks had no windshields in them because we had learned in Normandy that the reflected sunlight off the glass could give away our position. Not only was it raining but the weather had turned cold and we had not yet received much winter clothing from the Quartermaster. The supply convoys had been too busy trying to supply the front-line troops with ammunition and gasoline, so supplies like winter clothing had been stockpiled back in the rear areas. We had only received jackets that were lined with army blankets, and some khaki sweaters and helmet liners, so we were not really equipped to deal with the cold weather. Up to that time we'd had a lot of wet weather but it hadn't been terribly cold, and we had been in a fairly static situation where we had been able to take advantage of houses and

Surveying Aachen's destroyed skyline—the first time. The 2nd Armored Division later returned to the city after stopping the Germans during the Battle of the Bulge.

buildings for shelter. We hadn't been exposed to the kind of wet and cold weather for as long a period of time as we were about to experience.

The rate of march was set at only six miles an hour at night and twelve miles an hour during the day, which was fine because with the freezing rain the roads became very slick. We traveled under radio silence because we obviously didn't want the Germans to know that we were coming. This created problems for us as well because without radios we couldn't stay in contact with one another. Traveling under blackout conditions in miserable weather made it easy to take a wrong turn and get lost. So the solution was to employ the Military Police platoon of Division Headquarters and the 82nd Reconnaissance Battalion as traffic directors to mark the route. At every crossroads someone was always there to point the vehicles in the right direction. Because German paratroopers were known to be in the area dressed as American soldiers, some of those GIs directing traffic were subjected to stiff interrogation by some of the passing troops. Everybody was edgy and those M.P.s probably would have preferred to be somewhere else.

I rode in my "Peep" the whole way but was not at the head of my battalion. As was always my practice I rode out ahead of the column to a checkpoint and waited there for the column to come by. That way I could keep in contact with the column ahead of us and with Headquarters as well. Bill Bowers, my executive officer, led the column on this miserable road march. As I recall we traveled in the usual tactical formation with a reconnaissance element out in front followed by an advanced guard and then a battery of supporting artillery. The main body of the 92nd followed and the supply train vehicles, maintenance, and medical personnel brought up the rear.

This was the first night march we had experienced under these conditions. We had no idea where we were going, where the enemy was, or what we were getting into. Morale in the 2nd Armored Division had always been tops, but this massive German counteroffensive affected everyone, I think. Just days before we had been betting on the day the Germans would throw in the towel, only to discover that the enemy had not only recovered but also were apparently leaner and meaner than ever before. However, we knew that many of the troops the German offensive had steamrolled had been green and untested, not tough combat veterans like us. We weren't dispirited, just frustrated as hell that the war was going to go on for longer than we had anticipated.

We arrived at our new position three-quarters of a mile southwest of Forzee, Belgium, just before dark on 22 December, and for the first time since we arrived in Europe we quartered ourselves among the people who lived there. Until that time we had always used houses and buildings that had been abandoned to shelter ourselves, but it had begun to snow and the weather was so cold and miserable that we just imposed ourselves on the local population. Fortunately, most of the people were friendly and were happy to help us out. I located my headquarters in a château and the elderly woman who lived there offered us coffee, which turned out to be the lousiest cup of coffee I drank during the war because it was ersatz. I don't know what it was made of, perhaps ground-up bark or parched grain, but it was just awful. Nevertheless, we drank it down and pretended to enjoy it. From then until the end of the war we made extensive use of existing houses and buildings whether there were people living there or not.

The next day Combat Command A was ordered to seize the town of Ciney to prevent the Germans from getting between the Meuse River and us. Seizing the bridges over the Meuse was one of the key German objectives in their whole counteroffensive plan. The very tip of the German spearhead, composed of the 2nd Panzer and 116th Panzer Divisions, was approaching. They had little warning that CCA was already there. Just after 1800 hours I was ordered to move the 92nd thirteen miles to a new position near Havelange, Belgium. Our mission was to help the 14th Armored Field Artillery Battalion provide CCA with artillery support for their attack south toward Leignon. CCA began to move south toward Leignon early the next morning and had several clashes with enemy reconnaissance units. By the end of the day Leignon was secured, and I received orders at 1530 hours to move the 92nd twenty miles to a position just outside of Haid, Belgium, where the main German column was expected the following day. I had all three of my batteries fire two rounds of adjustment fire on the line of approach that the German tanks would have to take. Then we sat and waited.

On the morning of 25 December Combat Command B along with Task Force A of CCA launched an attack on Celles, where the leading elements of the 2nd Panzer Division were coiled up because they were short on fuel. This battle turned out to be the turning point in the Ardennes Offensive. Celles lay in a valley flanked by two ridges. General I.D. White divided CCB into two task forces, with each assigned to one of the ridges. The idea was to drive down the ridges and force the Germans into Celles, and then both task forces would meet up again to the rear of Celles to prevent the Germans from reinforcing the 2nd Panzer Division. Combat Command A's mission was to cut back behind the enemy's spearhead and seal off the troops that had advanced beyond Havrenne, Humain, and Buissonville. The enemy forces around this area were much stronger than those that had advanced to Celles, so once again the fighting that CCA became engaged in was much more vicious and fierce than what CCB experienced. The Panzer Lehr Division was located in Humain. They proved that the town's name was a misnomer and gave us all the fight we wanted. Panzer Lehr had been one of Hitler's crack demonstration units, and we had faced them before in Normandy and bloodied their nose. I think once they knew we were the opposing force they wanted a little revenge. The battle for Humain was the second largest tank battle on the western front during the war, ranking just behind the battle for Puffendorf.

The advance by CCA on Humain began at 0900 on Christmas Day. General Collier had divided CCA into four task forces: A, B, C, and D. The 92nd was teamed with the 14th Armored Field Artillery Battalion in providing support for the operation. Throughout the war the 14th was almost always assigned to Combat Command A, and the 78th Armored Field Artillery was assigned to CCB. The 92nd was utilized as the weighting element for the combat command that needed the most help. Since CCA was given the more difficult tasks during the Ardennes Offensive, the 92nd was assigned to it.

Task Force A and Task Force B led the attack in two separate columns. Task Force A jumped off without any problems, but four Panther tanks with supporting infantry attacked Task Force B before it even got started. One of the forward observers from the 14th Armored Field Artillery Battalion assigned to the 2nd Battalion of the 66th Armored Tank Regiment made things even worse by calling in the wrong coordinates, and the 14th ended up shelling some of our own troops. But eventually they got zeroed in and drove off the enemy while inflicting heavy casualties. Later on in the day the Reconnaissance Company of the 66th Armored Tank Regiment ambushed a German column near Verre and the 92nd supported the ambush with artillery fire. We fired on the rear of the column to prevent reinforcements from reaching the trapped Germans while the tanks destroyed the column itself. We ended up firing over eighteen hundred rounds that day to support CCA's advance on Humain, and at 1600 hours I moved the battalion two miles closer to a position just outside of Haversin.

During this operation I spent most of my time at the command post of Col. Lindsey Herkness, the commander of the 2nd Battalion of the 66th Armored Tank Regiment. Lindsey was a former classmate of mine at the Military Academy and a good friend. He was at his command post receiving reports from his units as they advanced, and he would give them instructions on what to do and where to go. Based on that information I always tried to keep at least one battery of the 92nd within four to eight thousand yards of Lindsey's attacking tanks. During the day the snow arrived and it became bitterly cold. Once it began snowing I don't think we saw the ground again until March.

I had also been given the task of supporting the 24th Cavalry Squadron that had been assigned the task of patrolling the area between CCA and CCB as well as occupying Humain. After driving a small German garrison out of Humain around 0230 the morning of 26 December, the 24th was counterattacked at 0700 hours and had to pull back. After being reinforced, the 24th and 4th Cavalry Squadrons twice tried to retake the town but by 1600 hours that afternoon, after some of the most bitter and savage fighting of the war, it was still in German hands. The 92nd fired almost three thousand rounds in support of the 24th and 4th Cavalry Squadrons.

We found out that evening that the Germans had been reinforced by elements of the 9th and 130th Panzer divisions that initially had been instructed to reinforce the 2nd Panzer Division at Celles. Because the German position at Celles seemed hopeless, these Tiger and Panther tanks had been diverted to the fighting at Humain. After holding defensive positions during the night, the Germans launched the first of three counterattacks at 0750 the morning of 27 December. The first attack was directed at Havrenne and consisted of fifteen tanks and a battalion of infantry. The Germans got within one hundred yards of our lines before our artillery fire drove them back. In addition to destroying eight Panther tanks and a self-propelled gun, we also disabled four German half-tracks, including one that contained a map that indicated that the German attack consisted of two prongs. The second attack was to occur at 0830, so an ambush was laid and when the enemy were within spitting distance of our tanks and tank destroyers, we all opened up and totally destroyed their formations. The third attack later in the day was aimed at Frandeux, and once again we helped break it up with artillery fire.

With German reinforcements for Humain repulsed, General Collier then committed CCA's reserves, and by 1620 hours most of the town was in our hands and the situation was well under control. During the day I moved the 92nd three miles to a position near Buissonville, where the battalion fired close to two thousand rounds to help break up the German attacks and to support the attack on Humain. The last German defenders, holed up in a castle, surrendered around sundown after watching a demonstration put on by a few British flame-throwing tanks serving with the 2nd Armored Division on detached duty. After the tanks had scorched a large tree located in front of the castle, two hundred German soldiers emerged with their hands in the air. They made a wise decision. The battle for Celles and Humain was over, and this proved to be the high-water mark of the Germans' Ardennes Offensive. From now on the Germans would no longer be advancing, but retreating. Much has been written about the 101st Airborne's heroic defense of Bastogne and of Third Army's mad dash to break the German encirclement. Bastogne is where Gen. Anthony McAuliffe uttered his famous reply of "Nuts!" to the German commander's demand that he surrender. To set the record straight, I really don't think he used the word "Nuts!" but probably something earthier. However, it was the 2nd Armored Division that actually stopped the German spearhead cold and prevented them from reaching the Meuse River.

Once the Germans were stopped, we knew that our mission was not yet over. We did need a rest, though, and so on 28 December the 2nd Armored Division, except the 82nd Reconnaissance Battalion and the artillery, was relieved in the line by the 83rd Infantry Division, whose mission was to retake Rochefort. Again, the men in the artillery rarely ever got any relief because you just don't keep artillery in reserve. For the next three days the 92nd remained in position near Buissonville and supported the 329th Infantry Regiment of the 83rd Infantry Division by firing a total of twenty-four hundred rounds. On 31 December the British XXX Corps finally relieved us, and I received orders to move the 92nd to the assembly area, a mile and a half southeast of Evalette, Belgium, to rejoin the rest of the Division. We spent New Year's Day 1945 cleaning and servicing our equipment and vehicles.

My command post was located in the lovely home of one of the members of the Belgian royal family. The family was still living there but moved their quarters upstairs so that we could have the first floor. Unfortunately, they had no coal to heat the huge house. But it had an enormous fireplace in the ballroom, and we built the biggest fire that you ever saw. That was the only heat we had in the house, so we kept that fire going. During the day we received our traditional Christmas and New Year's turkey dinner. The Army always attempted to serve their line forces holiday rations in an effort to keep morale up. We had been told that we would have a week to ten days to rest and prepare for the next operation.

That afternoon I received word that there was a meeting of all Division battalion commanders scheduled for 2100 hours. Because of some of the slickest and iciest roads I have ever encountered, it took me three hours to get from my command post to Division Headquarters. It was also as cold a time as I can remember. I don't recall what the temperature was, but it was certainly well below ten degrees without factoring in the wind chill. I was a little bit more prepared for the cold than some of my fellow officers because I had a very aggressive supply officer who had made some judicious trades with some Army Air Corps officers. I think it may have cost me a few bottles of Kentucky bourbon that Mildred managed surreptitiously to supply me with through the mail. To the envy of my fellow officers I owned a sheepskin-lined leather jacket, pants, and flight boots that the Air Corps crews wore on their high-altitude missions. I was by no means toasty warm, but I was definitely more comfortable wearing that clothing than if I had stuck to the meager winter clothing the Quartermaster had been able to forward to us.

At the meeting the upcoming operation was explained to us. The Division's mission was to attack south to the town of Houffalize, where we were to join elements of the Third Army to seal the German Ardennes Offensive salient. The Germans had a lot of troops committed in the Houffalize area, and we were to try to cut them off before they retreated. I think the German High Command realized that the offensive had failed and that the best thing for them to do was to "get the hell out of Dodge" before it was too late. Hitler, however, issued his stand and fight order, which cost the Germans many good troops. My good friend, Col. Carl Hutton, was now the Division Artillery commander, and he made the artillery battalion assignments. The 92nd and the 14th Armored Field Artillery battalions were told to remain in support of Combat Command A that was to spearhead the Division's attack. Instead of a week or ten days of rest and preparation time, we were told that the operation was to begin the next day!

Early on 2 January, a bitterly cold and blustery day, the 92nd hit the road again, and by 1445 hours had advanced thirty-two miles to a position near Ny, Belgium. Once in position we fired over two hundred rounds of harassment fire at enemy positions. "H-Hour" was set for 0900 the next day, and at 0830 we participated in a preparatory artillery barrage to support the attack. Visibility was poor due to foggy and snowy conditions, and in places the snowdrifts were waist deep. We were attacking on a two-tank front because there were only two roads that led to Houffalize. The 84th Infantry Division was attached to the 2nd Armored Division for this operation and the foot soldiers rode on top of the tanks. The plan was for the tanks to advance until the enemy stopped them, then the infantry would dismount and outflank the enemy's roadblock and eliminate it. This went against all conventional theory regarding the use of armor in combat. Armor was supposed to break through the enemy's defenses and get out into open ground to disrupt the enemy's communication and supply lines. It was the infantry's job to stay behind and mop up.

The roads leading to Houffalize were narrow with a high crown, and the icy conditions presented serious problems for our attacking tanks and half-tracks. Many of our tracked vehicles had rubber treads, but the replacement tanks and M-7s we received came equipped with steel tracks. The armored vehicles with the steel tracks simply could not stay on the icy roads. It was frustrating and funny at the same time to see them trying to maneuver. They looked like drunken mosquitoes on a pond. The British had no rubber-treaded tanks at all, and it was almost impossible for them to negotiate the roads. Time and time again I witnessed our tracked vehicles slide off the road and down an embankment, sometimes tipping over in the process. This often led to a disruption in our communications because it was standard practice for telephone lines to be laid down alongside the roads. When a tracked vehicle would slide off the road and then try to get back up the embankment, its steel track would just churn and chew up all of the telephone lines. Some of these telephone lines were six to eight inches in diameter, so it is easy to imagine how many lines of communication were cut when that happened. The engineers quickly learned to get the telephone lines out of the ditches and onto poles.

The first day of the attack went slow but steady. We used our POZIT antipersonnel rounds for the first time, and reports from our forward observers indicated that the results were excellent. I had forward observers with all four task forces, A through D, and I also had line officers with the 41st Armored Infantry Regiment, the 84th Division Artillery, and at CCA's command post. Task Force A attacked toward Trinal and Beffe and by evening had secured their objectives.

At 0445 on the morning of 4 January the Germans counterattacked with at least six tanks supported by infantry. We fired stonks on the enemy, and by 0645 the attackers had been driven back and the situation was again under control. One of my forward observers claimed that fire from our battalion had knocked out two of the attacking tanks and had inflicted heavy casualties among the infantry. After the counterattack CCA pushed forward but made little progress because of the weather conditions, minefields, and German roadblocks. A favorite German tactic was to fell several large trees to block the road, plant mines in among the felled trees, and then cover the roadblock with mortar and small-arms fire. In the afternoon I moved the 92nd three miles to a new position two hundred yards north of Ny. During the day we had fired almost three thousand rounds at the enemy.

Courtesy U.S. Signal Corps

M-7 awaiting action during the Battle of the Bulge, January 1945.

There were not very many buildings in this area that we were able to use for shelter, so we spent most of our time at night in our tents trying to keep from freezing to death. On one occasion I had selected the remains of a building for my command post, but Division Headquarters personnel arrived and decided to put their forward command post at that location so I was forced to move. I finally established my command post in a barn, where I slept in the loft that night. That had to have been the coldest night I have ever spent in my life because the temperature was around zero and we had nothing with which to build a decent fire. At least I was off the frozen ground and out of the elements. In fact, I don't remember ever sleeping at all during a combat operation. After all the orders for the next day's operation had been issued, all of the assignments made for the forward observers, and all the batteries located, I might have tried to get some sleep around midnight or one or two o'clock in the morning. I would nod off until five or six o'clock or until things began to stir. In many cases it was quieter during the day than it was at night, so during lulls in the action I would sometimes take a catnap. I know I didn't get a normal night's sleep during the entire Ardennes Counteroffensive. I don't know if the grueling hours and the stress of command were beginning to affect my physical appearance or not, but the men began to call me "The Old Man." I was twenty-eight years old.

The gun crews had become very adept at protecting themselves from the elements. As soon as we established a position they would construct little huts or dugouts for themselves. On several occasions they built little igloos and constructed small coal- or gasoline-fired stoves to keep warm. I'm sure these stoves were dangerous, but when you're literally in danger of freez-

"The Germans got within one hundred yards of our lines before our artillery fire drove them back."

ing to death, you throw caution to the wind. The troops also cut up Army blankets and lined their shoes with them. We had not been issued winter boots, and some of the men began to suffer from frostbite and exposure. We never did get adequate winter clothing from the Quartermaster. (We had nothing like the clothing the troops in Korea received during the Korean War.)

On 5 January we fired twenty-one hundred rounds to support CCA's Task Force C's attack toward Devantave and Consy. I moved my battalion a mile and a half to a position near Amorines, Belgium. The next day we continued the attack on Consy. At 0330 hours Task Force C attacked but failed to dislodge the enemy. The attack resumed at 0830, this time with Task Force B leading the charge, but they too were turned back by stiff enemy resistance. Task Force B then decided to bypass Consy and move on to the town of Devantave. Around 1100 hours a forward observer from my battalion entered Devantave with the forward elements of Task Force B. By noon the town was ours. The 92nd fired over three thousand rounds to support our attacks that day.

On 7 January Task Force A attacked the town of Dochamps, which it secured by 1645 hours. One of the key objectives in this drive to Houffalize was the town of Samree, overlooking the routes of Task Forces A and B. We knew it—and so did the Germans. We wanted it; they wanted to keep it. Several enemy infantry battalions and twenty Panther tanks defended it. After three brutal days of fighting, we finally took it. The 92nd fired almost five thousand rounds to support our attacks on Samree. I remember that on 10 January during the height of this battle I personally fired the 100,000th round our battalion had fired since we landed in Normandy. That day the 92nd was credited with a direct hit on a Panther tank that destroyed it. At 1200 hours I was ordered to advance the battalion two miles to a position three hundred yards south of the town of Lamormenil. By the end of the day Samree was ours, and the next day we fired nine hundred rounds in defensive fire missions as the rest of the Division recuperated. For the next three days we stayed in and around the town of Samree, firing a total of thirty-six hundred rounds. The most disconcerting thing that happened to us during this period us was that on 14 January one of my batteries displaced in a snow-covered meadow and fired ninety-six rounds to support one of our columns. After they packed up and hit the road again, we discovered that they had been smack in the middle of a German minefield! How they managed to get in and get out without detonating any mines was just dumb luck, I guess.

We began taking a lot of prisoners as the German soldiers, weak from hunger and cold, and tired of our constant shelling, just gave up. The advancing units didn't have the infantry to spare to escort the prisoners back to the rear areas so they would just pass them back up the column. Some of the tankers in the Division were still pretty upset about the Malmedy massacre and with the German troops who had disguised themselves in American uniforms as part of Otto Skorzeny's commando operation behind our lines. Consequently, any German soldier captured wearing any article of American clothing was treated pretty roughly at times. On one occasion a German prisoner who was walking by one of our tank columns was observed to have on American combat boots. A tanker who was standing next to one of my forward observers calmly took out his pistol and shot the German dead on the spot. This forward observer of mine had been in the line for the entire advance, and this event pushed him over the edge. He went all to pieces and we had to replace him. He was later diagnosed as a victim of combat fatigue.

Early in the morning of 15 January I was ordered to move the 92nd to a position one thousand yards west of Wilbrin, Belgium. By the end of the day our patrols entered Houffalize. Over the next two days we fired less than three hundred rounds as the German resistance began to weaken noticeably. It had taken us fifteen days to advance about fifteen miles. After we took Houffalize the Division was ordered not to cross the L'Ourthe River and pursue the enemy. The Ardennes Counteroffensive was over, and on 19 January the Division was released from VII Corps control, put back under control of XIX Corps, and ordered back north to the vicinity of Liege. On that same day General Harmon was given command of the XXII Corps and General White took charge of the 2nd Armored Division.

The "Battle of the Bulge" has been described by some as a turning point in the war, but for those who participated in it, I think we remember it more for the conditions in which it was fought than for its overall strategic significance. We had thought that Germany was beaten, only to find out that the enemy didn't know that. Germany, at this time, was the most defeated country in the history of the world that had not stopped fighting. The German soldier was bloodied and bandaged but not yet defeated. We couldn't wait to get back to the Roer River so we could launch the offensive that would terminate on Hitler's doorstep. Nothing could get between Germany's industrial heartland, the Ruhr Valley, and us now.

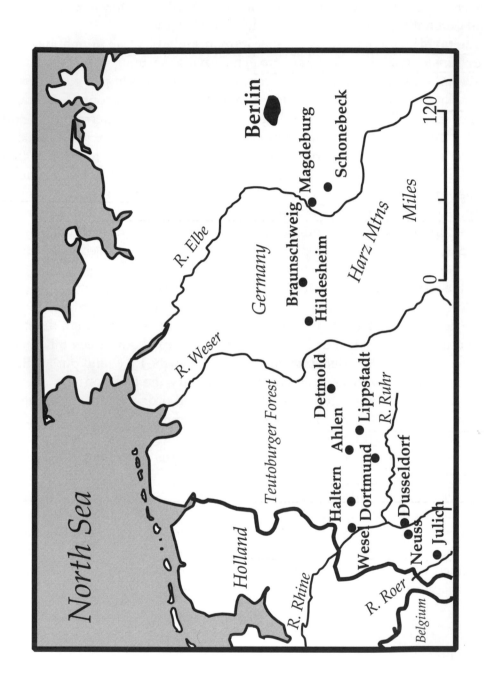

CHAPTER TEN: CROSSING THE ROER

To establish beachheads across the Rhine in early February 1945, the Allies developed a three-pronged plan of attack. British Field Marshal Montgomery would command British and Canadian forces and would launch an attack to the north in Holland. Canadian Gen. Henry D. Crerar would attack the Germans at Nijmegan. Gen. Omar Bradley, commander of American forces in the south, would attack across the Roer Valley and advance through the Frankfurt-Kassel region. Anticipating the American attack in the south, the Germans destroyed several dams on the Roer and flooded the valley. This prevented Bradley's forces from moving toward the Rhine or coming to the aid of General Crerar, whose troops faced the greatest concentration of German defenses.

It took two weeks for the Roer River waters to recede sufficiently for the 2nd Armored Division to launch its attack. Reminiscent of the break-out at St. Lo, the American attack across the Roer partially enveloped the German forces facing the Canadians under General Crerar. The 92nd Armored Field Artillery Battalion provided artillery support for the Division's attack all the way to the Nord Canal. The next immediate goal was the capture of the Adolf Hitler Bridge, which crossed the Rhine at Uerdingen-Krefeld. The enemy, however, was able to destroy the bridge before the Americans could gain control of it.

On 27 March 1945 the 92nd Armored Field Artillery Battalion crossed the Rhine near Wesel as the 2nd Armored Division attacked to the north to assist in trapping 300,000 German troops in the Ruhr Valley, Germany's industrial heartland. Once this objective was accomplished, the race was on to see who would reach Berlin first—the Allies in the west or the Russians attacking from the east. Just on the brink of winning the race, General Eisenhower inexplicably ordered the 2nd Armored Division to stop. Having decided to leave Berlin to the Russians, he ordered the 2nd Armored Division to destroy any remaining German opposition to the east and south of the Elbe River. On 22 April 1945 the 92nd Armored Field Artillery Battalion fired its last shot of the war.

Gen. William H. Simpson commanded the XIX Corps for Operation Grenade, the crossing of the Roer River. He was a stranger to me. I had normally known through personal contact or other means of association most of the top Army commanders because they had been in the old Army and I had run into them at one time or another. But General Simpson had come up through the ranks of the National Guard. He was a tall, gaunt man with very sharp features. He kept his head shaved and looked every inch the soldier. He reminded me of the characters in Bill Mauldin's 'Willie and Joe' cartoons.

The 92nd stayed in the vicinity of Wilbrin for seven days until I received orders to move the battalion to a position one hundred and fifty yards west of Dolenbreux, Belgium, for a week of rest and relaxation. During this period we were able to take hot showers, get hot meals, and perform maintenance on our equipment. Intensive training also took place for newly arrived replacements who were recent graduates of basic training back in the States. All of them received additional weapons training; some were trained as forward observers. To keep the men from getting bored, even the veterans were required to attend some of the classes taught by my officers. Some of them had been college professors before the war and were excellent teachers. Others were no good at all. Dealing with my officers was particularly difficult for me. The majority of the officers under my command had been with the 92nd since Fort Benning. I personally liked them all. I knew their strengths and weaknesses. Some of them stayed lieutenants all the way through the war because, in my mind, they were not capable of handling the addi-

The remains of an M-7 from the 92nd Armored Field Artillery Battalion after a German artillery barrage near Altdorf, Germany.

tional responsibility that would accompany a promotion. Some functioned fine as supply or motor pool officers, but I felt that they were not suited for tactical combat assignments so I could not promote them. Some of these people were the ones I liked the most, so that made it very difficult for me emotionally.

I took advantage of the lull in activity to get a pass and go to Paris. I went with a liaison officer from the French Army who served with the 2nd Armored Division. His home was in Paris, and he took me to all the famous places throughout the city. We went to "Pig Alley" and the M.P. Officers Club most of the time for our meals. I ran into quite a few American officers I hadn't seen since the States and renewed a lot of old friendships. I had a delightful time and, frankly, probably needed the time off. You don't realize the stress you're under as a commander until you get away from it. I got to be a tourist for a few days, and when I returned to the 92nd at 1700 hours on 2 February I felt renewed. It was good timing on my part because that evening we received orders to remove our 2nd Armored Division shoulder patches and to cover the Division markings on our vehicles with paint, so I knew that the new operation was about to begin. The next day we made a fourteen-mile night march to Verviers, Belgium, followed immediately by another night march thirty miles to Pesacken, Holland. We traveled at night to keep the Germans guessing about our location and intentions. The next day we covered another twenty-four miles to Inden, Germany, and finally on 9 February we passed back through Aachen and arrived in Altdorf, Germany, where we spent the next two weeks waiting for orders to attack. The offensive was supposed to begin on the ninth, but the Germans had destroyed the sluice gates to the Swannameul Dam on the Roer River that allowed the river to reach flood stage. Thus we had to wait for the water to recede before the attack could commence. This gave the Germans more time to prepare a welcome for us.

We had several close calls during this waiting period that added some unwanted excitement to our lives. Early in the evening of 14 February the Germans shelled our area, managing to land thirty-five rounds smack in the middle of Baker Battery. I had just returned from a reconnaissance patrol and gone into my command post when the attack began. My driver had pulled into a little building beside the command post and had gotten out of the Peep when the first round landed right in front of it and just demolished it. Another round hit one of the M-7s and blew it to smithereens. Three men were seriously wounded and were evacuated. We also lost a couple of trucks in the attack. And on the morning of 22 February I got my first glimpse of a German jet aircraft. An explosion awakened me, and I rushed outside to witness this odd-looking aircraft making a strafing pass on one of my batteries. It flew around for a few minutes alternately starting its engine and then gliding for awhile and then starting the engine again before it was finally shot down. We had two men wounded during that incident, which was exciting, to say the least, and added to everyone's anxiety.

The Roer Offensive finally began the next day with a pre-dawn artillery bombardment. Our position near Altdorf was far forward on the line, not more than three or four thousand yards from the Roer. The 92nd was well ahead of the Army and Corps Artillery, where all of the heavy guns like the 240mm mortars and 8-inch guns were located. The preparatory bombardment began at 0245. The bombardment was tremendous, and being in a position ahead of the bigger guns I got to witness their destructive power. When they fired, you would first feel the ground shake and hear sort of a thump, and then you would hear a swish and a crack as the shell passed overhead. So it was just a series of thump, swish, crack, thump, swish, crack, thump, swish, and crack. It conjured up visions of an enormous black bullwhip. And when the shell landed, the ground really shook. The ground was jumping up and down from the firing and then the explosions. It really was an experience. We had been far forward during the St. Lo breakout bombardment, but that paled in comparison to this.

The 30th Infantry Division led the attack, and we supported them with our guns. The 92nd had been reassigned to support Combat Command B, now commanded by Col. Sidney Hinds, of the 2nd Armored Division. Colonel Hinds had been in charge of the 41st Armored Infantry Regiment, and when General White took over the 2nd Armored Division after General Harmon left, Colonel Hinds was given command of CCB. Hinds was a soldier's soldier. He reminded me a great deal of Gen. Omar Bradley in that he had the same kind of leadership ability and quiet manner. With Hinds the soldiers who served under him came first. He was very solicitous of their welfare and did not put them in circumstances in which he himself was not willing to go. More than once he unnecessarily exposed himself in combat just to get a firsthand impression of a situation. He was not the most intelligent officer in the 2nd Armored Division, but he was tactically and technically sound when it came to the employment of infantry and the supporting armor. He knew what the job was all about.

The thing that I appreciated most about Colonel Hinds' style of command was the fact that he let his subordinate commanders run their own outfits. In particular, he didn't dictate to the artillery commanders how to employ their batteries. He would present you with a problem and what he wanted, and then he would let you work out your own maneuvers and deployments to carry it out. This style of command was directly opposite of General White's. He and I had had some disagreements over the deployment of the 92nd, disagreements he naturally won. In one particular instance during our assault on the Siegfried Line, General White ordered me to put one of my batteries across a river without the area's having first been cleared of the enemy and without supporting infantry. The next morning the battery awoke to find the enemy only one hundred yards away and a severe firefight ensued. The battery commander was so shook up by the incident that I had to replace him. But I enjoyed working with Colonel Hinds and was happy to be reassigned to Combat Command B.

Since CCB was not involved in the initial attack to cross the Roer, we were providing support for the 30th Infantry Division. The Army Air Corps also supported the attack with waves of P-47 Thunderbolt fighter-bombers. The Germans had set up three major defensive lines in an effort to keep us out of the Ruhr Valley. The 30th Infantry Division's mission was to breach this first line of defense. By 0425 Selgersdorf had been taken, and by 1300 hours Doubenrath had been secured. The enemy resisted the attack with artillery fire, mortars, mines, and booby traps. We observed that the German soldiers who were captured were very young. By the end of the day Hambach had been seized, several footbridges and one or two vehicle bridges had been laid across the river by the Army Engineers, and the attack was proceeding well. All in all, opposition by the Germans was classified as light. The 92nd fired almost four thousand rounds to support the 30th Infantry Division's attack.

By 0100 the next morning the town of Neiderzier had been cleared of the enemy; by 0845 hours a bridge that would support our armor had been built across the Roer at Krauthausen. We remained in position supporting the attack until 26 February, when the 92nd received orders from XIX Corps Headquarters to follow CCB across the Roer using a bridge built at Julich that had a railroad-marshaling yard. The whole town was nothing but rubble. Our mission was to protect the right flank of the 30th Infantry Division until the arrival of other units. By 1700 hours we had crossed the Roer, driven through Julich, and established a new position at Steinstrass, Germany. Here we fired about five hundred rounds in defense of roadblocks set up by CCB. The next day CCB was detached from the 30th Infantry Division and our positions defending their right flank were taken over by the 3rd Armored Division.

The Germans' second line of defense was located on the east bank of the Erft Canal. After being relieved by the 3rd Armored Division, CCB turned northeast. This was the natural route of advance. The Rhine River was on our right flank and a marshy area between Holland and Germany on our left. The corridor we used was a classic plain for the use of armor. CCB's mission was to strike out for the Rhine River as quickly as possible in order to seize as many bridges as we could before the Germans had a chance to blow them up. The Germans' third defensive line was located on the eastside of the Rhine.

On 27 February we moved twenty miles to a new position near Kalrath, Germany, firing over eighteen hundred rounds along the way to support CCB's attack. The next day CCB attacked through the 29th and 30th Infantry Divisions to secure crossings at the Nord Canal. We tried to stay as close as we could to the assault units and fired over seventeen hundred rounds to support their attack. In fact, we stayed so close that my batteries at times became part of the assault force. Around noon one of my batteries actually overran a three-gun German 105mm howitzer battery! By the end of the day we had traveled seventeen miles to a new position near Gubberath and had been shelled three different times. Some of the shelling we received was direct fire because the terrain was flat and you could see for miles. I recall that I had sent one of our motorcyclists to the rear to guide our kitchen trucks to our position so my men could have a hot meal. The driver of the leading kitchen truck told me that as the motorcyclist led the column toward our position, he suddenly just disappeared and then there was an explosion. The driver said the only thing he could figure out was that the motorcyclist had been hit by an 88mm round on a flat trajectory and had simply disintegrated. Naturally, the trucks kept on going without stopping to check it out because an 88mm multipurpose gun would make short work out of a stopped column. The enemy also continued their habit of shelling the main roads at regular intervals. Their harassing fire was annoying to us but, except in a few cases, it was relatively ineffective.

On 1 March we crossed the Nord Canal and advanced eleven miles toward Uerdingen-Krefeld, firing over one thousand rounds to support CCB's attack. The next day we traveled another eight miles to a position in Wielerhof, Germany. One of the things I remember about advancing into Germany was the accuracy of the enemy maps we had captured. They were just fantastic because every fence line, building, and terrain feature was indicated so accurately that we were able to locate a target and deliver our first rounds within ten yards of it within two or three minutes. On our way to Wielerhof we displaced several times and fired over two thousand rounds in counterbattery and direct support fire. On several occasions that day we had a scare thrown into us when the Germans fired over our heads near the town of Kaarst. Luckily, they did not possess POZIT rounds like we did but were still using timed fuses. They'd cut the fuses too short so the rounds went off too high overhead to do any damage to us.

The 2nd Armored Division's mission was to capture the city of Uerdingen-Krefeld and secure, intact, the Adolf Hitler Bridge that crossed the Rhine there. As we approached the city and our infantry began battling their way in, we fired harassing fire on both ends of the bridge to prevent enemy traffic from crossing it. We also fired POZIT rounds over the bridge itself in an attempt to keep the German engineers away so they couldn't blow it up. General Simpson, commander of Ninth Army, decided to keep the zones of operation between the different Corps a little flexible because the main objective was the seizure of the bridge. The 5th Armored Division, which was in XIII Corps, was on our immediate left, and the capture of the bridge became a competition between them and us. CCB won the race by mere minutes, much to the chagrin of the 5th Armored.

Our Division attacked with Combat Command A on the left and Combat Command B on the right. CCB attacked toward Neuss and Dusseldorf and met more resistance than did CCA because the Germans were using existing structures and buildings as defensive strongpoints and our route had more of those. The enemy would position panzerfaust (the German bazooka) teams in the buildings, and we would have to blast them out with high-explosive rounds. The infantry would pick off the survivors as they were driven out of the buildings. As we entered Uerdingen-Krefeld it degenerated into desperate house-to-house fighting, with the infantry having to clear out each house as they moved up a street. On 3 March at 0300 hours CCB launched the final assault to capture the Adolf Hitler Bridge. The 92nd was given the mission of firing on the far end of the bridge to prevent the Germans from setting off demolition charges and to keep their heads down while one of our patrols raced across it to establish a bridgehead. We fired for more than twenty-nine hours over a two-day period while the battle raged, amounting to more than fifty-six hundred rounds in support of the attack. During the battle Baker Battery spotted a ferryboat on the river that was being used by the retreating Germans and promptly sank it.

I had a perfect view of the battle from one of our forward observation points so I was able continuously to adjust and readjust our fire. The first patrol to make it across the bridge determined that it was already damaged too severely to support tank traffic. Colonel Hinds decided to try to put a battalion of infantry across with the hope that once a bridgehead had been established the engineers would be able to repair it. Around eight o'clock on the evening of 3 March a large explosion on the north end of the bridge created a crater thirteen feet across that all but eliminated the span's usefulness, even by infantry. The next day the Germans blew up their end of the bridge either by demolition charges or by parking several trucks on it that were loaded with explosives and then blowing them up. That settled the issue. The infantry spent the next several days eliminating pockets of resistance in the Uerdingen-Krefeld area. After that task was completed, most of the units in the 2nd Armored got to rest and recreate while other units of First Army established bridgeheads across the Rhine. The artillery, however, was kept employed defending our sector of the Rhine River from Dusseldorf to Uerdingen.

On 9 March we received word that the Russians were only twenty-eight miles from Berlin. Two days later we moved south to the Schlicherum area across the Rhine from Dusseldorf. Over the next three weeks we fired in and around Dusseldorf, expending over thirty-four hundred rounds of ammunition on targets identified by prisoners, German civilians, or our own air observers. We were supporting the patrols of the 125th Cavalry Squadron. This was a period for training, maintenance, and leave. Back in Hasselt, Belgium, the 2nd Armored Division was honored for having liberated that city. The green silk flag given to the Division as an award now hangs in the Division's museum at Fort Hood. The French awarded me the Croix de Guerre with Palm at Division Headquarters, and on 8 March I got a three-day pass to go to Brussels. I had a delightful time and really enjoyed Brussels more than Paris. The Belgian people were much friendlier and not so commercially aggressive as the French. They seemed to be genuinely glad that we were there. While I was in Brussels I learned that the Remagen Bridge had fallen intact into American hands.

When I returned to the 92nd on 27 March the battalion had moved to the vicinity of Glehn, Germany, about twenty or thirty miles north of Uerdingen-Krefeld near Wesel. The British had established a bridgehead across the Rhine in that area, and we were going to cross the river there. The 92nd crossed the Rhine at midnight on 29 March. The 2nd Armored Division's mission was to surround the Ruhr Valley by linking up in the area of Lippstadt with the 3rd Armored Division, which had crossed the Rhine farther south, thus depriving Germany of its main industrial area. The Ruhr Valley was basically a 35-mile wide by 60-mile deep area. Then we were to attack through the Teutoburger Wald (forest), cross the Elbe River, and beat the Russians to Berlin. After crossing the Rhine we stopped at Friedrichsfeld.

The next day we advanced thirty-three miles to Haltern, Germany, the outer limits of the bridgehead area. We encountered only slight resistance and the battalion fired only about one hundred and fifty rounds that day. For the attack the next day the Division again was divided into two columns, CCA on the north and CCB to the south. Our orders were to skirt the main industrial areas of the Ruhr Valley, where we could have gotten bogged down in house-to-house fighting for months, and push on through the Teutoburger Forest to Lippstadt. On 30 March we advanced fifteen miles to the Dortmund-Ems Canal, which we crossed after a short and spirited fight by dug-in infantry and a 20mm flak gun. When the 92nd was called on to provide support for an infantry attack across the canal, we responded by covering the area with over two hundred rounds. The following day, after a road march of over thirty-four miles, we came to the town of Ahlen, a military hospital town that housed about five thousand convalescing German soldiers. We fired propaganda shells containing leaflets that stated that unless the town surrendered, we would level it with artillery fire. Ahlen surrendered without a fight.

Many of the civilians we encountered as we drove through Germany during the last days of the war were completely unaware of the nearness of the American forces and the fact that we were even across the Rhine. When we approached a town of any size, we would often fire a few propaganda shells into the town to inform the people that we were coming in and if we encountered any resistance we were going to pull back and then level the town with artillery fire. Consequently, almost as soon as the leading tanks would enter a town or village, white flags would start popping out of the windows and doorways in surrender. We wouldn't actually see anybody. We had very little contact with the German people. Unless contact was necessary for conducting official business, we were ordered not to fraternize with the civilians, not that we had time anyway or that the civilians wanted to fraternize with us. Generally speaking, the

German civilians remained closed up in their homes or shops and stayed off the streets and out of our way because this was a hostile environment.

We did most of our traveling at night during this period because we could make more progress. During the day the Germans would construct roadblocks, and resistance was much stiffer. For some reason they just didn't like to fight at night, and often we would catch them by surprise. However, after a while it began to wear us down physically and psychologically because we weren't getting adequate sleep or rest and our biological clocks were thrown out of rhythm. We lived on catnaps, coffee, cigarettes, and canned food for about a month.

During the evening of 31 March, as we waited on the outskirts of Ahlen for orders to continue our advance that night, one of the most bizarre episodes of the war happened to the 92nd. At around 1900 hours we received a hurried message over the radio that a German train loaded with infantry, antiaircraft guns, and armor had just passed through the town and was headed toward the 92nd's position. We got "A" and "C" Batteries turned toward the railroad tracks and prepared to fire. "B" Battery was too far away to assist. No sooner had we got turned around when this train comes chugging by at a distance of fewer than one hundred yards. It was impossible to miss at that range with direct fire from our 105mm howitzers and every .50 caliber machine gun we had. We just absolutely tore that train to pieces. In all we destroyed the following: ten flatcars, eight antiaircraft cars containing multi-barreled 20mm antiaircraft guns in concrete turrets, one supply boxcar, eighteen boxcars carrying maintenance equipment, one 18-inch railroad gun that took four flatcars to carry, three ammunition cars, numerous troop-quartering cars, and several boxcars loaded with over one million antipersonnel landmines. It was a turkey shoot—and very satisfying.

That evening Colonel Hinds and his staff were having dinner at a gasthaus outside Ahlen when one of his officers decided, as a joke, to try to contact someone in authority at the next day's objective, Beckum, to demand the town's surrender. Lo and behold, the call went through to the German garrison commander, and Colonel Hinds decided to bluff it out. When the German commander refused the demand for the town's surrender, Hinds told him that the 2nd Armored Division would be on the outskirts of Beckum by midnight and if any resistance was encountered the Division's artillery would level the town. He immediately issued a march order for CCB. When we arrived at Beckum in the early morning hours, the German garrison had pulled out. This act of bravado on the part of Colonel Hinds undoubtedly saved us some time and casualties in achieving our objective.

On 1 April we closed the trap on the Ruhr Valley by advancing twenty-four miles to Lippstadt. At 1615 hours one of my patrols made contact with elements of the 3rd Armored Division. At that moment, trapped inside the Ruhr Valley were three hundred and fifty thousand German troops and Germany's industrial might. We set up roadblocks and fired over five hundred rounds at German troops who were attempting to flee the trap. At 0415 the next morning we began moving toward the Teutoburger Wald, the most direct route to Berlin, and an hour and a half later we ran into three hundred German soldiers who were no longer interested in dying for Hitler. After sending them back toward the rear we continued our advance for twenty-seven miles until we stopped at Haustenbeck. The leading elements of both CCA to the north, and CCB to the south, had run into stiff resistance in the Teutoburger Wald. The Teutoburger Wald is a low, densely wooded mountain range that afforded good defensive positions that the enemy used to their advantage. Antitank guns, tanks, and small-arms fire easily defended the few passes through the woods. The German defenders were SS officer candidates from the Panzer school located at Detmold.

During the fighting I lost one of my new forward observers. The life expectancy of a forward observer was not very long, and we went through forward observers pretty rapidly. It was a dangerous job that took guts. On this occasion the forward observer was so green that he got confused regarding the location of our guns. Instead of giving the command that would have angled our guns away from his position, he gave the wrong command. The barrage landed right on top of him, killing him and about a dozen of the infantrymen he was trying to support. It was a tragedy, but these things happen during the confusion of combat.

On 4 April CCB launched an all-out assault to break through the German defenses. For this operation we were attached to Task Force Disney, led by Col. Paul Disney. This proved to be a very interesting day for me. To observe Disney's attack better, I decided to take a ride in our observation plane and be the air observer for an hour or so. At one point during the flight I had the pilot land at General Hinds' headquarters—he had just been promoted—to discuss the operation with him. I found him standing in front of the operational map wondering where in the world CCA—the column on the left—was because they had fallen behind schedule. I probably wasn't thinking very clearly at the time because before I knew it I had volunteered to fly over CCA's intended route to find them. My pilot and I took off and began flying over the proposed route of the right column of CCA. We had flown for about ten minutes when we began to hear what sounded like popcorn popping. I looked out and could see holes appearing in the wings of our little Cub airplane. The realization that we were being fired at from the ground by enemy troops hit us simultaneously. The pilot quickly took evasive action, and we got the hell out of there.

On the way back to General Hinds' headquarters we flew over a long column of men marching along a road toward CCA's avenue of approach. Naturally, we initially thought they were German troops, but there was something odd about them that aroused my curiosity. I asked the pilot to circle back and take us down for a closer look. These men were ragtag-looking and were not marching in any kind of formation. As we passed overhead many of them began waving up at us, and I realized that these men were Allied prisoners of war who had been released or had somehow gotten free. About a minute later we located the leading elements of CCA and radioed that information back to General Hinds at Headquarters. After we landed we counted half a dozen holes in the wings of our little Cub aircraft and were very happy about our good fortune. During the operation that day the 92nd fired over eighteen hundred rounds in support of Colonel Disney's successful flanking attack. It took us more than two days of hard fighting to get through the Teutoburger Wald, the last major obstacle between the 2nd Armored Division and the Elbe River.

The next day we advanced thirty-six miles to the vicinity of Latferde. The retreating Germans had blown up all of the bridges across the Weser River so we had to wait for the engineers to lay new ones across, which they did by the end of the day. On 6 April we were given orders to proceed to Hildesheim as part of Task Force Disney and by the end of the next day we had reached the outskirts of the city. By 1750 that day Hildesheim capitulated. Three hours later that evening we were bombed and strafed by enemy aircraft, which resulted in half a dozen of my men being wounded.

During this period we were taking large numbers of prisoners. Between 7 April and 8 April Task Force Disney received over five thousand German prisoners, including more than three hundred taken by the 92nd. We were taking so many prisoners so fast that we couldn't process them fast enough. I had hastily constructed a prisoner-of-war cage to put the prisoners in so that they wouldn't go wandering all over the countryside. The prisoners we took said they would have surrendered much sooner but our intense artillery fire kept them from doing so. We were told that to the south of us whole towns were surrendering.

We stayed around the Hildesheim area for several days with really nothing to do, and this perplexed most of us. German resistance was dwindling; any that we encountered was being quickly overcome. We knew that our reconnaissance patrols were probing far to the east and were encountering little opposition, so many of us were befuddled by the delay. We knew that once we reached Berlin the war would be over, and we were anxious to end it. It was not until after the war when I was assigned to the Pentagon that I learned the reason the 2nd Armored Division had been halted by SHAEF in Hildesheim. Hildesheim was actually the location in Germany where we were to have met up with the Russians, not one hundred miles farther to the east at the Elbe River. However, the Russians were not advancing as quickly as they had predicted—and no wonder. Hitler was feeding his best forces into the meat grinder on the eastern front, trying to keep the Red Army out of Berlin. The 2nd Armored Division, at this time, was not facing the elite of the German Army. Those forces had been stripped from the western front and were deployed against the Russians. The troops we were encountering across Germany were mainly Home Guard troops, SS Officer Candidate School trainees, and Hitler Youth. The SS troops and the Hitler Youth were still fanatical defenders, but the Home Guard troops were mostly old men (many of them veterans of World War I), or physically unfit soldiers who had seen enough fighting and were anxious to give up.

We finally received the go-ahead from SHAEF Headquarters to continue on to the Elbe on 9 April. The launching of the final offensive was scheduled for the next day. Combat Command B broke into two columns after we left Hildesheim, and the 92nd was given the mission of supporting the southern column. We advanced over twenty miles that day and fired over sixteen hundred rounds to support the attack. CCA to the north had to move through the more industrialized area around Braunschweig and Immendorf, where the Hermann Goering Steel Works were located. The Goering Steel Works were surrounded by dozens of multi-purpose antiaircraft guns that had to be eliminated in order for Immendorf to be secured. The steel works were operated by slave labor conscripted by the Germans from conquered countries, and these displaced people were still there at the time of our attack. There were several Allied prisoner of war camps in the area that had been abandoned by their German guards, so these men had to be cared for as well. Consequently, CCA had a much tougher time advancing than did CCB.

As CCB's advance continued on 11 April, the first stiff fight that occurred involved the 92nd Battalion. As the leading elements of the battalion were passing through the town of Oscherleben, they received panzerfaust fire from one of the buildings. The shot hit my executive officer's half-track, destroying it and wounding eight men. Bill Bowers, the executive officer, was blown out of the half-track by the explosion and suffered a broken arm. As soon as he gathered his wits he ordered Battery "B" to come forward and fire at point-blank range at any possible defensive position in the town. After firing forty-four rounds and practically leveling the town, we continued the advance.

I was not there at the time of this incident. I was up front with the 82nd Reconnaissance Battalion, which was leading CCB's attack, and about to get involved in another adventure of my own. A new airfield beside the road east of Oschersleben had just been secured and our observation planes had been brought up. We had two planes, one of which was kept up in the air all the time, weather permitting. One would fly an hour and land, and then the other would take off and stay up an hour, and so on. When my driver drove by the airstrip around 1500 hours, I stopped by to see how things were going and found that one of the observers had become quite ill and could not fly. Consequently, the other observer had to fly both shifts without a break and was suffering from fatigue. I decided to fly the next shift to give the observer a break.

The pilot and I took off in the little L-4 to fly cover for our advancing column. It was a fascinating hour. I would observe our troops enter a small village and the white flags of surrender would almost simultaneously begin popping out of windows and doors. On one occasion I noticed a bus come into a town from the opposite direction of our advance. As they saw one of our tanks drive through the intersection on a diagonal course, the bus stopped, the doors flew open, and all of the people in the bus piled out and hid facedown in the ditch alongside the road. I don't know how long they stayed there, but every time we passed over during my flight they were still in the ditch. On the same flight we flew over another village that was still occupied by German troops. As the people looked up, I saw them point at us and then run into their houses and buildings. I swear you could hear the doors slamming shut! The German troops scrambled into their vehicles and began moving forward and backward, slamming into one another as they tried to turn around to leave the town. It was sort of like watching a Keystone Kops comedy routine. But as often happens in combat, the shoe can shift to the other foot in a hurry.

We had just flown over Wanzleben, the last sizeable town before you get to Magdeburg, when I spotted an installation of some kind off to the left several miles. I figured it had to be an antiaircraft installation because the Army Air Corps had reported that they had run into a lot of flak around the Magdeburg area on their bomb runs to Berlin. I assumed that they were 88mm antiaircraft guns, but they turned out to be 128mm rifles. I contacted our forward observer with the 82nd Reconnaissance Battalion, who happened to be the commander of Battery "C," Capt. William R. "Thumper" Carey, and told him that there was a fairly large antiaircraft installation off to his left. He replied that they were moving too fast to fire at anything themselves but to keep him informed. I had just spotted an airfield and the Elbe River in the distance when the antiaircraft guns began to fire at us. The first flak burst was an "over" and the second a "short," but they were close enough that the L-4 shivered and shook violently. The pilot dove straight down and leveled out at one hundred feet in an effort to avoid the flak, but we

A German 88mm multi-purpose rifle captured near Magdeburg, Germany, April 1945.

started hearing that popcorn-popping sound once again.

I looked out my window and noticed little puffs of smoke coming from the gardens and rows of buildings on the outskirts of Magdeburg and realized that they were firing at us. The pilot banked the plane to turn us around, and we were about to get away when "Thumper" called on the radio to warn me that there were enemy aircraft in the area. I looked up as we were banking and saw three Me-109Fs up above us and knew that if they spotted us they would come in and tear us to pieces. After a very short conversation, the pilot and I decided that the best thing to do was to find a place to land and wait until the fighters left. We landed in a field about a mile and a half from the road that our column was advancing on and immediately abandoned the plane in case the fighters spotted it and came in for strafing runs. As I left the plane I grabbed my map. While we waited I plotted the exact location of the antiaircraft installation that had been shooting at us. When the Messerschmitts left after about five minutes of snooping around, we got back in the L-4 and took off again. As soon as we got in the air I radioed in the coordinates of the German installation to my battalion, which by this time had moved through Oschersleben, and ordered them to deploy and fire at the antiaircraft guns. Five minutes later I watched as the whole area where the installation was located was pounded to smithereens. Afterward, we flew over the area and found that we had completely destroyed four of the heavy guns and had killed dozens of the gun crews.

On this flight I may have been the first member of the ground forces to see the Elbe River. We were flying out ahead of the reconnaissance elements and were probably being more daring than we should have. After the flight was over the pilot and I felt very fortunate to have survived. The destruction of the German antiaircraft installation allowed the leading tank elements of CCB to enter the outskirts of Magdeburg. On 12 April the 92nd was one of the first units to reach the Elbe River. By 2130 hours one of our forward observers, 1st Lt. Stephen Kaloropolos, had accompanied a patrol of the 119th Infantry Regiment across the river. The 41st Armored Infantry Regiment was also ferried across to establish a bridgehead.

The enemy still held the city of Magdeburg, but we were determined to cross the river anyway. The Germans had blown up the bridge located at Schonebeck, so the 17th Engineer Battalion was given the mission of building a new one that night. The 41st Armored Infantry Regiment was sent across the Elbe to secure a bridgehead so the engineers could proceed. Unfortunately, no antitank weapons were sent with them because with the construction of the bridge that night it was thought that the tanks and tank destroyers would go across the following morning. However, just as the engineers were about to complete the bridge early the next morning, the Germans began shelling it with deadly accurate fire and by the middle of the afternoon had destroyed it, leaving the infantry stranded on the other side of the river. We had tried unsuccessfully all day to silence the German batteries with counterbattery fire, expending over two thousand rounds.

Late that same day we received word that President Roosevelt had died. The death of FDR was a tremendous shock to all of us. We had finally reached the Elbe River and knew that the war was almost over, and this news just took the wind out of our sails. Roosevelt was much more of a national hero to us out in the combat areas than he was to a lot of people back home. To us he was more than just our commander in chief. To many of us he was a father figure, a man's man, an inspiration, a hero. Here we were on the verge of victory, and for him to die just before we finished the job seemed terribly unfair. FDR's death cast a pall over the whole Army. None of us knew anything about Vice President Harry S Truman other than he was a little guy from Missouri noted for uttering cornball expressions. I don't think any of us thought that he was anything like the caliber of leader we needed at this particular time. Fortunately, he proved us wrong and carved out his own legacy.

As much as we were saddened by the news of Roosevelt's death, we still had a crisis of our own to deal with, namely, extricating the 41st Armored Infantry Regiment from the east side of the Elbe. At 0500 on the morning of 14 April the Germans counterattacked our infantry on the east side of the river with infantry and tanks. The men of the 41st had no antitank weapons and were quickly overrun, and by 1130 that morning the bridgehead had been completely surrounded and was in danger of annihilation. Two of the three battalions on the east side of the river had been wiped out, and Colonel Disney had been seriously wounded during the fighting. The decision was made at Headquarters to build another bridge across the river farther south out of the vision of the German artillery spotters so that we could put some tanks and tank destroyers across to relieve the pressure on the bridgehead area. However, that position too was shelled by the Germans, forcing General Hinds to consider using a bridge established by the 83rd Infantry Division farther south. At that point General White, commander of the 2nd Armored Division, decided that discretion was the better part of valor and ordered the withdrawal of the remaining troops on the east side of the Elbe. Under the cover of a smoke screen fired by the 92nd, many of the survivors were ferried back to the west bank or swam across the river to safety. One of those to make it back alive was our forward observer, Steve Kaloropolos.

It seems that the position of the 119th Infantry Regiment unit to which Kaloropolos had been attached had been overrun by the German counterattack, and he and about sixty other men had found safety in a basement of a house in the town of Elbenau. A German doctor and his nurse who lived in the house promised to keep quiet about the Americans' location if they were allowed to leave to tend to German casualties. The Americans agreed, and the German doctor and nurse kept their word. We had given up Kaloropolos for dead and were very happy to see him. I think he had nine lives because he had been wounded in action twice before but had always come back to the battalion after he recovered. He was a good forward observer and a brave man.

In fact, not all of the troops did withdraw from the east side of the river. We maintained a small bridgehead there not from which to launch an attack, but to stop the Germans from attempting a crossing themselves. While the battle raged on the east side of the Elbe, General Simpson, commander of XIX Corps, was summoned to General Bradley's headquarters. There he was told that the XIX Corps was to stop at the Elbe and not continue the drive to Berlin. Simpson himself delivered the bad news to General White at 2nd Armored Division Headquarters. For the next six days we stayed in the Magdeburg area harassing the Germans on the other side of the Elbe with Time-On-Target attacks, counterbattery fire, and interdiction fire. We fired over eight thousand rounds across the Elbe River during those six days, and at 1604 hours on 19 April, I personally fired the 92nd Battalion's 150,000 round since we landed in Normandy. Magdeburg itself had finally fallen the day before to Combat Command A and the 30th Infantry Division after the city had received a massive artillery bombardment and air strike.

On 20 April the 2nd Armored Division was ordered to turn over our sector to the 30th Infantry Division and was given a new mission. A large enemy force including fifty tanks was reported to be escaping to the Harz Mountains, and CCB was sent in pursuit. The 92nd was attached to Combat Command Reserve during this operation. Just before we turned over our position to elements of the 30th Infantry Division, several Junkers 88 bombers bombed our area but, fortunately, although they came close, no one was injured. That day we traveled eighty-four miles to a position near Kl-Rhuden, Germany. On 22 April the 92nd fired a stonk on a contingent of "Werewolves," which was an organization of Hitler Youth and Nazi Party members forming for an attack on Seehausen. Our fire broke up the attack. By 23 April our division's area of responsibility had been cleared of all enemy combatants. We didn't know it at the time, but the 92nd Armored Field Artillery Battalion had fired its last round of the war.

With the drive to Berlin cancelled, the 2nd Armored Division turned its attention to police duty. Our mission was to insure that the civil governments continued to operate to help maintain utility services and law and order for the local population. Our job was to reestablish civil control and to keep the economy going as smoothly as possible. We did not want German society to suffer a total breakdown because chaos would have resulted. We did not want roving bands of angry Germans creating problems with our lines of communication or supply lines.

Instead we allowed the local governmental leaders to continue in their positions, even if they were known Nazis. Criminal proceedings and retribution were not part of our mission. There would be plenty of time for criminal proceedings later. Our approach in dealing with the Germans seemed to work, for we encountered few problems. In several instances we even helped repair their own transportation and communication systems, and we also made sure that they had enough food and that it was distributed properly. The 92nd was given responsibility for three towns: Germshiem, Kl-Rhuden, and Bornhausen.

I personally had little contact with the German population, but my staff officers did because they were given direct control of the towns under our jurisdiction. We worked with the Division G-5, who sent his staff members down to supervise the entire operation. We were assigned police duty for only about three weeks. During this time the decision was made by SHAEF that the 2nd Armored Division would be the American unit that would occupy the American sector of Berlin after Germany surrendered. Hitler had not yet capitulated, and his fanatical, and costly, battle to keep the Russians out of Berlin continued to rage.

Gen. I.D. White pins Silver Star on Lt. Col. William R. Buster at Alfeld, Germany, 4 May 1945.

CHAPTER ELEVEN: BERLIN AND HOME

The Russians, who had embarked on a massive offensive in January, captured Berlin on 2 May 1945. On the seventh, Germany, a nation physically, materially, and emotionally shattered, surrendered unconditionally. An occupied and divided Germany provided the Russians with little incentive to maintain their alliance with France, Great Britain, and the United States. With their hard-won territories in eastern Europe to administer and pillage, Russia found itself suddenly back at economic and political odds with its former allies. Berlin became one of the centers of friction. With postwar meetings to determine the rules of occupation between the former allies looming, the 2nd Armored Division was chosen by General Eisenhower as the American occupation force to create an impressive military presence in Berlin.

Once in Berlin, Buster, promoted to Division Artillery commander, viewed the war-torn city firsthand. He was able to visit the Brandenburg Gate and Hitler's bunker as well as other Berlin attractions. During July and August, Buster's unit was chosen to provide security for the Potsdam Conference. He was able to get a glimpse of Winston Churchill, Joseph Stalin, and Harry S Truman as the Allied leaders reviewed the troops. Not long after the surrender of Japan on 15 August 1945, the Kentuckian was ordered to report to the Pentagon in Washington. Following a welcome leave spent with his family, he returned to the Pentagon to take on a number of important postwar assignments. In 1948 Buster resigned from the Army to manage the family farm in Midway, Kentucky.

MY BIRTHDAY day 15, 1917

I believe Eisenhower chose the 2nd Armored Division for the Berlin assignment for both military and political reasons. Militarily, the 2nd Armored was a powerful, heavyweight armored division with tremendous offensive and defensive capabilities. With Germany out of the way, I don't think Eisenhower was sure Stalin would willingly allow U.S. troops into Berlin. The 2nd Armored was selected to make sure that happened, one way or another. Second, choosing a heavyweight armored division to be the occupying force made a forceful political statement to Stalin that the American presence in Berlin would be a permanent one. Stalin got the message.

Around midnight on 1 May we received the news that the world had been waiting six long years to hear. That night the BBC reported that Adolf Hitler, the s.o.b. who had started all of this, had taken the coward's way out and committed suicide. In retrospect I think many people would have preferred that Hitler had been taken alive and put on trial for his crimes against humanity. As we crossed Germany we had gotten some information about the horrors some of the American and British troops had discovered in the various concentration camps they had entered. But most of us in the 2nd Armored had not seen this ourselves. So when the news reached us that Hitler was dead, we were glad and would have been happy to have been the ones to put a bullet in his head. The reaction in my battalion was one of great satisfaction and celebration. Class 6 rations were drawn and we all drank a toast to the departure from this world of dear old Adolf.

Following news of Hitler's suicide we began receiving reports by radio that surrender negotiations had been initiated by his successor, Adm. Karl Donitz, so we knew that the German surrender was just days or hours away. Germany's official surrender occurred early in the morning of 7 May. The next day we were relieved of our police duty and were pulled back to an assembly area near Salzgitter preparatory to our move to Berlin. We stayed in Salzgitter for a period of almost two months while negotiations between our government, Great Britain, France, and Russia continued. We spent the time cleaning up and repainting all of our equipment and

"We finally entered Berlin 4 July 1945. Berlin looked like a giant honeycomb with most of the buildings and homes gutted and without roofs. The central part of Berlin was just pulverized."

received new uniforms. We were expected to put on a good show for the Russians.

Also beginning at this time we began sending men back to the States on rotation. We used the point system. Each soldier had earned a certain number of points depending upon how long he had been in the service, how long he had been overseas, and how many battle stars he had received. Consequently, once the fighting stopped our high-point men became eligible to be sent back home. Over the next several months quite a few of the veterans of the 92nd Battalion returned to the States. Some of them, I'm sure, would have loved to have been there when we marched into Berlin, but I couldn't blame them for wanting to go back home as soon as possible. Many of the senior officers of the 2nd Armored Division were also rotated out and sent back to the States.

On 28 May the 92nd was chosen by Gen. I.D. White to be a demonstration unit at Brunswick, Germany, for a visiting Russian general. We fired a fifteen-gun salute in his honor. The reviewing stand was actually just a raised platform, and as we were passing in review a flight of P-47 Thunderbolts flew over. These experienced pilots came in so low that I thought they were going to take the tip off the antenna on my half-track. It scared the Russians to death—I saw them duck down as the planes roared by! The Russian general and General White were so impressed by my unit's appearance and the entire demonstration that General White and his successor, General Collier, continued to use my battalion exclusively for these exercises for the next several months. It was quite an honor, and I was very proud of my men.

On 22 June the 2nd Armored Division was placed under the control of the 7th U.S. Army. That same day Colonel Hutton was given command of Combat Command A and I was promoted to Division Artillery commander. Division Artillery was assigned to CCA, and CCA was selected to lead the 2nd Armored Division into Berlin. We finally received word to begin moving toward the capital the last few days of June. That's when the Russians began playing cute with us, which justified Eisenhower's choice of the 2nd Armored Division as the American occupation force. The Russians controlled the bridge across the Elbe River that we were supposed to use. Several times we received orders to cross the Elbe using this bridge and to continue down the Autobahn into Berlin. When we would arrive at the bridge we would find that the Russians had torn up the planking during the night for "repairs." They rejected the offers by our engineers to help them with the "repairs." After several attempts at this location we decided that they were just not going to allow us to cross the bridge, so we found another point farther south a number of miles out of our way. We crossed the Elbe there and then went on into Berlin by a more circuitous route. The story that we got later was that the Russian troops in Berlin at that time were not high-quality troops, not the kind of elite troops Stalin wanted there when we arrived. They were having a hard time rounding up all of these rag-tag troops, who had been raping and looting the city of everything, so they were playing for time in delaying our advance into the city. But that was really just the first in a series of incidents perpetrated by the Russians in order to interfere with us, and certainly a portent of future events like the Berlin airlift. Stalin was testing our resolve, and I'm sure he didn't like the answer he received.

It was an interesting trip to Berlin. We met a lot of run-of-the-mill Russian soldiers for the first time. They were still using a lot of horse-drawn artillery and wagons. Where one of our batteries consisted of about fifty vehicles, theirs had maybe five, many of which were American-made. They would have a command car plus an American deuce and a half pulling four guns. Most of their other stuff was horse-drawn. The crudity of their equipment and their ragged appearance made us realize what a tough fight they had had against the elite troops the Germans had thrown against them. They had suffered enormous casualties driving the enemy back to Germany. We had a great deal of respect for the bravery of the Russian soldiers. Of course, we also felt that we would have kicked their butts if the need had arisen.

We didn't know much about them until we got to know them while in Berlin. We found the average Russian soldier to be very naïve. We were told that when their elite troops got to Berlin they were paid for the first time in many months. They were paid in occupation marks and they had lots and lots of money. They had so much money that they had to carry it around in little bags that they slung over their shoulder. They would buy anything American. Some enterprising GIs were selling them cheap PX watches for around six hundred dollars each. We had to chastise some of our pilots for flying back to Brussels and loading up their planes with these cheap watches and other goods in order to make a killing on the black market selling to the Russians. So many Americans were getting rich in Berlin that the military authorities found it necessary to implement currency controls. Up to this time the Russian and American occupation marks were each made by their own government, only the Russian marks were not backed by hard currency as the American marks were. Our GIs almost broke the American economy by cashing in these worthless Russian marks and receiving good U.S. money for them. Currency control was finally instituted and everyone was given a pay record. When I left Germany, no one was allowed to cash in more occupation marks than they had received as pay. But before this system was implemented a lot of enterprising American officers and soldiers had sent lots and lots of money home.

We finally entered Berlin on 4 July 1945. The streets were deserted when we arrived. We were assigned the southern third of West Berlin. The British sector was right next to us; the French sector to the north. The American occupation zone was actually the elite residential section of the city. Our zone was located south of Unter den Linden, which had been spared much of the heavy bombing by the Allied planes because there were few factories located there. The rest of Berlin looked like a giant honeycomb with most of the buildings and homes gutted and without roofs. The central part of Berlin was just pulverized.

While stationed in Berlin I took the opportunity to see the Brandenburg Gate, the Reichstag, and the old Adlon Hotel. As Division Artillery commander I was also permitted to visit Hitler's bunker, including the room where he blew his brains out. Russian soldiers guarded the bunker complex, and I had to part with some cigarettes before they would let me in. Amazingly, the Russians had left things pretty much the way they had been when Hitler was holed up in there, and I was able to "liberate" some of Hitler's personal stationery. I donated the stationery to the Kentucky Military History Museum in Frankfort, where it can be viewed today.

The trees in the once-beautiful Tiergarten had been reduced to stumps by the bombing. The cleanliness, orderliness, and frugality of the Berlin residents impressed me. After a severe thunderstorm that blew down many of the trees in our section of Berlin, the residents came out and within thirty minutes everything had been cleaned up. You would never have guessed that there had been a storm at all. I learned later that the people used the wood for fuel because that's all they had after the war. They had no heating oil or gas. The forests surrounding Berlin were immaculate. The traditional German folktales always referred to people of the forests as fagot gatherers and from what I saw there was more than a grain of truth to them. The paths in the forests were totally devoid of twigs and branches and were just a delight to walk through. Part of our mission in Berlin was to clear the streets of debris caused by our bombing, but we found that this took very little effort. When we supplied the vehicles, the native Berliners were more than happy to load the debris with their bare hands and have us haul it away. I found the Germans to be very pragmatic people. The war over, they were anxious to get on with their lives and rebuild their city.

I managed to tour the whole city and found it a very moving experience to drive down some of the streets that had been totally wiped out. The rubble had been swept to the side and all of the streets were passable, but there was the unmistakable odor of death over the whole city. Undoubtedly, many of Berlin's citizens had been buried in the rubble during the bombing and were still there awaiting proper burial. The smell of death has a very peculiar odor, one that soldiers never forget. It's a very distinctive smell, not like the odor of decaying livestock or vegetation. It hung over Berlin like a cloud.

After I returned to the States and was assigned to the Pentagon, I was given an assignment that took me back to Berlin in the early part of 1946. In that short six-month period I found that the Tiergarten had been replanted and West Berlin had been cleared of all the rubble. Many of the buildings were still without roofs, but most of the homes had been restored and it began to look like a thriving city again. East Berlin was a different story. The Russians had not done much at all and it still looked like a bombed-out city. The only "improvements" the Russians had made in East Berlin were to erect large billboards and placards with Stalin's picture and Communist slogans on them throughout their half of the city. Even at that early date the contrast between West and East Berlin was striking.

One of our major assignments in Berlin was to provide security for the Potsdam Conference, which was held in Berlin from 17 July to 2 August and was attended by Truman, Stalin, and Churchill. This was a spit-and-polish operation for us, and we had to provide reviews for each leader individually. These reviews were different from typical reviews because instead of all of the troops marching past a reviewing stand, a mobile reviewing stand passed by the troops, who stood at attention along the side of the Autobahn. I got to see all of the Allied leaders firsthand. It was a very interesting time because we all realized that they were deciding what the geopolitical map was going to look like for years to come.

The 2nd Armored Division was actually only supposed to be assigned occupation duty for a period of two months, just long enough to make the point to Stalin that the United States intended to stay in West Berlin. We were to be relieved by the 82nd Airborne Division at the end of August and sent to the south of France to begin intensive training for the invasion of Japan. Of course, these plans were called off after we dropped the atomic bombs on Hiroshima and Nagasaki on 6 and 9 August, and Japan wisely surrendered five days later. When we heard the news about the destructive power of the atomic bomb, our reaction was "Hooray!" because we all had had our fill of the war by that time, and the thought of having to go to the Pacific made us all sick. We were for anything that would end the war over there quickly so that we wouldn't have to go. We experienced a tremendous feeling of relief when we finally received word that Japan had surrendered and that the war was really over. We all had a tremendous sense of satisfaction that we had accomplished our mission and would soon be going home.

The 2nd Armored Division provided the Honor Guard for the "Big Three" conference at Potsdam. "I got to see all of the Allied leaders firsthand. It was a very interesting time because we realized that they were deciding what the geopolitical map was going to look like for years to come."

Shortly after the atomic bombs had been dropped on Japan but before they surrendered, I received orders transferring me from the 2nd Armored Division to a new assignment in the European Section of the Operations Planning Division (OPD) in the Pentagon. Later named the Plans and Operation Division, this agency coordinated the activities of the other War Department General Staff agencies. This was the agency that really gave a boost to Eisenhower's career. He was the one who was given the assignment of creating and setting up the OPD before the United States became militarily involved in the war. Ike was just a lieutenant colonel when he set up the agency, and we all know how his career took off after that.

When I received my transfer orders, General Collier, commander of the 2nd Armored Division, called me into his office and made me stand at attention in front of his desk for twenty minutes while he outlined the reasons why I should stay in the outfit. He didn't invite me to sit down and didn't talk to me like a Dutch uncle. He practically demanded that I stay with him as Division Artillery commander and suggested that I would be disloyal if I left. He then told me to think about it and dismissed me. I didn't have to think very long. I had been overseas almost three years, had a wife I hadn't seen in three years, a son I had never seen, and I thought that the new assignment in the Pentagon would be a splendid opportunity if I wanted to further my military career. I also knew that Col. Hugh Exton, who had previously commanded the 78th Armored Field Artillery Battalion but had been sent home on rotation, had been assigned to the OPD and that he had undoubtedly put in a good word for me. I knew Hugh had probably pulled some strings and called in some markers to get me transferred. After all, there were a lot of lieutenant colonels the Army could have chosen for that assignment and I had no particular connections to speak of. I felt that under those circumstances I ought to accept the transfer—and did. The 2nd Armored Division itself arrived back in the United States in January 1946, so I wasn't too far ahead of the rest of the Division.

I left the Division near the end of August and flew to one of our airbases in Prestwick, Scotland, where I stayed for several days because the airport got socked in by fog. I then flew on to New York, where I was surprised to find a Red Cross station for returning servicemen. Overseas soldiers often discuss what they miss the most being away from home and the first thing they'll eat when they get back to the States. Most say steak and eggs or something of that nature. The first thing I asked for was a glass of milk. I hadn't had a glass of milk for three years and that's all I could think of. That glass of milk in the airport in New York was the most refreshing I've ever drunk. I quickly followed that with a glass of Coca-Cola and a fresh garden salad. A strange first meal back home, to be sure, but that's exactly what I wanted!

I had been given a high-priority transportation rating so I was able to board the next available train heading to Washington, D.C. Upon my arrival I took a cab straight to the Mayflower Hotel, where a room had been reserved for me. I reported for duty at the Pentagon the next day, 29 August 1945. I was immediately given forty-five days R&R and was able to finagle a seat on the "George Washington" that evening that was heading for Lexington, Kentucky. Mildred met me at the old railroad station on Main Street in downtown Lexington, and I saw my two-and-a-half-year-old son for the first time. He and I had an interesting time getting acquainted. Mildred slid in behind the wheel to drive us home, and my son was sitting in the front seat between us. I put my arm across the seat and laid it on Mildred's shoulder. My son looked at me and picked my arm up and put it back over on my side! He was not too sure about the stranger in the car! But we got acquainted and became pretty good friends soon after that. Mildred and I spent the next forty-five days getting reacquainted ourselves. We drove down to Ponte Vedra, Florida, and enjoyed some three weeks there soaking up the sun and relaxing. Mildred had spent the war in Midway with her mother and had not had an opportunity to go anywhere, what with all the rationing and travel restrictions that had been necessary. She needed the time away, too.

After my days of R&R were up, we rented a house in the Chevy Chase area of Washington, and I reported back to duty to begin my assignment in the Operations and Planning Division. It was very interesting work. The Operations Section was, in effect, the Washington headquarters for all of the overseas commands, and all operations that were being conducted anywhere in the world were coordinated through the OPD. The European Section where I was assigned consisted of twelve officers in addition to a sizeable staff. We were responsible for the coordination of the activities of all U.S. forces in the European Theatre. We were in constant communication with the various European headquarters by teleconference, cable, and correspondence. We had to coordinate the demobilization of the Army so that it remained a balanced force. We coordinated the logistics of the demobilization effort such as arranging for the transportation and mustering out of the returning troops. This was a massive effort and took a lot of planning and coordination of various resources.

(Above) *2nd Armored Division on review for President Harry S Truman on 24 July 1945, during the "Big Three" meetings at Potsdam. (Below) President Truman uncovers during the playing of the National Anthem by 2nd Armored Division Band.*

One of the more interesting challenges we faced every day was the preparation of briefings for the higher-ups. Every morning the European Theatre chief, the chief of OPD, and the Chief of Staff for the Joint Chiefs all had to be updated on what had happened at the various European headquarters during the night. We rotated this duty among the twelve officers, and when my turn came up I'd get down to my office in the Pentagon by 2:00 a.m. and begin my preparation. I'd go by the message center to collect all of the cables that had come in during the night and study those and pick out the most interesting ones. I would then take these and go over to the cartography section and they would update the situation map. At eight o'clock I would first brief my superior officer and then I would brief the European Theatre chief, then the chief of OPD, and then the Chief of Staff. At the briefings with the chief of OPD and the Chief of Staff there would be briefings by the South American and the Pacific Theatre sections as well. So I was aware of what was going on in the other theatres. We generally worked six and a half days a week, but at times it was all day and all night when we were dealing with crisis situations, like when the Communists in Yugoslavia shot down one of our C-47s. During that crisis the 82nd Airborne in Berlin was put on alert for a possible invasion of Yugoslavia. Fortunately, that situation resolved itself without the commitment of combat troops. The Yugoslavian crisis was known as a "Green Hornet," which actually was an action paper that had a green cover on it and required an answer within twenty-four hours. When a "Green Hornet " came in you were required to stay there until you had the answers, and if it arrived on a Friday it might take you all weekend. This was not a 9:00 to 5:00 job.

One of our main concerns in the European Section of the OPD was the refugee situation. The refugee problem greatly affected the location, billeting, and movement of our troops in Europe. The United States was obligated to take care of the refugees to a certain extent because many of them were located in our zone of occupation. We had to provide them with transportation to get them back to their homes, and we had to house, clothe, and feed them, as well as provide them with medical attention until then. As the Army demobilized, the staff in the Pentagon was down-sized as well, and although I didn't have direct responsibility for the displaced persons problem initially, as personnel in our section were discharged it got to the point where I became the "expert" on displaced persons. When President Truman decided that the United States should relax the laws on immigration, he appointed a presidential commission in December 1945, consisting of representatives from the State, Army, and Immigration departments to study the problem.

The commission decided that it needed more facts before it could draw any conclusions, so it appointed a three-man panel to travel to Europe on a fact-finding mission. I was chosen to represent the War Department. I accompanied Ugo Carusi, commissioner of immigration, and Undersecretary of State Howard Travers. We left on 21 January 1946 and were gone for three months. We stopped in London, Paris, Berlin, Munich, Heidelberg, Vienna, Geneva, Bern, Zurich, Lugano, Milan, Genoa, Rome, and Naples and discussed the refugee situation with officials in those cities. In Tidworth, England, we heard about the plight of the war brides, English women who had married GIs during the war and couldn't join their husbands when they were rotated back to the States. We helped solve that problem for them by eliminating some of the red tape they had to go through. In Rome we had an audience with Pope Pius XII in the Vatican. He had a wonderful presence. You could just feel his personality and his strength. He was kind and quiet. He read a prepared speech to us thanking us for coming and for our humanitarian mission. After that we just chatted for about thirty minutes. It was quite an experience. After that we went back to Paris and then flew home.

I had enjoyed the time I spent at the Pentagon. It was interesting and important work. Had everything worked out, I had planned to make the Army a career. However, back home in Kentucky I had another, more important obligation awaiting me. Mildred's family owned a farm in Midway, and at the time the farm was without a manager. Deep down I knew that Mildred was not cut out to be an Army wife. She really wanted me to come home and take over the farm. With the war over, I felt I had no real reason not to go home. With the Army demobilizing, the opportunities for promotion would become few and far between once again just as before in the prewar Army, although with my experience and connections I felt that I would have been successful. So I went to my superior in the Plans and Operation Division and explained the situation at the farm and that I felt I needed to do something about it. I told him that I would like to take a leave of absence without pay to try to work it out. To my surprise he readily agreed and asked me how

In January 1946, Buster (second from right) *was one of three officials appointed to undertake a three-month fact-finding mission to Europe to study the problems of displaced persons. Among the highlights of the trip was an audience with Pope Pius XII.*

long I needed. I told him it might take up to a year to get the farm situation straightened out. He replied that he would do everything he could to get it approved. The paperwork sailed right through, the only hitch being that they told me it was against regulations for an officer to be deprived of his pay except in the event of a court-martial and that I would have to accept half-pay. Consequently, I went on leave on 15 December 1947 at half-pay.

Once I got home it didn't take me long to realize that the farm was going to take all of my efforts to manage it successfully. More important, I realized that I enjoyed the work and being home with my family. So in March 1948 I submitted my resignation to the Army and by the time it wound its way through the appropriate channels, it didn't take effect until 1 December.

I had enjoyed my life in the regular Army and had been proud to serve my country. I was able to continue my association with the military after the war by joining the Army Reserve and later the Kentucky National Guard. In a sense I was able to have my cake and eat it, too. It seemed to me that I had come full circle, back to the home of my ancestors, the Busters and Nooes and Lillards, almost like the hands of a clock. For me, Time really was On Target.

AFTERWORD

William R. Buster's commitment to public service did not end in December 1948, with his retirement from active duty. Though he found managing the family farm near Midway a satisfying and fulltime job, the father of three agreed in 1953, at age thirty-seven, to join the Kentucky National Guard and organize the 23rd Corps Artillery as assistant commander. He held that position until 1960, when he was named corps artillery commander. On 15 March 1960, he accepted Governor Bert Combs's offer to become assistant adjutant general of the Commonwealth of Kentucky, a position he would hold until December 1967. On 16 November 1960, he was federally recognized as a brigadier general of the line. He retired from the armed forces on 15 July 1969, having rendered thirty years of service. He remained keenly interested in the men with whom he had served, however, and enjoyed attending reunions with his comrades in arms as his schedule permitted. For a number of years, beginning in 1972, he served as president of the Hell on Wheels Association.

Whether a uniformed officer or a civilian, Buster was repeatedly asked to give of his time and talents to civic causes. He rarely refused the call. A Mercer countian by birth, he quickly embraced the native county of his wife, Mildred, and involved himself in every aspect of its community life. He was elected to leadership positions in the Midway Lions Club, the Woodford County Farm Bureau, the American Red Cross, and New Union Christian Church. Buster was named a director of two local financial institutions, Home Federal Savings and Loan and the United Bank and Trust Company. He lavished particular attention on Midway College, on whose board of trustees he served for twenty-eight years; for eight of those years he was chairman of the board.

Ironically, the combat veteran who emerged from World War II physically unscathed sustained a serious injury less than fifty miles from his farm. Driving home from a civic meeting one rainy evening in 1954, he came upon a road construction site in Shelby County. As he held his arm out the window to signal his intention to turn, an approaching truck struck the car and severely wounded Buster, who lost his left arm. "My two immediate concerns," he recalled later, "were whether I would still be able to fish and stay in the National Guard." Both questions were answered in the affirmative. The secretary of the army granted a special waiver that allowed Buster to remain in the Guard, and the avid outdoorsman continued to enjoy fishing trips the rest of his life. At age sixty-five, he journeyed to the Central American nation of Belize, where he caught a fifty-pound tarpon.

Always interested in history and historic preservation, Buster in 1972 agreed to assist the Kentucky Historical Society, which was undertaking an extensive renovation of the Old State Capitol and its adjacent annex in Frankfort. As coordinator of the society, he oversaw both the renovation of those historic buildings and the creation of a military museum that would be housed in the State Arsenal. He planned to be at the society for one year. But when KHS Director George M. Chinn decided to retire in November 1973, the organization's executive committee unanimously voted to offer Buster the position, and he accepted.

Under William R. Buster's ten-year leadership, the Kentucky Historical Society emerged as one of the finest historical societies in the nation. He extended the operation of the traditionally Frankfort-based organization to every corner of the commonwealth. The traveling Historymobile program, for example, visited schools, fairs, and festivals in each of the state's 120 counties. The historical markers program oversaw the placement of more than three hundred markers along the state's highways, and the oral history, museum, and publications activities of the society received numerous commendations from such groups as the American Association for State and Local History.

Those of us who were privileged to work at the society with "WRB," as he invariably signed in-house memos, treasure the experience. Buster's long-time administrative assistant, Edna Flowers, has commented that she knew of no one on the staff who did not admire him. He was "truly a charismatic leader … an inspiration." "He's the only person in the world I would change my lifestyle for," Robert B. Kinnaird, his deputy and successor, once declared. "I used to spend my time hunting and fishing and reading history. General Buster asked me to come work for him, and now I am so busy working for the society that I don't have time to hunt and fish." Kinnaird concluded: "It has been a personal privilege and richly rewarding to work with General Buster." James C. Klotter, who served as publications editor throughout the Buster years and later as KHS director, recently remarked that "General Buster was, first and foremost, a good man, and people throughout Kentucky recognized that. For a leader that is an important attribute." Klotter added: "He also gained support for the cause of history because he had the respect of those around him on his staff. He brought in talented professionals, told them his expectations, and then let them do their jobs. The result was a professionally run and widely admired organization. When he retired he left behind a much better institution than the one he found on his arrival."

On 1 November 1983, Buster's resignation from the society became official. In laying down his duties, he made a characteristically gracious offer. "As always," he said, "I stand ready to assist in any way that I can." He then turned his full attention to Audubon Farm, where he raised tobacco and beef cattle and started breeding and raising thoroughbred horses. He also continued to enjoy fishing and hunting dove and quail. Following a short illness, he died on 15 December 1995, at the age of seventy-nine. A "service of worship and thanksgiving" was held three days later on the campus of his beloved Midway College.

October 1999   Thomas H. Appleton Jr.

A FINAL TRIBUTE

As a non-commissioned officer, it was my honor to serve with Gen. William R. Buster for almost five years.

While I was in the 14th Field Artillery, one year before the war, and learning to be an artilleryman, Bill Buster was a first lieutenant. With our obsolete and hazardous equipment, we trained continuously. In 1942, the 92nd Armored Field Artillery was formed and there was still more training. Lieutenant Buster told us that the training would save our lives someday, and the record shows that he was right.

During combat in Europe, then-Lieutenant Colonel Buster was always visible. He seemed to be everywhere, checking on his men and equipment, giving guidance and assurance to all of us.

Since the war, General Buster was very active in the Hell On Wheels Association. For the last twenty-five years of my contact with him, he was always available, giving advice to the members or serving in some capacity. I always found him to be a gentleman, as did all the members of the Association. He was a soldier's soldier.

Robert C. Pryor
Chairman of the Board
Hell On Wheels Association

Robert and his wife were good friends of Leona and me.

Index